Physical Education Association
of Great Britain and Northern Ireland

New
Directions
in
Physical
Education
Volume 2

Editor

Neil Armstrong, PhD
University of Exeter

Human Kinetics Books

ISBN: 0-87322-367-5

ISSN: 1048-6224

Acquisitions Editor: George McKinney
Managing Editor: Julia Anderson
Assistant Editors: Elizabeth Bridgett, Moyra Knight, Julie Swadener
Copyeditor: Wendy Nelson
Proofreader: Kari Nelson
Indexer: Sheila Ary
Production Director: Ernie Noa
Typesetting and Text Layout: Yvonne Winsor
Text Design: Keith Blomberg
Cover Design: Jack Davis
Interior Art: Gretchen Walters
Printer: Versa Press

Printed in the United States of America

10   9   8   7   6   5   4   3   2   1

Human Kinetics Publishers
  (Europe) Ltd.
P.O. Box IW14
Leeds LS16 6TR
England
0532-781708

U.S. Office:
Human Kinetics Publishers, Inc.
Box 5076, Champaign, IL 61825-5076
1-800-747-4457

Canada Office:
Human Kinetics Publishers, Inc.
P.O. Box 2503, Windsor, ON N8Y 4S2
1-800-465-7301 (in Canada only)

Contents

Series Preface

New Directions in Physical Education is a series of books initiated by the Physical Education Association Research Centre and edited by the Centre Director in association with the Physical Education Association of Great Britain and Northern Ireland.

Each edition of *New Directions in Physical Education* includes relevant contributions from recognized leaders in the field of physical education on topics of current interest in sport, dance, and physical, health, and outdoor education. Contributors are selected by the editor in consultation with officers of the Physical Education Association, but, of course, the views expressed are those of the authors and not necessarily those of the Physical Education Association of Great Britain and Northern Ireland. Suggestions of suitable topics worthy of inclusion in future volumes and of potential contributors would be welcomed by the editor. Correspondence should be addressed directly to Dr Neil Armstrong, PEA Research Centre, University of Exeter, Exeter, EX1 2LU, United Kingdom.

Preface

Section 1 of the Education Reform Act (ERA) of 1988 places a statutory responsibility upon schools to provide a broad and balanced education for all pupils, providing progression and continuity from age 5 to age 16 and beyond. The ERA defines the National Curriculum as consisting of religious education, English, mathematics, science, technology, history, geography, a modern foreign language, art, music and physical education that must

- promote the spiritual, moral, cultural, mental and physical development of pupils at the school and of society, and
- prepare pupils for the opportunities, responsibilities and experiences of adult life.

The ERA empowers the Secretary of State to specify, as he or she considers appropriate for each foundation subject, including physical education, attainment target (objectives) and programmes of study (means of achieving attainment targets). Attainment targets and programmes of study provide the basis for assessing a student's performance in relation both to expected attainment and to the next steps needed for the student's development.

In the case of physical education, the Secretary of State has decided that the attainment target and programmes of study should not be prescribed in as much detail as for other foundation subjects. He believes that schools and teachers should have substantial scope to develop their own schemes of work. The National Curriculum Working Group for Physical Education was therefore set up to advise on a statutory framework that is sufficiently broad and flexible to allow schools wide discretion in relation to matters to be studied.

New Directions in Physical Education, Volume 2, has been prepared in the light of the information described and, with the subtitle *Towards a National Curriculum*, and the papers have been drawn together at the height of the discussions following the communication of the National Curriculum Working Group's advice to the Secretary of State.

The objective (attainment target) of this book is, therefore, to document this debate as much as to inform and enrich the debate at a critical moment in the development of physical education in schools. To do this the country's leading authorities have been asked to consider their own specialist areas of the physical education programme in the context of physical education in the National Curriculum. The result is a unique source of information, comment and discussion on the potential role of health-related physical activity, track and field, gymnastics, dance and outdoor education in the National Curriculum. In addition to specialist-area inputs, other experts have been invited to contribute chapters that address key issues underpinning the formulation and delivery of physical education from age 5 to age 16 and beyond.

In chapter 1, Dr Andrew Sparkes gives a broad overview of the rapidly changing landscape in education and argues that teachers need to be viewed as workers engaged in a labour process. To illustrate the point, he provides details regarding the growth of school governors' powers and links this to case-study material highlighting the impact this has had on the life of a female physical education teacher. This teacher's troubles are explored in terms of the wider social context in which physical educators' work is now being defined, and it is suggested that physical educators need to develop appropriate rhetorics as part of a political strategy to promote their subject in school and gain control of their curriculum.

In chapter 2, Dr Kenneth Fox summarizes relevant concepts in self-esteem theory, with particular reference to the physical domain, pointing out that self-esteem has many underlying dimensions and that self-perceptions seem to play an important role in the physical environment. Dr Fox discusses the relationships among specific contents of self-perceptions, such as self-efficacy, perceived ability, and perceived competence, in terms of a possible hierarchial self-esteem structure. He addresses developmental aspects of self-esteem in children and the mechanisms by which individuals promote their own self-esteem, and concludes by examining the implications of his work for teaching styles and curricular content in PE.

The recent explosion of knowledge in information technology has resulted in the formulation of an Information Technology Capability attainment target. Dr David Brodie and Mike Skinsley, in chapter 3, consider the role of information technology within physical education. They review current applications of information technology in administration, data analysis, communication, and assessment and evaluation. Future applications, such as interactive video, kinematics, voice-activated input, and smartcards are discussed, and the implications for physical education are clearly identified.

In chapter 4, the first of the specialist chapters, Dr Neil Armstrong and Dr Stuart Biddle examine the role of health-related physical activity (HRPA) in the National Curriculum. They analyse contemporary research findings in paediatric exercise science from a multidisciplinary perspective and support their case for HRPA with the results of Dr Armstrong's research into children's physical activity patterns. They discuss physiological and psychological outcomes of HRPA and strategies for promoting HRPA. They conclude their contribution by emphasizing that HRPA should underpin the PE programme and that PE teachers must explicitly address the problem of children's low levels of physical activity.

In chapters 5 and 6, Richard Fisher and John Wright consider the potential contribution of track and field and gymnastics to the National Curriculum. They focus, in their own ways, on the child as a decision maker and not simply the imitator of movement patterns as part of the received curriculum. Their approach is practical, and they present well-thought-out programmes of study built around key stages, with an abundance of practical examples drawn from their wide experience of working with children.

In chapter 7, Sarah Stevens examines the development of dance in the school curriculum and the dilemma dance specialists face in meeting the National Curriculum requirement that the subject be considered within physical education for all key stages. She discusses current curriculum models from a dance perspective and suggests ways of further enhancing the study of dance, within the National Curriculum, as a formed and performed art.

Like dance, outdoor education is not a named subject area in the National Curriculum. Dr Barbara Humberstone argues, in chapter 8, the final specialist chapter, that outdoor education has considerable cross-curricular implications and can provide powerful media for personal and social development and change.

This volume of *New Directions in Physical Education* concludes with Bob Laventure's comprehensive and insightful chapter on the vital relationship between the physical education curriculum and postschool participation in HRPA, sport and active recreation of young people. Bob overviews recent research into young peoples' lifestyles and local provision of facilities and develops from personal experience a rationale for increasing links between school and community. This edition therefore closes appropriately with the thought that 'long-term partnerships between the school and the community will develop, founded upon the belief that all parties have the lifelong sporting, health and recreational needs of young people as their primary concern.'

The publication of this volume would not have been possible without the tremendous support of the authors, the publishers and the staff of the Physical Education Association Research Centre. My thanks to all concerned.

Neil Armstrong, PhD, FPEA, FIBiol
University of Exeter
United Kingdom

Contributors

Neil Armstrong, PhD, FPEA, FIBiol
Reader in Exercise Science
Director of the PEA Research Centre
University of Exeter
Exeter EX1 2LU

Stuart Biddle, PhD, FPEA
Lecturer in Education
Associate Director of the PEA Research Centre
University of Exeter
Exeter EX1 2LU

David A. Brodie, PhD
Professor of Physical Education and Movement Science
University of Liverpool
Liverpool P69 3BX

Richard J. Fisher, FPEA
President of the Physical Education Association
  of Great Britain and Northern Ireland
Dean of Science
St Mary's College
London TW1 4SX

Kenneth R. Fox, PhD, FPEA
Lecturer in Education
Associate Director of the PEA Research Centre
University of Exeter
Exeter EX1 2LU

Barbara Humberstone, PhD
Lecturer in Physical Education
University of Southampton
Southampton SO4 2GJ

Bob Laventure
Inspector of Physical Education
Coventry Local Education Authority
Coventry CV1 2LQ

Michael Skinsley, FPEA
Head of Physical Education
Hartcliffe School
Bristol

Andrew C. Sparkes, PhD
Lecturer in Education
Associate Director of the PEA Research Centre
University of Exeter
Exeter EX1 2LU

Sarah E. Stevens
Head of Dance
Bedford College of Higher Education
Bedfordshire MK40 2BZ

John Wright, FPEA
Former Principle Lecturer in Physcial Education
Nonnington College of Physical Education
Kent CT13 0JG

Chapter 1

The Changing Nature of Teachers' Work: School Governors and Curriculum Control in Physical Education

Andrew C. Sparkes

The Changing Educational Landscape

'When I first started teaching, you were highly respected. You were proud to announce you were a teacher. Now you do anything to avoid it. It's been a gradual change over the last 20 years. Certainly when I left in 1970 to have kids, I was still proud to be a teacher, and parents respected you. Probably when I went back 5 years later it had changed a bit' (personal communication). These are the words of Sally, a physical education (PE) teacher in her late 40s, who is concerned about the way her job has changed in the last 20 years. More will be heard from her later on.

Apparently, Sally is not alone in her concerns, and many physical educators feel that their subject is not valued in schools (see Sparkes, Templin and Schempp, 1990). Nor is the problem confined to PE teachers. An interview study of 300 secondary teachers conducted in 1989 suggests that there is considerable malaise among professionals in the classroom. Commenting upon the study, its deputy director Dr Pamela Robinson, cited in Price (1990, p. C3), commented that many felt overwhelmed by the pace of change in schools and that they perceived that 'the job they were trained to do, as teachers in front of children, marking books, preparing lessons, has dramatically and quickly changed'. Likewise, Sikes and Aspinwall (1990) comment that teachers, at all career stages and working in all types of schools, are experiencing uncertainty and exhaustion and feel that 'it is becoming increasingly difficult for them to be the sort of teacher they want to be and be seen as being' (p. 2).

Not surprisingly teachers feel stressed. The findings of a questionnaire survey of 1,782 teachers conducted by Travers and Cooper (1990) found that in comparison to other highly stressed groups, such as tax officers, general practitioners, dentists and nurses, teachers were experiencing significantly lower levels of job satisfaction and suffering from significantly higher levels of mental ill-health. In particular, the survey indicated that teachers were dissatisfied with their jobs in terms of the opportunities available to use their abilities, their hours of work, their physical working conditions, industrial relations between management and teachers in their school, the recognition they got for good work, the ways their schools were managed, chances of promotion and—most of all—their rate of pay. Sixty-six per cent of the sample had actively considered leaving the teaching profession in the last 5 years. Twenty-eight per cent were currently looking for alternative employment, and 13% were seeking premature retirement.

The 10 major sources of job pressure for teachers, according to Travers and Cooper (1990), are these:

1. Lack of support from the government
2. Constant changes taking place within the profession
3. Lack of information as to how the changes are to be implemented
4. Society's diminishing respect for the teaching profession
5. The move towards a National Curriculum
6. Salaries that are out of proportion to work load
7. Having to produce assessments of pupils
8. Dealing with basic behavioural problems
9. Lack of noncontact time
10. The fact that being a good teacher does not necessarily mean promotion

Others, such as Kyriacou (1989), Freeman (1989) and Capel (1989), note that an important source of stress for teachers is the feeling that they are not in control of the situation in which they have to operate. In relation to this, Cole (1989) notes,

Teachers have always had a relatively low degree of control over the child's development, but the effect of government policy in the 1980s is to reduce that control even further. Central control of the curriculum and examinations, reinforced by parental power at the local level, will reduce teachers' control over exactly what they teach their pupils, how and when. Teachers' skills (and the pride taken in them) of adapting the curriculum and teaching methods to the particular needs of individuals and groups, and testing them appropriately, will be undermined. (p. 165)

In essence, teachers' work has undergone a fundamental reorganization in the last decade (see Apple, 1986, 1988; Shaw, in press). During this period the status of the teaching profession has been eroded by a variety of forces. The general public's image of teachers has changed considerably as they have born the brunt of a generalized criticism of the education system orchestrated by a range of government officials and the media. For example, the *London Times* article 'Teachers Back Call for Autumn Strikes' (Broom, 1990) was headed by a large photograph of a group of delegates at the National Union of Teachers annual conference in Bournemouth. This small group of delegates are apparently sitting together in the front of an otherwise empty hall, judging from the empty seats behind them. The photograph is angled to make one particular individual—we are left to assume it is a teacher—who is reading a newspaper its focal point. The cover page of the newspaper he is reading dominates the shot—it is the *Socialist Worker*. The message to the readership is clear and is symptomatic of the manner in which teachers have been portrayed in recent years. As Ball (1988) notes, 'In the media teachers are now readily portrayed as uncaring, improperly trained, resistant to change, politically suspect and mercenary, in short "unprofessional" ' (p. 296).

Teachers have been getting a bad press for quite some time now. The Black Papers on education issued in the late 1960s were a significant starting point in this process (see Cox and Dyson, 1969a, 1969b). More recently, publications by representatives of the 'New Right', such as the Hillgate Group (1989), Lawlor (1990), and O'Keefe (1990), have carried on this tradition. These populist critiques attempt to establish as 'fact' in the public consciousness a view of teachers as 'left wing' radicals who are to blame for declining academic standards, large-scale illiteracy, indisciplined students, and the failure of industry to compete with other countries. As Halpin (1990) comments, 'The teaching profession was an easy scapegoat, and the government wasted little time in putting much of the blame for the nation's economic difficulties on teachers who, it was alleged, not only didn't know how to teach but, worse, were teaching the wrong things' (p. 37).

The subject area of physical education has not avoided similar attention, and Evans (1990a) suggests that innumerable broadsides have been fired on PE teachers in recent years. For example, on July 11, 1986, the newspaper *Today* carried a leading front-page article, entitled 'Barmy Britain', that portrayed PE teachers as a bunch of radicals intent on seriously damaging the place and position of competition in the PE curriculum. Following this trend the BBC 'Panorama' programme screened in March 1987 contained a host of negative images of physical educators as anticompetition and 'trendy', thereby implicating them in the declining standards of national sport, students' health, and discipline in society, to name but a few. Indeed, as part of this 'moral panic', PE teachers were portrayed as a threat to the very social fabric of our society (see Evans, 1990b; Pollard, 1988). To this must be added the efforts of the 'sport lobby', who have been quick to blame PE teachers in schools for any poor performances given by individuals or teams at the national level (see Hardy and Sparkes, 1987; Williams, 1990).

These *socially constructed images* (often with little, if any, supporting evidence) have instigated a number of critical debates about the nature and state of schooling in Britain. As Evans and Davies (1988) realize, these debates 'have had a profound effect not only on the way in which outside "publics" (parents, employers) think about schools and teachers, but on the way teachers and pupils think about themselves, how they experience their jobs and schools as places of work' (p. 4). These experiences have developed, and are developing, within an ongoing 'conservative restoration' (cf. Apple and Teitelbaum, 1986) that involves two major thrusts. First, there is increased centralized control of the curriculum, as evidenced in the National Curriculum, the changing role of Her Majesty's Inspectorate (HMI), the increasing influence of the training agency, grant-related in-service training, and the increased emphasis placed upon public examinations and testing within the educational system[1]. Second, strenuous attempts have been made to introduce the philosophy of the marketplace to education in terms of competition, market forces and privatization in the form of Local Financial Management, opting out, city technical colleges, open enrolment, and the ill-fated voucher scheme[2]. Indeed, Bash (1989) claims, 'The *market* is now the dominant theme in the formulation of UK educational policy. Classical free-market economics is currently a major aspect of national politics and has been for about the past 10 years' (p. 19).

For Brown (1990) all this forms part of a 'third wave' in the sociohistorical development of British education that is characterized by the rise of the 'ideology of parentocracy', whereby 'a child's education is increasingly dependent upon the *wealth* and *wishes* of parents, rather than the *ability* and *effort* of pupils' (p. 66). This ideology is intimately associated with the ongoing privatization of education under the slogans of 'parental choice', 'educational standards' and the 'free market'[3]. Consequently, at first glance these policy thrusts appear paradoxical. In the first there is a tightening of the centralized grip on the educational policy-making process, whereas in the latter the state seems to be divesting its responsibilities for educational provision. However, Hargreaves and Reynolds (1989) argue that these processes are not contradictory, because 'a limited commitment to privatization is in many respects not at all in conflict with the centralized control of educational policy. As coordinated arms of educational policy, the two processes can, in fact, hold the course of educational change firmly within a powerful grip' (p. 7). It is within this shifting landscape that teachers now have to operate and make sense of their world of work in schools.

The Teacher as Worker[4]

Clearly, it is well beyond the scope of this chapter to engage in a detailed analysis of the many issues raised above. However, these recent events have highlighted the need to view educational institutions as political entities that shape, and are shaped by, their environmental and organizational contexts. Furthermore, these same events have sharpened the focus on the teacher as a worker in an organizational setting. Connell (1985) reminds us that 'teachers are workers, teaching is work, and the school is a workplace. These simple facts are often forgotten. Nevertheless they are workers, and in understanding them it is essential to analyse their work' (p. 69). He goes on to argue,

Teaching is a labour process without an object. At best, it has an object so intangible—the minds of the kids, or their capacity to learn—that it cannot be specified in any but vague and metaphorical ways. A great deal of work is done in schools, day in and day out, but this work does not produce any *things*. Nor does it, like other white-collar work, produce visible and quantifiable *effects*—so many pensions paid, so many dollars turned over, so many patients cured. The 'outcomes of teaching', to use the jargon of educational research, are notoriously difficult to measure. . . . The fact remains that it is always difficult to specify the object of teachers' labour, the raw material they are supposed to be working on. In consequence the definition of the task can expand and contract in quite alarming ways. . . . In practice, then, the labour-process-without-an-object is not an amorphous mess. It is very firmly shaped by circumstances and demands, both immediate and remote. (pp. 70-73)

These are issues of great importance, because it follows that the practice and definition of teachers' work can change according to local demand, national priorities, the historical period, and the teacher's own stance taken in relation to these changes (cf. Lawn, 1987). Conceptualizing teaching as a labour process allows some key questions to be asked—for example, 'What is happening to workers' control over their own work?' and 'What is happening to skill in work?'[5] As indicated, the relationships of authority in schools and school systems that have the potential to shape the character of teachers' work activities seem to be changing rapidly. Unfortunately, we have little information about how the changing contemporary educational scene has affected the lives of physical educators. As a consequence, Evans and Davies (1988) claim, 'we still need much more research as to how the opportunities for teachers can be structured by the perspectives and actions of others and how they experience conditions of control over their opportunities, careers and life-styles inside the institutional work place' (p. 8). With this in mind the rest of this chapter sets out to explore but one strand within the complex network of issues that have so recently impacted upon the lives of teachers, that is, the changing relationship between physical education teachers and school governors. By choosing this particular strand I hope to highlight the problematic nature of this emerging relationship and the manner in which the legal powers now available to governors enables them to influence the content of the school curriculum and the work conditions of teachers.

The Rise of Governor Power

Simply in terms of their numbers, governors are now an influential group within the educational system. In 1988 Mahoney claimed that there were over 300,000 school governors in England and Wales, but no one knew the exact number. Indeed, Wisker (1989), commenting upon one Local Education Authority (LEA), noted that it had more new governors than new teachers. Alongside their numerical growth, school governors have also been invested with greater legal powers. The Taylor Report of 1977 (Department of Education and Science, 1977), *A New Partnership for Our Schools*, argued strongly that governing bodies should be allowed to exercise their full authority as outlined in the 1944 Education Act in terms of determining the general conduct of the school. The responsibilities of governors were to cover all, or some aspects of, the appointment and dismissal of teachers and other staff, admission of pupils, *internal organization and the curriculum*, finance, care and upkeep of premises, and the fixing of certain holidays (see the Taylor Report, Department of Education and Science [DES], 1977, para 2.4, p. 6). Importantly, this report stressed the need for a *partnership*, in equal proportions, among all parties concerned with the school's success. However, it did make clear that the governors had a powerful voice in the general direction and the conduct of the curriculum in the school.

The role of the governors in terms of the curriculum was further strengthened by the 1986 Education Act, in which they were able to *consider* the secular curriculum policy of the LEA and make decisions regarding its modification for their particular school. In terms of sex education this act (section 18) enabled governors to decide if this issue should be included in the curriculum. Commenting on this, Mahoney (1988) suggests, 'This controversial clause establishes the precedent that for the first time governors have exclusive control over a specific named component of the secular curriculum' (p. 62). The powers of the governors have been extended by the 1988 Education Reform Act, particularly with regard to financial delegation, variously known as Local Financial Management (LFM) or Local Management of Schools (LMS). Since April 1, 1990, every primary and secondary school in England and Wales has been 'formula funded', with each school's budget being allocated according to the number of pupils and their ages. By April 1, 1993, all primary and secondary schools with 200 or more pupils will receive 'delegated budgets', the responsibility for which lies in the hands of the governing bodies. Within this framework the governing bodies will be responsible for the appointment of staff, staffing levels, implementation of the National Curriculum, the school's budget, and disciplinary and grievance procedures. Clough, Lee, Menter, Trodd and Whitty (1989) note, 'It is school governors, while having due regard for the requirements of national and local policy, who will determine the numbers of teaching and non-teaching staff that will be employed in their schools and the number of incentive allowances that will be paid. Effectively, they will have the right to hire and fire staff on behalf of the LEA' (pp. 37-38). These powers are even more immediate in schools that 'opt out' and draw their funds directly from the Department of Education and Science. In such schools, Broom (1989) stresses, 'Heads and governors will have complete control over budgets subject to the requirements of the National Curriculum, they will also be free to determine the school policy on everything from maths teaching to the purchase of toilet paper' (p. 21).

All these powers, together with the fact that teaching-staff costs take the greatest percentage from a school's budget, need to be considered in relation to the policy of 'open enrolment' that allows pupils to choose which school they attend, coupled with the fact that LEAs are no longer able to place entry ceilings or planned limits on particular schools. It has been suggested by Hargreaves and Reynolds (1989) that this policy may lead to high levels of competition among schools for pupils, with the more successful and popular schools becoming oversubscribed, while the less popular schools get less funding and eventually become 'sink schools'. They argue, 'Schools and secondary schools in particular, it seems, will be allowed to flourish or flounder according to the market dictates of parental choice. Schools are being and will increasingly be placed in the position of competitive enterprises bidding for parental custom' (p. 5). Fewer pupils will mean less money from the formula and will require schools to dismiss teachers in post. Not surprisingly, Thomas (1989) notes,

> in England and Wales, the Local Management of Schools initiative will give governors of schools a degree of independence on finance and on staffing which will be more extensive than any other system described here. Pupil-related funding formulae will emphasise the accountability of schools to parents, arising from the greater powers of school choice. The authority of governors over the appointment, suspension and dismissal of staff will strengthen the accountability of staff to governors. (p. 122)

The relationship between governors and teachers is clearly changing, and this has definite implications for the subject area of physical education. Unfortunately, there is little empirical evidence available concerning this changing relationship at the micro or individual level, where it is acted out in the daily life of the school. The following section draws upon data from a cross-cultural study that utilized the life-history method to investigate the lives and careers of physical education teachers (see Templin, Sparkes and Schempp, in press). Part of the documentary evidence provided in this study by one late-career teacher, called Sally, included a written reflective account of her experiences with governors in two contrasting historical periods and in two different types of schools. Extracts of this account are presented here in an attempt to highlight and make problematic the changing nature of this relationship prior to locating it in a wider social context and considering some of the implications for PE.

School Governorship in the 1960s:
A Grammar School Teacher's Perspective

These are the reflections of Sally on a period in the mid 1960s when she was employed as an assistant teacher of PE in an all-girls grammar school[6].

> The advent of the thrice yearly School Governor's meeting created little more than a ripple of interest in the school itself. The groundsman was instructed to tidy up the already immaculate front garden, while 'pressganged' sixthformers slaved to produce delectable morsels (suitable to tempt the governors' palate) in the cookery room. The caretaker was

summoned to re-arrange the furniture in the Headmistress's office, and the bone china tea cups appeared on the counter in the school office. Staff were directed in as sentries to keep chattering girls away from the front of the school, both when the governors arrived, and for the duration of the meeting. Occasionally, next morning the Headmistress would pass on some innocuous message from the governors to the staff, 'The school Governors are delighted with the excellent examination results gained this year, and wish that their congratulations be conveyed to the staff'. More often, however, the occasion elicited no comment, and as far as the school was concerned, only the trayful of dirty tea cups in the school office next morning bore witness to the fact that the meeting had indeed taken place. Governors' meetings were therefore something of a mystery to us lesser mortals. Held behind closed doors no one would dare ask what went on, and I doubt if even the Deputy Head was privy to any of the proceedings. How they filled the time was therefore only a subject for mere conjecture. For while it was understood that governors had to approve new staff appointments, and changes in the curriculum, we had it on good authority that they always complied with the wishes of our somewhat domineering Headmistress, making this exercise in all probability something of a mere formality, rather than the subject of rigorous debate.

Governors were always referred to by senior members of staff in those hushed tones which are synonymous with deference, and carefully shielded from the exigencies and unpleasantness of reality. Their only direct contact with the staff was at the post Speech Day tea party, and as far as I knew they never actually met the pupils. They were certainly never to be seen around the school, and even when attending the annual concert, carol service, and school opera—inordinate sense of duty again ensured a good turn out—they assembled in the Head's office to be shepherded to their reserved front row places only after everyone else had been seated. They also left immediately afterwards while the 'hoi polloi' waited patiently for them to wend their way again in the direction of the Head's office and a restorative glass of sherry.

It would be difficult to collectively describe this worthy band, for they were indeed a group of very different individuals. However, they did appear to share certain common characteristics. They were all 'well spoken', middle class, and middle aged citizens, acutely aware of the honour which member-ship of a small town grammar school governing body conferred. Many had 'connections' in the town, and although it might not be the 'done thing' for school governors to flout political beliefs in the course of duty, there was little doubt that their sympathies lay with the very Conservative County Council of the time. Above all they were considered honest, well thought of, and *eminently respectable.*

The respect and deference they commanded, along with the carefully preserved mystery which surrounded their activities, suggested at the time this privileged group of apparently distinguished human beings wielded influence and power. History has since revealed that it was indeed a hollow reign, behind an albeit splendid front. In reality these sixties governors, like so many of their predecessors, were merely relatively ineffectual trustees. The real balance of power resided within the grasp of a very capable, dynamic, and autocratic Headmistress. (Sparkes, 1990d, pp. 42-43)

School Governorship in the 1980s:
A Comprehensive Teacher's Perspective

By the late 1980s, Sally was a departmental head at a coeducational comprehensive school in a city where competition for pupils was becoming more and more intense due to falling rolls.

School Governors and their activities had, until recently, been something of a mystery to those outside the governing bodies. Members of a rather remote band of people who descended for the termly governors' meeting; they were somehow shrouded in mystery, and seen as a special species of person with whom one was expected to ingratiate oneself at school plays and the concert. The rare opportunity for mere teachers to 'hob nob' with these apparently eminent personages seemed reserved only for those whose recent activities merited special attention and reward. A carefully chosen few who were summoned to the Head's office to partake of sherry, and indulge in entertaining the governors with small talk as a preamble to some school function. It therefore came as something of a surprise when the Headmaster announced that each of the school governors had volunteered to take a special interest in each particular department, and would shortly be contacting the relevant heads of department. Mine, as it soon became apparent, had every intention of taking this responsibility seriously.

Determined to be positive about this unexpected turn of events, my hopes were raised. Perhaps my governor might be instrumental in updating our almost mediaeval equipment, and help resolve some of the more pressing departmental problems. This new style of school governorship might even mark the birth of that new partnership envisaged by the Taylor Report (Department of Education and Science [DES], 1977), nearly a decade before. The first inkling that my hopes might not be realised dawned as I became aware that the 'bloke' who kept 'dropping in' for a gossip with one of my junior colleagues in the department was in fact *my governor*. Already on familiar first name terms with everyone in the department except me, I remember feeling vaguely uncomfortable as he disappeared with a male colleague in the direction of the boys' changing room. This was hardly the mode of professional intercourse that I had expected!

It was soon evident that my preconceived hopes of a fruitful and supportive relationship were naive and hopelessly optimistic. My governor turned out to be a man with a mission, a man who saw it as his duty to become something of a messiah. Reason and rationality did not feature prominently in a single minded approach to his perception of the situation. His intent, it became clear, was not only to 'sort out the PE Department', but to save the school in the process as well. By revolutionising our facilities, and exhorting, supporting and extolling the virtues of the winning school teams he had conceptualised, he was to fulfill cherished ambitions to restore the school's somewhat tarnished public image.

His ambitions, no doubt fuelled by good intentions, were nonetheless supported by an intransigent attitude that permitted neither negotiation nor compromise, let alone consideration of alternative points of view. A situation no doubt exacerbated by the fact that he was obviously very 'chummy' with the reactionary element within the PE department. He heard only what he wanted to hear, and wanted no truck with anything unlikely to improve the school's public image. Matches, matches, and yet more matches were called for—especially against those schools who were enjoying greater popularity. Anything creative, aesthetic, or which would not attract public attention were dismissed as irrelevant. My comments such as, 'only fifteen per cent of the school population participate in competitive sports, don't you think we should offer activities in which all children can participate?', fell on stoney ground. He even suggested that the trampolining and dance club which were enjoying considerable popular support should be abandoned in favour of running more inter-school fixtures.

Since assuming responsibility for my department I have endeavoured to transform what had previously been an elitist, skills dominated, and very competitive regime into one more compatible with contemporary educational thinking. Thus equality of educational opportunity, and relevant experiences for all were becoming accepted as a justifiable approach to this subject. The added dimensions of personal and social development plus a health focus together not only ensured that pupils received the type of physical education to which they were *entitled* (DES, 1985), but came nearer to supporting official curricular views as set out in *The School Curriculum* (DES, 1981). As one colleague kindly commented, I had moved the department through 'light years' to a more enlightened and forward looking position. At one blow a school governor had dismissed all this innovation as not only irrelevant but undesirable. So much for the hopes of a prosperous new partnership! (Sparkes, 1990d, pp. 43-45)

Personal Troubles and Social Issues

The reflective account given by Sally provides important insights into her subjective reality regarding specific relationships with school governors in two historical periods. The passive stance of governors in the 1960s has been replaced, in her case at least, by an assertive interventionist approach in the 1980s. As if to emphasize this point, Angela Rumbold, the Minister of State for Education (cited in Doe, 1989, p. A1), told a conference of governor-trainers in May 1989, 'They [governors] are not there, as they so often were in the past, merely to rubber-stamp decisions taken by the local authority and the head. Governors are there to govern.' However, as Sally's experiences indicate, this newly emerging relationship will not be without its problems, and it has the potential to greatly affect the working conditions of physical educators in schools. This is particularly so in terms of their control over the curriculum. In Sally's case the governor with a 'special interest' in PE attempted to enhance the prestige of the school by advocating a curriculum geared to the production of successful school teams in order to attract pupils in a falling-rolls situation. His advocacy of a skewed curriculum based on elitist practices acted to directly negate the efforts of Sally, who, as departmental head, had attempted over the years to construct a balanced curriculum that provided a range of experiences for pupils of all abilities, based on the notion of entitlement. In essence, this struggle was over who controlled the curriculum[7].

Of course, it could be argued that what happened to Sally is just a one-off case. However, case studies of the particular are capable of illuminating issues of general importance. This is especially so when the personal truths of individuals are located in a wider sociohistorical context. In essence, Sally's account concerns her personal troubles with one particular governor. However, as Mills (1959) argued, these 'personal troubles' are intimately connected to 'social issues', that is, the troubles experienced by the individual arise in the context of broader social problems. Mills suggests that although the linkage may not be obvious on the surface, an individual's difficulties are almost always interconnected with other structures in a society. If Sally's personal troubles are to be treated with the seriousness they deserve, and if we are to understand the impact of increasing governor power on the educational process and the subject area of PE, then there is a need to activate what Mills called the 'sociological imagination' in an attempt to illuminate how these personal troubles and social issues relate to one another. Such a task requires that a 'relational' stance (see Apple, 1979) be adopted that moves beyond the level of the individual teacher and school to locate them within the wider social, political and economic landscape. The next section begins this exploration by considering the local social context in terms of the perspectives that governors may hold and the impact these can have in shaping the work of teachers in schools.

Local Social Context and Governor Perspectives

Schools, and the teachers who work in them, do not exist in a social vacuum. As Bell (1986) reminds us,

> Changes in the environment are transmitted from the outside world through the school to the department and its staff. . . . Changes in one aspect of that social system, even where these are changes in attitudes, priorities and

interpretations rather than the more substantial changes in structure, organization and resourcing, will all affect the department and its members in
some way or other, although these effects may be different and elicit different
responses for different people and at different times. (p. 113)

At the local level schools are part of a community that is made up of people who
may differ significantly in their social class positions, educational backgrounds,
religious beliefs, and views on the purpose of schooling. The parents and pupils
that teachers interact with on a regular basis are drawn from this community,
and they have the potential to shape the form and content of teachers' work.
Likewise, governors are also drawn from this community that exists beyond the
school gates and, as such, along with parents and pupils, form part of what
Arfwedson (1979), cited in Hatton (1987), has defined as the 'local social context'
(LSC). Arfwedson suggests that the LSC is capable of affecting teacher work in
three distinct ways. It directly constrains teachers' work (e.g. the involvement of
governors in the allocation of finances to purchase fitness-testing equipment for
a health-related fitness module), it directly constrains institutional structures (e.g.
governors may insist on the introduction of mixed-ability groupings), and it
directly affects teacher beliefs and hence indirectly teacher work (e.g. teachers
believe that governors have the power to influence their promotion prospects,
and so they respond in ways that they think governors define as appropriate).

Overt and Covert Power: Pressure Tactics and 'Good Intentions'

Australian studies by Hatton (1987) and Connell (1985) indicate how, in certain
conditions, factors outside the school can intrude into the classroom setting and
provide a strong limiting pressure on teachers' pedagogical practices. In both
cases powerful groups of parents exerted pressure upon teachers to conform to
their interpretation of legitimate teaching practices. For example, in Hatton's
(1987) study of Riverton School, the Parents and Citizens Committee (P&C) was
the overt means by which parents and citizens in the local area were given direct
input into school affairs. Hatton illustrates how the vocal and powerful P&C
influenced the purchasing of equipment for the school and the transfer and
promotion of teachers and how they exerted pressure to prevent a move by staff
to introduce team teaching in open-plan classroom situations. According to
Hatton,

Parents, regardless of their social background, typically engage in assessments of teacher competence. What was significant was that some parents,
particularly through the P&C which functioned as a steering group, had
sufficient and proven political and cultural power to act on their assessments
in ways which had implications for teachers' futures. A negative assessment
could result in a transfer to a less desirable situation. Conversely, a positive
assessment could provide security from an unwanted transfer. Just as it is
likely that teachers are motivated to teach in certain ways to gain the

approval of colleagues, so too it is equally likely that their practices will be shaped in particular ways to ensure the approval of parents, or at least, avoid parental disapproval, in contexts where parents have a demonstrated capacity to act on their assessments or where their right to intervene is a cultural given. (p. 466)

As was indicated earlier, governors in England and Wales now have the *legal right* to act upon their assessments of teachers, intervene in the curriculum process, appoint or dismiss staff and award incentive allowances. Therefore, governors, as part of the LSC, are able to exert strong pressures on teachers to comply with their wishes. This may be particularly so, as in the case of Sally, in situations of falling rolls, and many physical educators may be subjected to similar pressures in the future as schools vie for pupils. Of course, not all governors are of the kind described earlier. Indeed, if Sally and the governor in question had held similar visions of PE and its function within the school, then his interventions might have been defined by her as supportive rather than pressuring. Whether supportive or pressuring, it remains that governors are now capable of adopting, and legally empowered to adopt, a more active and interventionist stance regarding curriculum issues. Most would agree that a return to the passive form of governorship of the 1960s would be undesirable. The concept of an active partnership between governors and teachers as advocated in the Taylor Report (DES, 1977) is to be welcomed in a democratic society. However, the nature of this relationship and the form of the intervention into the curriculum by governors will vary from school to school.

The vast majority of governors are sensible, well-meaning and caring individuals with considerable personal integrity and are determined to do their best for the school in a reasonable and rational manner. Many respect the professionalism and expertise of the teachers, and all schools should welcome supportive and informed governors. Indeed, Golby and Brigley (1989), in a detailed study of parent governors in Devon, emphasized that the governors often formed close and productive relationships with the professionals in their schools, and noted that there were very few cases of friction among parents, heads and teachers and many of high-quality co-operation. But 'good intentions' and 'what is good for the school' are systematically ambiguous, leaving the nature of how these are defined and achieved unquestioned. No doubt the governor who caused so much stress for Sally had 'good intentions' and the 'interests of the school' at heart. Such terms form a 'symbolic canopy' (Popkewitz & Lind, 1989), based on a consensus view of school life that is central to the discourse of management, which masks elements of power and interests. As Mahoney (1988) points out to aspiring governors,

> Quite clearly, your motives for being a governor will decisively affect the way you perform your duties. . . . You are just one member of a very diverse group of people: some are there for political motives, others for professional, others religious, others educational, others social, others commercial, yet others parental. (p. 4)

Three Major Perspectives of Governors

It is important to recognize that governors enter the school not as empty vessels but with a range of motivations that are shaped by the contemporary sociopolitical climate and their own biographies. That is, they are guided by their own perspectives. According to Becker, Geer, Hughes and Strauss (1961), a perspective is a coordinated set of ideas and actions that a person uses in dealing with some problematic situation; it involves that person's ordinary way of thinking and feeling and acting. In their study of parent governors, Golby and Brigley (1989) identified three broad perspectives in action. Most of the parent governors held a traditionalist perspective that favoured the grammar school curriculum, methods and ethos.

A majority of the Devon respondents, representing over half of all secondary parent governors in the county, have experienced some form of selective education, private or grammar, and almost half hold qualifications from higher education. Some of them harbour nostalgia for the academic ethos of traditional grammar schools. Devon retains some working models which are accorded high esteem in some of the local folklore. Academic excellence, firm discipline and polite behaviour figure prominently in the language of these governors. There is also residual support for corporal punishment[8]. (p. 7)

The utilitarians were identified as a second and growing group that placed their emphasis on schools' relationship to employment and useful skills.

This viewpoint is coloured by employment in service, business and industrial positions and an education which has usually followed a path through secondary modern and/or technical schools to some form of further education or training. A broader view of the aims of education is taken. . . . The curriculum will be one which develops the potential of the whole range of pupils. It will centrally include moral and social education; careers and vocational education are valued. . . . The common belief is that schools are public institutions which should serve the community by producing eminently employable, well-socialised young people. . . . Local business, community figures and the policy emerge prominently on the educational landscape of such parent governors[8]. (p. 8-9)

Finally, there were the egalitarians, who formed the small minority and subscribed to a comprehensive, rather than a grammar or technical school, philosophy.

Egalitarian aims are usually described in more overt sociopolitical language. They are rooted in a more idealistic conception of society, unlike the traditional and utilitarian perspectives which tend to assume as given the demands upon schools and the form of society which produces them. Education in this egalitarian perspective is to contribute to the positive advancement of social justice for the whole community[8]. (p. 9)

Which perspective dominates a governing body may vary according to the kind of school and its geographical location. As yet, there is not enough information available regarding the composition of governing bodies in different parts of the country to enable an extensive comparative analysis. However, a recent study by Thody (1989) in Leicestershire indicated that the social composition of the governing bodies in this county did not correspond to the social composition of the rest of the country as a whole. For example, 34.4% of the governors had industrial or commercial backgrounds, 35% were in education-related occupations, and the governors came predominately from social classes I to III. Furthermore, Deem's (1989) study of 15 governing bodies indicates marked differences in the composition of governing bodies with regards to gender and race/ethnicity. Deem comments, 'The majority of all governors (250 in all 15 schools) in our study are male and middle-class. One-third of the 250 are women and 7% are black or Asian' (p. 252). Women were found to be more numerous in primary school governing boards, whereas secondary schools were much more male dominated. Only 1 of the governing bodies had more female than male governors, only 3 were chaired by women (all these were primary schools), and only one board had an Asian chair. Deem suggests that, as a consequence, school governing bodies are operating very much within a white, patriarchal and middle-class framework[9].

Neutrality Is Impossible: Reflections of a Parent Governor

A governor's background will affect the perspectives she or he holds, and it seems likely that the traditionalist and utilitarian perspectives are dominant at present. Although it is not the place of this chapter to debate the merits of these differing perspectives, their existence needs to be acknowledged because they indicate that there can be no such thing as a neutral governor. This claim is supported by Tipton (1989), who provides an appraisal of her own involvement in a governors' meeting in the role of parent governor. The problems of having the interests associated with one's own child being in the school are raised to illustrate how they can induce 'tunnel vision', that is, decisions are influenced by a concern for one's own child as opposed to the interests of the children en masse. The question of personal ideology is also raised.

> Am I supposed to somehow be apolitical? . . . And should I try to appear unaligned when I have a political position? . . . As matters stand nothing is asked of a parent governor candidate other than that a short paragraph be submitted with the nomination form outlining his or her case for being elected. . . . Herein emerges the problem of closet ideologies. . . . If there is no such thing as a collective ideology that can be drawn upon for parent government, how can anyone act as a parent governor other than through his or her existing framework of thought? (pp. 40-41)

This honest appraisal indicates that, even with the best intentions, it is impossible for governors not to adhere to some perspective that frames the way they interpret events. It is interesting to consider the implications of this for PE, should the traditionalist and utilitarian perspectives come to dominate and shape the world of governors as they did in the Devon study by Golby and Brigley (1989). Significantly, both these perspectives were found to be concerned crucially with the products of education and the close monitoring and assessment of teacher performance.

Assessment of the educational process is extremely complex and difficult. As Connell (1985) reminds us, teaching is a labour process without an object. Its products are intangible and vague. Duignan (1988) emphasizes this point and argues that 'many organisations, especially human service organisations such as schools, have unclear goals, uncertain technology and fluid participation. Connections between goals and activities are difficult to establish and cause and effect relationships are tentative, at best' (p. 119). This is particularly so for physical education. How does one measure aesthetic appreciation, feelings of competence or well-being, a love of physical activity, social responsibility and so on? What does it mean to be a good physical education teacher? What does it mean to be physically educated?

Proctor (1984) has commented on the amorphous nature of PE and the problems of definition in such a diverse and multifaceted subject area. For some, in terms of accountability, the observable, identifiable products of physical education are most easily associated with physical skills and their translation into team results (see Sparkes, 1989a). In this sense, there may be strong pressures exerted in the future by some governors for PE departments to commit their energies to the production of winning school teams at the expense of the more creative, aesthetic, and less tangible aspects of their curriculum. In tandem may also come pressures to include only those aspects that are seen to have relevance to industrial needs in terms of the production of a 'healthy' worker—again at the expense of the more aesthetic elements of the physical education curriculum (see Sparkes and Dickenson, 1989). Consequently, PE would become defined as valuable only insofar as it serves ends outside of itself, and the intrinsic value of many of the activities that take place within this subject would be denied.

Some of the most highly valued outcomes of schooling and PE, however, are not amenable to simplistic quantification, and this needs to be recognized. Sadly, as schools and departments are exhorted to become more efficient, accountable and productive, the instrumental tendency inherent in the traditionalist and utilitarian perspectives is likely to grow in strength. Of course, this is not to deny that schools should make every attempt to be efficient and economically viable, but this should not be at the expense of valuable aspects of the curriculum and the quality of children's learning experiences. As Duignan (1988) recognizes,

There is a danger that if education becomes driven by economic criteria only those outcomes that are measurable will be valued. There is an even greater danger that in the present econo-political climate the worthwhile will be submerged by the immediate, by the visible, and measurable, by the politically expedient. As Beare so eloquently stated 'the problem has always been that economically driven objectives will overwhelm the delicate, sensitively educational ones'. (p. 123)

PE as a Marketing Tool:
Who Loses When Governors Want Winning Teams?

In the context of Local Financial Management, scarce resources, falling rolls, opting out, open enrolment, the increased power of governors to influence staff appointments, and the dominance of the traditionalist and utilitarian perspectives, the emphasis and purpose of many PE departments may be forced to change radically in the future. For example, PE may become valued predominately for its marketing potential as the schools in an area compete with each other to attract pupils. Browning (1989) comments,

> Most chairmen (of governors) express a distaste for the inter-school rivalry that open enrolment will generate, but nevertheless, being pragmatic creatures, several have created subcommittees responsible for this area and named them the 'Marketing the School' committee. The 'School and Community' committee was an understated version of the same thing. (p. 26)

In such a situation, it is not impossible that future appointments to PE departments could be made predominately according to the candidate's ability to contribute to competitive sport rather than to the general education of children. Job descriptions could well include extracurricular activities as an essential item without linking them to the 'directed time' of teachers' contracts. Consequently, newly appointed physical educators, along with those already employed who have career ambitions, may be vulnerable to pressures from governors to develop successful school teams during extracurricular time, that is, to provide unpaid labour beyond their contractually agreed hours. More importantly, they may feel pressured to skew their curriculum in such a way that the educational experiences of pupils in their care become impoverished in the pursuit of interschool sporting success. Regarding teacher appraisal, success and failure on the games field could become an important part of the headteacher's report to school governors. Interschool sporting success, due to its high visibility, may become the main 'product' by which the PE department is judged when staff, resources and allowances are allocated. At worst, this would foreshadow, in a thinly disguised form, the return of the 'payment by results' schemes that operated in elementary schools at the beginning of the century.

To this scenario must be added the prospect of licensed teachers. It is not impossible that governors, to save on staffing costs, may choose to employ such people to coach the school teams. Several, each with a very high level of expertise in one particular sport, could be employed for less than the price of an experienced all-round PE specialist. Many interest groups involved in sport and coaching would like access to the school curriculum (see Hardy and Sparkes, 1987). For example, Dick (1986), the National Coach for Athletics, has argued forcefully that qualified sport *coaches* should be involved as support staff within the physical education programme. As the route to becoming a licensed teacher is made progressively easier—no probationary year, the possibility of being paid the qualified-teacher rate at the employer's discretion from the day they enter school, only 2 years' successfully completed full-time higher education (see Lodge, 1989)—many more people with coaching qualifications will be available for employment in schools and, having gained qualified teacher status after 2 years, will be able to exert their own powerful influence on the form and content of the PE curriculum.

Governors' and Teachers' Work in a Wider Context

Governors, just like teachers, may be involved in social processes that have consequences beyond the level of individual awareness (see Sparkes, 1989b, 1989c). In view of this, their emerging relationship with PE teachers needs to be placed in a wider sociohistorical context. According to Smith (1989) 'There is general agreement among writers on the political sociology of education that the 1980s have seen a marked shift of power towards central government departments, at the expense of local education authorities and teachers' associations' (p. 176). As such, the transformation of the relationship between governors and teachers, from passive acquiescence in the 1960s to active intervention in the 1980s, is illustrative of a shift in the relative autonomy of schools from 'licensed autonomy' to 'regulated autonomy'. According to Dale (1979), cited in Ball (1988), licensed autonomy prevailed when

> an implicit license was granted to the education system, which was renewable on the meeting of certain conditions. Just how those conditions could be met was again subject to certain broad limitations. . . . The educational expansion of the decade from the early sixties to the early seventies stretched the terms of the education system's license to new limits. . . . The major source of teachers' authority was that they could expect to be backed up by their employers and their representatives as long as they stayed within certain implicit boundaries of curriculum, pedagogy, and evaluation. (pp. 100-105)

In contrast, Dale (1979) explains that in regulated autonomy, 'control over the education system is to become tighter, largely through the codification and monitoring of processes and practices *previously left to teachers' professional judgement*, taken on trust or hallowed by tradition' (p. 104, emphasis added). Today, it would appear that indirect rule has been replaced by direct rule. In summarizing the contemporary situation, in which the freedom of teachers to manoeuvre is greatly reduced, Ball (1988) comments, 'Choices have been removed or preempted and certain functions have been withdrawn. In effect the lines of control are now visible rather than invisible, direct rather than indirect, explicit rather than implicit' (p. 291).

The subject area of PE has developed within, and been shaped by, this changing socioeconomic climate. Hoyle (1986), in an overview of curriculum development in PE during 2 decades, has defined the period from 1966 to 1975 as the decade of 'innovation' and the years 1976 to 1985 as the decade of 'accountability'. The cultural characteristics of the former period were relative affluence, increased leisure time and options, greater autonomy of lifestyles, and a belief that those who would be affected by decisions should participate in their making. Developments in PE mirrored some of these characteristics. For example, there was a growing emphasis on recreation, there was a trend towards educational gymnastics and dance, outdoor pursuits became more prevalent, discovery learning was advocated, there were more mixed-ability classes, and pupil choice was emphasized as wider participation became a major theme. During the decade of accountability the social climate changed significantly, and direct challenges were made to the autonomy of the educational system to determine the curriculum. Hoyle argues,

> Affluence was replaced by economic stringency. Demographic changes resulted in a reduction in the allocation of public funds to education. The numbers of unemployed increased substantially. . . . A new political ideology founded on monetarism emerged, in which the market was held to ensure that all activities were judged according to their contribution to the economy, and 'enterprise' was emphasized as a cultural theme. (p. 40)

Consequently, despite the growth of examinations and the emergence of health-related fitness and aerobics within the PE curriculum, many of the innovations that were initiated in the 1960s seem likely to be reversed. Importantly, teachers' freedom to experiment has been eroded, and Hoyle (1986) stresses how the autonomy of the earlier decade has now been supplanted by control in terms of the increasing influence of central government and the increased power of the consumer to have an impact upon educational issues. Clearly, these changing political, economic and social circumstances have had a marked effect upon the educational system and those who operate within it. They will continue to do so, and Saunders (1986), in his consideration of PE in the late 1980s and the 1990s, argues, 'Some will act as constraints, few will lead to greater freedom and control. Nevertheless, the curriculum of physical education will continue to be shaped by a number of forces both inside and outside schools' (p. 10).

Whether the long-term consequences and outcomes of decisions taken by governments, in terms of their actual impact on schools, are intended or otherwise is open to debate (see Smith, 1989). The impression remains, however, that a range of events during the last decade, including the allocation of greater legal powers to governing bodies, have acted to undermine the relative autonomy of the teacher. According to Rothman (1984),

> Autonomy refers to freedom from external social control over both the internal affairs of the profession and individual behaviour of the membership.

For the collective it involves the authority to establish, monitor, and enforce its own membership criteria and standards of conduct. *Autonomy at the individual level involves discretion to define the terms, conditions, pace and content of work. Autonomy is never without limits, since many external groups have the resources to impose restraints upon any occupational group.* (p. 186, emphasis added)

The work of Templin, Savage and Hagge (1986) identifies the loss of autonomy as a key element in the ongoing deprofessionalization of physical educators in North America. As illustrated earlier, school governors are enabled, by their increased powers, to directly influence the content of the curriculum, sometimes with dramatic effect. Such direct intervention reduces teacher autonomy, which in turn undermines the image of the teacher as a dedicated and expert practitioner capable of applying specialized skills and esoteric knowledge with judgement and care, that is, a professional. Indeed, Roy (1983) sees increasing state intervention into education as a direct attack on the freedom of teachers to do their jobs and 'a threat which represents the greatest challenge to the teaching profession since the introduction of state education in 1870' (p. 4). Likewise, Simons (1988), in her consideration of the implications of the National Curriculum for teacher professionalism, expresses the fear that 'the responsibility for curriculum experimentation, development, growth and change—the hallmark of educational professionalism—will no longer be the concern of teachers, schools or localities. They are destined to become the implementers of curricula, judged nevertheless by the success of the treatments they no longer devise' (p. 80).

In view of all of this, physical educators need to be wary and make every attempt to locate the happenings in their own school within the wider social and political framework. As such, they need to be critically aware of the changing nature of their relationship with school governors and the potential consequences this may have for their teaching skills and their ability to make decisions concerning the curriculum. This changing relationship has the potential to make a profound impact upon the nature of their work in schools. In Apple's (1982) terms, 'They embody a fundamentally changed relationship between a person's labor, skills, consciousness, products, and other people' (p. 34). With the 'conservative restoration' in full swing, school governors will have a profound impact upon how teachers do their jobs and who decides whether the job has been carried out successfully. Within the analytical framework suggested by Apple and Teitelbaum (1986), governors' growing ability to control the curriculum and influence the conditions of teachers' work may be seen as part of a wider social movement involving the large-scale deskilling of teachers. They argue that deskilling occurs when

individuals cease to plan and control a large portion of their work, the skills essential to doing these tasks self-reflectively and well atrophy and are forgotten. The skills that teachers have built up over decades of hard work—setting relevant curriculum goals, establishing content, designing lessons and instructional strategies, individualized instruction based on an intimate knowledge of students' desires and needs and so on—are lost. In many ways, given the centralization of authority and control they are simply no longer needed. (p. 182)

The end result of this process is teachers as 'technicians', that is, individuals who implement in the most efficient manner a limited set of procedures to match a range of criteria that are selected and defined for them by other groups. The teacher then becomes limited to 'how to do it?' questions, rather than asking the 'why?' questions that are so essential to the development of the creative and reflective practitioner. Such deskilling, if extensive, can lead to an occupational group becoming proletarianized. The worker's control over the work process is eroded, autonomy is reduced, work becomes fragmented, there is a separation of conception from execution, the relationship between employer and employee breaks down, and management controls are strengthened as craft skills and the craft ethic decline (see Braverman, 1974; Thompson, 1989). Most importantly, proletarianization is not just a limited technical process but involves alterations in worker consciousness. According to Lawn and Ozga (1988), this process has already operated with industrial workers, and now, due to the changing nature of capital, it is the turn of white-collar and service-sector workers to be proletarianized.

Facing the Challenge:
Advocacy and the Power of Rhetoric

According to Shaw (1987, in press), the rapid and determined incursion into schooling by the central authorities has raised teachers' awareness of control. Furthermore, he suggests that the prolonged industrial dispute has made teachers more professionally, though perhaps not much more politically, aware. Indeed, Williams (1990) argues that the limited ability of the PE profession to defend itself in recent years is the result of a lack of experience and a lack of expertise in manipulating the situation to their own advantage. This is worrying because the future development of PE depends upon those who teach it becoming politically astute in order to reassert the professional nature of their work in their relationships with governors, teachers from other subject areas, senior management and local industrialists.

This will not be achieved without some form of struggle. As Lawson (1985) reminds us, 'professional status is not gained by mere self proclamation. Rather, it is achieved through social negotiations, involving contests with other aspirants and existing professions as well as would be clients' (p. 9). This struggle will include negotiations over the nature of the work process in schools and who should determine the content and delivery of the curriculum. In their relationships with governors, teachers need to skilfully deploy the ideology of professionalism to improve their conditions of service, their social status, and their occupational autonomy. Ironically, it may be the parent governors themselves who are teachers' closest allies in this struggle; the parent governors in Golby and Brigley's (1989) study indicated

> a reluctance to become too embroiled in the school curriculum. They doubt their capacity to cope with the complex and technical detail of curriculum problems. There is a widespread recognition that, while lay perspectives on the curriculum are desirable, final decisions ought to rest with professional teachers. Some express their anxiety at the steady erosion of teachers' authority in curriculum matters. (p. 47)

At present, many governors are prepared to accept that the teachers are the professionals in the educational arena. How long this perception lasts is open to question. Governors, like other members in our society, need convincing, and as I have argued elsewhere (Sparkes, 1990a), physical educators need to become effective advocates for their subject. To become an effective advocate one must become a skilful user of rhetoric. This is a form of language that is geared towards an audience and readied for an occasion or adapted to its ends. Above all else, rhetoric is about persuasion; it is a pragmatic art and operates in the province of the nonprovable, the contingent, and in the realms of judgement rather than certainty (cf. Simons, 1989; Sparkes, 1991, 1990b; Williams, 1990). Too often rhetoric is defined in pejorative terms. However, as Williams and Jenkins (1988), in their consideration of the National Curriculum proposals and PE, note,

> it should be remembered that the art of the successful educator has always included the ability to use the rhetoric of the day to his or her advantage. Those in physical education who have been successful in securing a place within TVEI initiatives have had to do so through the rhetoric of personal and social education or life skills. There is much in the current proposals which could be used to the advantage or disadvantage of physical educa-tion. . . . It is up to the physical education profession to ensure that we capitalise on the possibilities. (p. 131)

Physical educators need to be aware of the perspectives of their school governors along with those of other significant publics who are able to influence their subject in schools. Appropriate rhetorics can then be developed to align the organizational categories (internally structured forms and activities) used by teachers operating within the context of a particular subject with the institutional categories held by other significant groups, such as school governors (see Reid, 1984; Sparkes, 1990c, 1988, 1987; Sparkes et al. 1990; Williams, 1985).

If too great a mismatch occurs between the two kinds of categories, then the prospects for the survival of the subject become bleak, as the demise of Latin and Greek illustrates. Consequently, there is a need for physical educators to be aware of the rhetorics available to them. For example, Williams (1990) empha-sizes that the rhetoric of the physical is extremely powerful insofar as many others recognize that this is the one essential feature of PE that distinguishes it from other subjects. She goes on to point out that other rhetorics are available and notes, 'It is therefore important that the teacher understands not only the nature of physical education and its relation to sport and to recreation, but also the rhetoric of sport, recreation and health' (p. 5). To this must be added the moral dimension of teaching and PE's potential to contribute to a more just and equitable society.

Of course, it could be argued that such rhetorics depend upon instrumental justifications that are weak at the philosophical level of analysis. Indeed, this might well be the case, but pragmatically these forms of justification, when tailored to specific audiences, may lead to short-term gains in staffing and resources that can provide a firm foundation and an initial tactical advantage that might lead to more substantial status gains in the future. As Parry (1988) recognizes, at various times certain forms of justification are required to act as a means of self-defence or self-promotion. He comments,

> In the real world outside the door there are people who would casually disembowel the PE profession if they could. Even if some people may never be persuaded by our arguments we must seek to address the widest constituency so as to persuade more people than just ourselves of its worth. . . . The present political climate constrains us and we must act opportunistically within it to the extent that our principles allow. . . . I have no grievance against being politically astute nor against the presentation of the values of the subject to suit a particular purpose or audience. We should seize the moment and the opportunity to demonstrate instrumental value and contingent benefits if this will suit our purposes. (pp. 107-111)

Of course, this is not to suggest that individuals sell their souls on the altar of short-term gain. Nor does it excuse physical educators from engaging in some hard and serious thinking about the nature of their subject and its intrinsic justifications. Indeed, every opportunity should be taken to convince governors of the intrinsic value of the subject and to indicate to them the complexities of this subject as it is taught in schools today. The ability to understand, create and utilize a range of rhetorics is essential for physical educators in challenging and transforming the views of others. This is an important issue, and Newby (1990) reminds us that those who control the rhetoric control the higher ground. He notes,

> I think we have to gain control over our own language. Much of the rhetoric which now bespeaks the work that we do has been imposed on us from elsewhere. . . . We are easily encumbered by a discourse which belongs in the market-place and in industrial production. Talk of course delivery systems, of bolt-on components in modular programmes, of clients and providers is a far-remove from the organic language which used to characterise the discourse of teaching and learning. . . . I believe we have been brow-beaten into submitting to this DIT-speak too easily. The politics of such language runs deep: if passing governments are not pressed, when dealing with important

educational matters, to try to do so in the language of those who work with those matters daily, then they will naturally enough use language with which they are themselves more familiar—and expect us to do likewise. I'm all for refreshing the language, but not when it distorts the subject of its discourse. We need to regain control of our words. Then maybe we can feel more secure in controlling our own intentions and practices[10]. (p. 11)

Gaining control of our words will not be easy in the prevailing political climate. However, the struggle over words is crucial to how teachers define themselves and how they act in relation to others, which in turn influences the role teachers play in sculpting the educational landscape of the future and controlling their work within schools. If teachers define themselves, or let others define them, in ways that are limiting, then the chances are greatly increased that their actions and visions will also become limited.

New possibilities are opening up for physical educators in their emerging relationship with governors and other significant publics. At this stage there is everything to play for. As Williams and Jenkins (1988) remind us, 'We should bear in mind that it is apathy not hostility that is our worst enemy. We are working at a time which, while fraught with difficulty, offers unparalleled opportunity' (p. 131).

Likewise, Golby (1989) argues that as governorship moves from the ceremonial and generally supportive function it has traditionally served towards the governorship of tomorrow, new opportunities will arise. To make the best of these opportunities, physical educators need to be proactive in helping governors understand the school system, its complexities, and the nature of teaching and learning in their subject. However, if physical educators do not reassert, and provide evidence of, their professional status and expertise over others in physically educating children, then the fears expressed by Templin et al. (1986), that school PE and physical educators may become an anachronism, may materialize into a painful reality. Of course, the changing relationship between physical educators and school governors in terms of the impact it has on the nature of their work is in need of further research. How this relationship evolves, and its effects, can be unraveled only as the future unfolds. One thing is for sure: Physical education teachers cannot ignore this issue. They must confront it with a sense of political realism if they are to maintain control of their work and promote their subject in schools.

Notes

1. More detailed considerations of the many issues associated with increased centralized control of the curriculum are provided by Campbell (1989), Chitty (1989), Evans and Davies (1987), Hargreaves and Reynolds (1989), Kirk (1989), Sparkes and Dickenson (1989), Thomas (1989), and Wragg (1987).

2. The implications of introducing a marketplace philosophy to education have been discussed by Bash and Coulby (1989), Chitty (1989), Hargreaves and Reynolds (1989), Pring (1987), Saunders and Harris (1990), and Wragg (1988).

3. In relation to the policies associated with this 'third wave', Brown (1990) emphasizes that these will not only reinforce educational inequalities but actually *increase* them. He also points out that the ideology of parentocracy did not emerge as a result of a ground swell of popular demand for radical educational reform among the majority of parents. Rather, it has been the state, and not parents, that has strengthened its control over what is taught in schools.

4. From 'The Changing Nature of Teacher's Work: Reflecting on Governor Power in Different Historical Periods' by A. Sparkes, 1990, *Physical Education Review*, **13**, pp. 39-47 and from 'The Emerging Relationship Between Physical Education Teachers and School Governors: A Sociological Review' by A. Sparkes, 1990, *Physical Education Review,* **13**, pp. 128-137. Adapted by permission of the North Western Counties Physical Education Association.

5. For a more detailed analysis of the labour process, see Braverman (1974) and Thompson (1989).

6. Sally's views are presented in more detail in Sparkes (1990d, 1990e).

7. There is a powerful gender dimension to the interaction between Sally and this male governor. However, it is beyond the scope of this chapter to consider this issue in greater detail.

8. From *Parents as School Governors* (p. 11) by M. Golby and S. Brigley, 1989, Tiverton, Devon: Fair Way. Adapted by permission of Fair Way Publications.

9. The work of Deem (1989, in press) also provides powerful insights into the dynamics of how school governing bodies operate in relation to gender, class, and race/ethnicity. Within the existing frameworks for the exercise of power, it is evident that women, blacks and working-class governors of any gender and ethnicity have a difficult time getting their points of view heard or their personal agendas listened to.

10. From 'Educating Teachers: Leave Your Minds Outside the Door' by M. Newby. In *The Exeter Society for Curriculum Studies—Proceedings of the Autumn Conference 1989* (pp. 1-14) by S. Brigley (Ed.), 1990, Exeter: Exeter Society for Curriculum Studies. Adapted by permission of the Exeter Society for Curriculum Studies.

References

Apple, M. (1979). *Ideology and curriculum*. London: Routledge & Kegan Paul.

Apple, M. (1982). *Education and power*. London: ARK.

Apple, M. (1986). *Teachers and texts*. New York: Routledge & Kegan Paul.

Apple, M. (1988). Work, class and teaching. In J. Ozga (Ed.), *Schoolwork* (pp. 99-115). Lewes: Falmer Press.

Apple, M., & Teitelbaum, K. (1986). Are teachers losing control of their skills and curriculum? *Journal of Curriculum Studies*, **18**, 177-184.

Arfwedson, G. (1979). Teachers' work. In U. Lundgren & S. Patterson (Eds.), *Code, context and curriculum processes* (pp. 80-106). Stockholm: Gleerup.

Ball, S. (1988). Staff relations during the teachers' industrial action: Context, conflict and proletarianization. *British Journal of Sociology of Education*, **9**, 289-306.

Bash, L. (1989). Education goes to market. In L. Bash & D. Coulby (Eds.), *The Education Reform Act* (pp. 19-30). London: Cassell.

Bash, L., & Coulby, D. (Eds.) (1989). *The Education Reform Act*. London: Cassell.

Becker, H., Geer, B., Hughes, E., & Strauss, A. (1961). *Boys in white*. Chicago: University of Chicago Press.

Bell, L. (1986). Managing to survive in secondary school physical education. In J. Evans (Ed.), *Physical education, sport and schooling* (pp. 95-115). Lewes: Falmer Press.

Braverman, H. (1974). *Labor and monopoly capital*. London: Routledge & Kegan Paul.

Broom, D. (1989, August 28). The blackboard revolution. *The London Times*, p. 21.

Broom, D. (1990, April 19). Teachers back call for autumn strikes. *The London Times*, p. 2.

Brown, P. (1990). The 'third wave': Education and the ideology of parentocracy. *British Journal of Sociology of Education*, **11**, 65-85.

Browning, E. (1989, June 30). The spice of life. *London Times Educational Supplement*, p. 26.

Campbell, R. (1989). HMI and aspects of public policy for the primary school curriculum. In A. Hargreaves & D. Reynolds (Eds.), *Education policies: Controversies and critiques* (pp. 161-177). Lewes: Falmer Press.

Capel, S. (1989). Stress and burnout in secondary teachers: Some causal factors. In M. Cole & S. Walker (Eds.), *Teaching and stress* (pp. 36-48). Milton Keynes: Open University Press.

Chitty, C. (1989). *Towards a new education system: The victory of the new right?* Lewes: Falmer Press.

Clough, N., Lee, V., Menter, I., Trodd, T., & Whitty, G. (1989). Restructuring the education system? In L. Bash & D. Coulby (Eds.), *The Education Reform Act* (pp. 31-53). London: Cassell.

Cole, M. (1989). The politics of stress in teaching. In M. Cole & S. Walker (Eds.), *Teaching and stress* (pp. 161-170). Milton Keynes: Open University Press.

Connell, R. (1985). *Teachers' work*. London: George Allen & Unwin.

Cox, C., & Dyson, A. (Eds.) (1969a). *Fight for education: A black paper*. London: Critical Quarterly Society.

Cox, C., & Dyson, A. (Eds.) (1969b). *Black paper two: The crisis in education*. London: Critical Quarterly Society.

Dale, R. (1979). The politicisation of school deviance: Reactions to William Tyndale. In L. Barton & R. Meighan (Eds.), *Schools, pupils and deviance* (pp. 95-113). Driffield: Nafferton.

Deem, R. (1989). The new school governing bodies—are gender and race on the agenda? *Gender and Education, 1*, 247-260.

Deem, R. (in press). Governing by gender? School governing bodies after the Education Reform Act. In P. Abbot & C. Wallace (Eds.), *Gender, sexuality and power*. London: Macmillan.

Department of Education and Science. (1977). *A new partnership for our schools* (The Taylor Report). London: Her Majesty's Stationery Office.

Department of Education and Science. (1981). *The school curriculum*. London: Her Majesty's Stationery Office.

Department of Education and Science. (1985). *Better schools*. London: Her Majesty's Stationery Office.

Dick, F. (1986). Physical education and sport coaching. *British Journal of Physical Education, 17*, 199-201.

Doe, B. (1989, May 26). Rumbold lightens load on weary governors. *London Times Educational Supplement*, p. A1.

Duignan, P. (1988). The politicisation of administrative reform in Australian education. *Educational Management and Administration, 16*, 115-132.

Evans, J. (1990a). Defining a subject: The rise and rise of the new PE? *British Journal of Sociology of Education, 11*, 155-169.

Evans, J. (1990b). Ability, position and privilege in school physical education. In D. Kirk & R. Tinning (Eds.), *Physical education, curriculum and culture: Critical issues in the contemporary crisis* (pp. 139-167). Lewes: Falmer Press.

Evans, J., & Davies, B. (1987). Fixing the mix in vocational initiatives. In S. Walker & L. Barton (Eds.), *Changing policies: Changing teachers* (pp. 96-116). Milton Keynes: Open University Press.

Evans, J., & Davies, B. (1988). Introduction: Teachers, teaching and control. In J. Evans (Ed.), *Teachers, teaching and control in physical education* (pp. 1-19). Lewes: Falmer Press.

Freeman, A. (1989). Coping and SEN: Challenging idealism. In M. Cole & S. Walker (Eds.), *Teaching and stress* (pp. 48-68). Milton Keynes: Open University Press.

Golby, M. (1989). *Supporting democratic governors*. Unpublished paper, School of Education, Exeter University.

Golby, M., & Brigley, S. (1989). *Parents as school governors*. Tiverton, Devon: Fair Way.

Halpin, D. (1990). Making sense of the National Curriculum. *Forum, 32*, 36-38.

Hardy, C., & Sparkes, A. (1987). School sport and the control of the physical education curriculum. *Bulletin of Physical Education, 23*, 28-31.

Hargreaves, A., & Reynolds, D. (1989). Introduction: Decomprehensivization. In A. Hargreaves & D. Reynolds (Eds.), *Education policies: Controversies and critiques* (pp. 1-32). Lewes: Falmer Press.

Hatton, E. (1987). Hidden pedagogy as an account of pedagogical conservatism. *Journal of Curriculum Studies*, **19**, 457-470.

Hillgate Group. (1989). *Learning to teach*. London: Claridge Press.

Hoyle, E. (1986). Curriculum development in physical education 1966-1985. In *Trends and developments in physical education* (pp. 35-45). Proceedings of the 8th Commonwealth and International Conference on Sport, Physical Education, Dance, Recreation and Health. London: Spon.

Kirk, G. (1989). The growth of central influence on the curriculum. In B. Cosin, M. Flude, & M. Hales (Eds.), *School, work and equality* (pp. 12-33). Milton Keynes: Open University Press.

Kyriacou, C. (1989). The nature and prevalance of teacher stress. In M. Cole & S. Walker (Eds.), *Teaching and stress* (pp. 27-34). Milton Keynes: Open University Press.

Lawlor, S. (1990). *Teachers mistaught: Training in theories or education in subjects?* London: Centre for Policy Studies.

Lawn, M. (1987). What is the teacher's job? Work and welfare in elementary teaching, 1940-1945. In M. Lawn & G. Grace (Eds.), *Teachers: The culture and politics of work* (pp. 50-64). Lewes: Falmer Press.

Lawn, M., & Ozga, J. (1988). The educational worker? A reassessment of teachers. In J. Ozga (Ed.), *Schoolwork: Approaches to the labour process of teaching* (pp. 81-98). Milton Keynes: Open University Press.

Lawson, H. (1985). Knowledge for work in the physical education profession. *Sociology of Sport Journal*, **2**, 9-24.

Lodge, B. (1989, May 19). Probation year rule to be lifted for licensees. *London Times Educational Supplement*, p. A4.

Mahoney, T. (1988). *Governing schools: Powers, issues and practice*. London: Macmillan.

Mills, C. (1959). *The sociological imagination*. Oxford: Oxford University Press.

Newby, M. (1990). Educating teachers: Leave your minds outside the door. In Brigley (Ed.), *The Exeter Society for Curriculum Studies—Proceedings of the Autumn Conference 1989* (pp. 1-14). Exeter: Exeter Society for Curriculum Studies.

O'Keefe, D. (1990). *The wayward elite: A critique of British teacher-education*. London: Adam Smith Institute.

Parry, J. (1988). Physical education, justification and the National Curriculum. *Physical Education Review*, **11**, 106-118.

Pollard, A. (1988). Physical education, competition and control in the primary school. In J. Evans (Ed.), *Teachers, teaching and control in physical education* (pp. 109-123). Lewes: Falmer Press.

Popkewitz, T., & Lind, K. (1989). Teacher incentives as reforms: Teachers' work and the changing control mechanism in education. *Teachers College Record*, **90**, 575-594.

Price, C. (1990, May 4). True confessions. *London Times Educational Supplement*, p. C2.

Pring, R. (1987). Privatization in education. *Journal of Educational Policy*, **2**, 289-299.

Proctor, N. (1984). Problems facing physical education after the great debate. *Physical Education Review*, **7**, 4-11.

Reid, W. (1984). Curricular topics as institutional categories: Implications for theory and research in the history and sociology of school subjects. In I. Goodson & S. Ball (Eds.), *Defining the curriculum* (pp. 67-75). Lewes: Falmer Press.

Rothman, R. (1984). Deprofessionalization: The case of law in America. *Work and Occupations*, **11**, 183-206.

Roy, W. (1983). *Teaching under attack*. London: Croom Helm.

Saunders, E. (1986). Trends and developments in physical education: An overview. In *Trends and developments in physical education* (pp. 7-21). Proceedings of the 8th Commonwealth and International Conference on Sport, Physical Education, Dance, Recreation and Health. London: Spon.

Saunders, P., & Harris, C. (1990). Privatization and the consumer. *Sociology*, **24**, 57-75.

Shaw, K. (1987). Skills, control and the mass professions. *Sociological Review*, **35**, 775-794.

Shaw, K. (in press). Ideology, control and the teaching profession. *Policy and Politics*.

Sikes, P., & Aspinwall, K. (1990, April). *Time to reflect: Biographical study, personal insight and professional development*. Paper presented at the annual meeting of the American Educational Research Association, Boston, MA.

Simons, H. (1988). Teacher professionalism and the National Curriculum. In D. Lawton & C. Chitty (Eds.), *The National Curriculum* (pp. 78-90). Bedford Way Papers 33. London: Institute of Education, University of London.

Simons, H. (Ed.) (1989). *Rhetoric in the human sciences*. London: Sage.

Smith, D. (1989). Unintended transformations of control over education: A process of structuring. *British Journal of Sociology of Education*, **10**, 175-193.

Sparkes, A. (1987). Strategic rhetoric: A constraint in changing the practice of teachers. *British Journal of Sociology of Education*, **8**, 37-54.

Sparkes, A. (1988). The micropolitics of innovation in the physical education curriculum. In J. Evans (Ed.), *Teachers, teaching and control in physical education* (pp. 315-338). Lewes: Falmer Press.

Sparkes, A. (1989a). The achievement orientation and its influence upon innovation in physical education. *Physical Education Review*, **12**, 36-43.

Sparkes, A. (1989b). Culture and ideology in physical education. In T. Templin & P. Schempp (Eds.), *Socialization into physical education: Learning to teach* (pp. 315-338). Indianapolis: Benchmark Press.

Sparkes, A. (1989c). Health-related fitness and the pervasive ideology of individualism. In C. Raymond (Ed.), *Physical education today* (Perspectives 41, pp. 37-45). Exeter: University of Exeter.

Sparkes, A. (1990a). School governors and physical education in the 1990s: On the need for effective advocacy. *British Journal of Physical Education*, **21**, 236-238.

Sparkes, A. (1990b). The power of rhetoric in gaining the higher ground: Some questions. In S. Brigley (Ed.), *The Exeter Society for Curriculum Studies—Proceedings of the Autumn Conference 1989* (pp. 17-18). Exeter: Exeter Society for Curriculum Studies.

Sparkes, A. (1990c). *Curriculum change and physical education: Towards a micropolitical understanding.* Deakin: Deakin University Press.

Sparkes, A. (1990d). The changing nature of teachers' work: Reflecting on governor power in different historical periods. *Physical Education Review,* **13**, 39-47.

Sparkes, A. (1990e). The emerging relationship between physical education teachers and school governors: A sociological analysis. *Physical Education Review,* **13**, 128-137.

Sparkes, A. (1991). Towards understanding, dialogue and polyvocality in the research community: Extending the boundaries of the paradigms debate. *Journal of Teaching in Physical Education,* **10**, 103-133.

Sparkes, A., & Dickenson, B. (1989). The many faces of TVEI: Some possibilities and problems for physical education. *British Journal of Physical Education,* **20**, 31-34.

Sparkes, A., Templin, T., & Schempp, P. (1990). The problematic nature of a career in a marginal subject: Some implications for teacher education programmes. *Journal of Education for Teaching,* **16**, 3-26.

Templin, T., Savage, M., & Hagge, M. (1986). Deprofessionalization and the physical educator. In *Trends and developments in physical education* (pp. 322-327). Proceedings of the 8th Commonwealth and International Conference on Sport, Physical Education, Dance, Recreation and Health. London: Spon.

Templin, T., Sparkes, A., & Schempp, P. (in press). *Physical education teachers: A cross-cultural analysis.* Indiana: Benchmark Press.

Thody, A. (1989). Who are the governors? *Educational Management and Administration,* **17**, 139-146.

Thomas, H. (1989). Local management of schools. In B. Cosin, M. Flude, & M. Hales (Eds.), *School, work and equality* (pp. 114-122). Milton Keynes: Open University Press.

Thompson, P. (1989). *The nature of work.* London: Macmillan.

Tipton, B. (1989). Reflections of a parent governor. *Educational Management and Administration,* **17**, 39-42.

Travers, C., & Cooper, C. (1990). *Survey on occupational stress among teachers in the United Kingdom: A summary of the major findings.* Manchester: School of Management, Manchester University Institute of Science and Technology.

Williams, E. (1985). Understanding constraints on innovation in physical education. *Journal of Curriculum Studies,* **17**, 407-413.

Williams, E. (1990, January). *Physical education in the 1990s.* Paper presented at the Commonwealth and International Conference on Physical Education, Sport, Health, Dance, Recreation & Leisure. Auckland, New Zealand.

Williams, E., & Jenkins, C. (1988). Reaction to reform—the National Curriculum proposals and physical education. *Physical Education Review*, **11**, 123-132.

Wisker, J. (1989, May). *The role of the LEA in the new era.* Invited address, Summer Conference, Exeter Society for Curriculum Studies, School of Education, Exeter University.

Wragg, E. (1988). *Education in the market place: The ideology behind the 1988 education bill.* Hamilton House, London: National Union of Teachers, Jason Press.

Wragg, E. (1987). The slippery road to statethink. In P. Preece (Ed.), *Perspectives on the National Curriculum* (Perspectives 32, pp. 23-28). Exeter: University of Exeter.

Chapter 2

Physical Education and the Development of Self-Esteem in Children

Kenneth R. Fox

The self as an object of conscious thought has consistently been a central issue for philosophers, psychologists, and child developmentalists. As early as 1892, James dedicated a large portion of his psychology text to the nature of self-concept, and Cooley (1902) and Mead (1934), through symbolic interactionism, went on to describe the self in terms of an individual's social experience. Although the pervasiveness of behaviourism caused a lull in the study of self-esteem in the 1930s and 1940s, Maslow's theory of self-actualization (1954) and Erikson's work with the development of identity (1968) went on to establish the search for a sense of self as fundamental to healthy human development. In 1959, Combs and Snygg wrote, 'As the central point in the perceptual field, the phenomenal self is the point of orientation for the individual's every behaviour' (p. 145). More recently, Campbell (1984) has declared the desire to enhance self-esteem as the First Law of Human Behaviour, suggesting that motivation, beyond the basic biological requirements, can be explained by a human desire to experience good feelings about the self. Situations are constantly sought out that maximize subjective success and minimize failure.

These notions are consistent with many other theories of motivation. The appreciation that conscious thought-processes regarding the self and its abilities are responsible for directing much of our behaviour underlies self-efficacy theory (Bandura, 1982) and effectance or competence motivation theory (Harter, 1978; White, 1959). According to these theories, the view we have of ourselves and of our capabilities has a great influence over our choice of and persistence in, behaviours.

As a consequence, self-esteem as a construct has increasingly been used as the primary indicator for mental and social life adjustment. Research has indicated that self-esteem has strong associations with a host of positive achievement- and social-related behaviours. A person who is well-balanced emotionally, for example, is happier, more satisfied, less anxious, and more likely to perform well academically and physically and to demonstrate qualities such as leadership

(Wylie, 1979). This is usually accompanied by a generally higher level of well-being (Diener, 1984). Conversely, in psychiatric intervention, feelings of worthlessness are considered characteristic of psychopathology, with low levels of self-esteem closely related to depression, a sense of hopelessness and thoughts of suicide (Harter & Marold, 1990).

Self-Esteem Enhancement Through Physical Education

Given the apparent dual role of the objective self as (a) an index of emotional welfare and (b) a mediator of behaviour, it is not surprising that self-esteem has attracted the attention of educators and educational researchers. Self-esteem has been widely chosen as a worthy curricular end-product in itself, and programmes have been designed and delivered with a view to its promotion.

Rightfully, physical educators have also staked a claim in self-esteem enhancement in children. The early traditions of physical education that emerged through the British public school system were founded on a belief in the 'character-building' qualities of competitive team sport. The pervasiveness of this athleticism is still apparent today in physical education, with team sports dominating the curriculum in almost all secondary and some primary schools. Surveys published in 1974 and 1987 (Physical Education Association of Great Britain and Northern Ireland [PEA] 1987) have revealed that teachers consistently place self-realization as one of the three top priorities of their educational objectives. Also frequently included as important objectives are the promotion of related psychological constructs such as social competence, moral development and emotional stability.

The notion of self-esteem development through physical education is widespread, and Gruber (1986) has drawn attention to the fact that almost all foundational physical education texts include a section on mental health and self-esteem issues. Reports by Her Majesty's Inspectorate consistently call for greater consideration for the whole child and particularly the promotion of self-esteem in all children. Typical is a statement of aims of physical education from the recent document *Physical Education From 5 to 16* (Department of Education & Science [DES] 1989a). Among the 11 aims suggested are that physical education should foster self-esteem through the acquisition of physical competence and poise and develop self-confidence through understanding the capabilities and limitations of oneself and others (p. 2). Self-esteem-related goals are also apparent in similar documents on health education and personal and social education (DES, 1989b, 1989c). The National Curriculum objectives for physical education have yet to be announced, but input from a related working party in physical education (British Council of Physical Education, 1990) has indicated an underlying theme of personal development, confidence and achievement through the improvement of physical competencies and skills.

Psychological Theory Links Physical Activity With Self-Worth

This concern for psychological development through physical education is not unrealistic or without foundation. There are some formidable supporters outside physical education who have argued for the importance of the physical environment in the progression of self-concept. Developmentalists such as Piaget (1969) have described how the body, through its movement, serves as an instrument of cognitive development in infants and young children. White (1959) saw that healthy mental growth in the young child was, to a large degree, dependent on a sense of physical competence and control over its environment. More recently, Harter (1985a, 1985b) has provided empirical evidence to show that for young children, physical experiences provide salient information for the development of self-worth. Additionally, constructs such as body image and perceived attractiveness, which are related to physical activity, fitness, and health, are also emerging as powerful and influential determinants of self-esteem from an early age and throughout the life span.

Furthermore, the role of self-evaluation as a mediating factor in sport and exercise behaviour has been the subject of many investigations by sport psychologists. A multitude of self-constructs such as perceived competence, perceived ability, physical estimation, sport confidence, movement confidence, and self-efficacy have been studied in search of a more complete understanding of motivation in the physical setting. Some of these constructs have been used to focus on the improvement of performance in sport. More recently, there has been a trend towards the promotion of lifetime involvement in sport and exercise as leisure and health-related activity. It is clear that perceived competence in sport is closely linked to voluntary participation in sport in children (Weiss, 1987) and adults (Fox & Corbin, 1989).

The potential for the nurturing of a healthy sense of self and related behaviours through physical education appears to be impressive. From the early years, curricular experiences might be engineered that, through encounters with movement and exposure to the expertise of physical educators, will develop a sound physical self-concept and contribute to a global sense of worth. Indeed, reviews that have focused on the effect of exercise and fitness on self-esteem in adults (Sonstroem, 1984; Sonstroem & Morgan, 1989) have concluded that even a few weeks of exposure to physical activity programmes can result in improved self-esteem. Additionally, Gruber (1986), when reviewing investigations into the impact of primary school PE programmes on children's self-esteem, has reported a generally positive effect, particularly with those youngsters with initially low levels of self-esteem, with fitness-related programmes resulting in the most success.

Unfortunately, mechanisms for these changes have been difficult to isolate. Despite a proliferation of research in the 1960s and 1970s, many studies suffered from design weaknesses and vague instrumentation that lacked a firm theoretical base (Wylie, 1979). Sonstroem (1984) concluded, 'At this time it is not known why or in what manner exercise programmes affect self-esteem, or which people are responsive' (p. 150).

This absence of substantive directives from research makes curricular policy-making in physical education quite difficult. Although there is strong intuition among teachers that self- esteem can and should be enhanced by their programmes, the generally poor understanding of the complexities underlying self-esteem structure and formation tends to make the best programme design and delivery a hit-or-miss affair.

Similarly, the aims and objectives of formal curriculum documents regarding self-esteem development may be gallant and forward looking but are characteristic of the vagaries that seem to be a feature of this area. Understandably, they choose not to define or operationalize self-esteem and are unable to identify strategies for meeting self-esteem targets. At best there is an optimistic belief that kids feel better about themselves simply through exposure to achievement-related experiences in the physical domain. Studies designed to investigate the negative impact of poorly conducted PE programmes on self-esteem are not attempted, because they would be unethical. Practice and retrospective self-report strongly suggest, however, that physical education can have a depressing effect on the self-esteem of some youngsters. It is critical, therefore, that the relationship between self-esteem change and teaching styles, methods and curriculum content be better understood.

Research of the 1980s has brought a new lease of life to the study of self-esteem and related aspects of motivation. Although as yet there are no clear answers, theoretical advancements have been made that have allowed a richer insight into the content and organization of the self-esteem construct. It is the purpose of this chapter to outline some of this progress and relate it to the context of the physical education curriculum, in the hope that future programme design will be better informed. A 5-to-16 national physical education curriculum presents a golden opportunity to establish guidelines for age-appropriate experiences for our youngsters. These directives should reflect current thinking regarding the mental as well as the physical well-being of the child. Specifically, this chapter presents examples of contemporary self-esteem theory that have implications for future curriculum policy-making in physical education.

Definition of Self-Esteem

A problem that has plagued the progress of self-esteem research is the multitude of terms used and the apparent ease with which they are interchanged. Already this chapter has used the terms *self-worth*, *self-realization*, *self-actualization*, *self-concept*, and *identity*, among others, to indicate constructs used by researchers that are closely related to self-esteem. The literature is littered with many others, such as *self-acceptance* and *self-confidence*. This leads to difficulties, because often to psychologists the constructs are conceptually quite different. Specific definitions are required that are constant over time and across studies before meaningful discussion and comparison can take place. This has been dealt with elsewhere (Fox, 1988), and there now appears to be some general agreement among the two most frequently used terms. *Self-concept* merely refers to self-description, whereby a series of statements are used, such as 'I am male', 'I am a student', to formulate a multifaceted personal picture. *Self-esteem* (used in this chapter and generally elsewhere as synonymous with *self-worth*), on the other hand, carries an evaluative global judgement of self on whatever criteria the individuals in question consider important to them. Campbell (1984) describes self-esteem as 'the awareness of good possessed by oneself' (p. 9). The terms of reference for 'good' will in part be determined by pervading societal values. For instance, some Western cultures appear to be heavily dominated by measures of achievement and appearance, whereas the values of other cultures may be more deeply rooted in the quality of social or spiritual relationships. These normative influences are constantly present, so that self-esteem is rarely formulated in a social vacuum. However, there is scope for individuals to personalize what matters to them, and this will be discussed later in this chapter.

Similarly, the 'good' mentioned in the definition need not reflect the moral tone of society. Some individuals may adopt the values of alternative subgroups. In the context of physical education, for example, a youngster may choose to smoke in order to be an accepted member of a gang, and a temporary sense of worth might arise from the ability to appear 'cool'. In effect, self-esteem is about feeling an OK person and is dependent on what the individual interprets as being OK. Understanding value systems of individual children and their subgroups, as well as of the society they live in, becomes very important, as these will tend to drive behaviours.

Assessing Self-Esteem

The notion that self-esteem is made up of self-perceptions from several different domains of life has recently become well established. Traditionally, psychologists have derived self-esteem scores from paper-and-pencil inventories that have elicited responses about attributes and abilities in a wide range of settings. Self-esteem on some instruments, such as the Piers-Harris Children's Self-Concept Scale (Piers, 1969) or the Coopersmith inventory (Coopersmith, 1967), is represented by the total score of these diverse items. This approach to measurement has been heavily criticized (Harter, 1985b; Rosenberg, 1979) for its failure to take into account that individuals attach different significance to the various aspects of self in order to reach a global judgement. Rosenberg's (1965) Self-Esteem Scale has taken a different line, avoiding reference to specific domains and using general items such as 'On the whole I am satisfied with myself.' The result is an explicit global estimate of self-worth.

Self-Perception Profiles

Contemporary attempts at self-esteem assessment have combined this latter approach with self-perception profiles. These are made up of several separate subscales, each designed to tap feelings about the self in different domains of life. For instance, Harter's (1985a) Self-Perception Profile for Children includes scholastic ability, athletic competence, appearance, behavioural conduct, and social competence facets, alongside global self-worth. Research has shown that children's self-perceptions show signs of this differentiation from ages as early as 5 or 6 (Harter & Pike, 1984; Soule, Drummond, & McIntire, 1981).

Profiles become increasingly complex with cognitive maturation, so that 8 subscales for adolescents and 11 for adults are used in order to adequately represent self-perceptions. Marsh and O'Neill (1984) have found a similar need with their Self-Description Questionnaire series, which for preadolescents includes subscales for three academic areas (reading, maths and general school ability) and four nonacademic areas (peer relations, parent relations, physical appearance and physical ability). After a series of studies, Marsh and Shavelson (1985) concluded, 'Each of the studies provided clear support for the multifaceted nature of self-concept. The structure of self-concept and the relationship between self-concept and other constructs cannot be adequately understood if this multidimensionality is ignored' (p. 122).

This multidimensional approach to the study and assessment of self-esteem has allowed us to draw a much richer picture of each individual's self-perceptions. It is now possible, for example, to compare self-perceptions across subdomains and to test the contribution of each domain to global self-esteem. A youngster who feels physically competent may at the same time feel socially inept or unpopular, and this may result in lower self-esteem than might be expected, particularly if friendship is highly valued and desired.

The Physical Domain in Self-Perception

Fortunately for physical educators, the physical domain is well represented in self-perception content in young children and appears to continue throughout the life span. Typically in self-perception profiles, it has been divided into physical appearance and physical ability constructs, as these may draw quite different perceptual responses. Harter's instrument, for example, includes an athletic-competence subscale that assesses perceived ability in sport and games, and a physical-appearance subscale that taps general feelings about looks but also face and hair, height and weight. Several instruments are also available that individually assess more specific aspects of the physical self such as body cathexis (Secord & Jourard, 1953), physical ability or estimation (Sonstroem, 1976), sport confidence (Vealey, 1986), and movement confidence (Griffin & Crawford, 1989).

It is interesting to note that although perceptions of physical abilities are always present in some form, physical appearance dominates the physical self-concept and is more closely related to global self-esteem. In other words, certainly from early adolescence, youngsters are more concerned about what they physically look like than what they can physically do (Harter, 1990b). This is not surprising, as physical appearance may affect perceptions and performance in other domains, such as friendships, to a greater extent than sport competence. Some physical competencies and fitness components such as coordination, strength, and fatness are likely to be incorporated into perceptions of physical appearance. In effect, appearance represents the interface of the self with the world, and such is its importance that Harter has come to view physical appearance as the 'public' self (Harter, 1990b).

Organization of the Self-Perception Complex: The Hierarchical Model

With the recognition of the coexistence of multidimensional self-perceptions and global self-esteem, there remains the question of the relationships among different constructs and, in particular, the mechanisms by which global self-esteem promotion may be initiated through domain-specific perceptions. From a PE perspective, for instance, how does an improved sense of physical competence or fitness translate to the more stable core of self-esteem?

Self-Esteem as a Construction of Perceptions

The most appealing models to explain these relationships have been generated by theorists who see self-esteem as a construction of perceptions. These models generally represent a hierarchically organized selection of specific dimensions or categories of self that feed into a global self-construct at the apex. Epstein (1973) was among the first to propose such a structure and envisaged global self-esteem as a superordinate construct overlying four second-order dimensions— competence, moral self-approval, power, and love worthiness. The competence dimension was further divided into specific mental and physical abilities.

Shavelson, Hubner, and Stanton (1976) produced an education-oriented model that also presents an apex of global self-esteem, subsumed by academic, social, emotional, and physical domains of self-perception. These are further segmented into underlying subdomains, such as ability in English or maths in the academic domain, so that perceptions of increasing specificity and decreasing stability make up the roots. Marsh and colleagues confirmed this structure through several studies using hierarchical factor analysis techniques (see Marsh, 1987). The hierarchical nature of the structure was supported, but it appears that complex links between some domains exist, and dimensionality becomes increasingly dominant, and the hierarchical structure weakens, with age.

Physical Self-Perceptions

Our own research has been tied up with the identification of content and structure of self-perceptions in the physical domain and their relationship with global self-esteem (Fox, 1990; Fox & Corbin, 1989). Focusing initially on an American college student population, through open-ended questionnaire analysis, four subdomains of important content were identified. These were sport competence, physical conditioning and fitness, physical strength, and physical attractiveness.

The Physical Self-Perception Profile was developed, which includes 6-item subscales for each of these subdomains. A physical self-worth subscale was also added, which was seen as a construct representing the combined outcome of subdomain content in the hierarchical structure illustrated in Figure 2.1. This structure has been consistently supported in several studies using different populations across the United States. Clearly, a physical self exists by late adolescence, which although closely related to self-esteem, is a separate entity that is strongly influenced by several subdomains concerned with physical accomplishment and appearance.

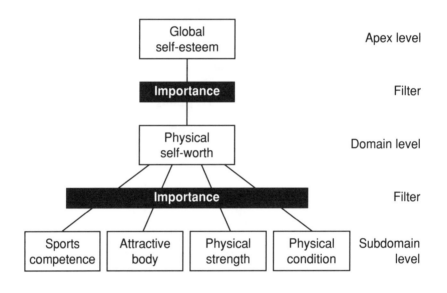

Figure 2.1   A hierarchical structure of self-perceptions in the physical domain. *Note. From The Physical Self-Perception Profile Manual* (p. 14) by K.R. Fox, 1990, DeKalb, IL: Office for Health Promotion, Northern Illinois University. Reprinted by permission.

Unfortunately, as yet this content has been less convincingly demonstrated with adolescents in Britain, as the dimensions are not clearly defined. We do not know whether this is a result of less sophisticated self-perception differentiation or problems with the inability of the measuring instrument to make the trans-Atlantic language transfer. Currently, we are attempting to identify physical self-perception content once again at source, using open-ended interviews with early adolescent British children, with a view to tracking developmental change through the teen years.

The hierarchical model is an important concept for educators, as it provides a possible mechanism by which the day-to-day occurrences at school might filter upwards to formulate and modify more global estimates of competence. Using the physical domain as an example, Figure 2.2 illustrates several levels of self-perception, which range from state ('right now') feelings of competence or adequacy to a generalized physical self-esteem and finally a global self-esteem. Although this model has not been adequately tested through research, intuitively it seems that several repeated exposures to success in football lessons would eventually produce an increased sense of football competence. This in turn, if combined with similar experiences in other sports, might promote feelings of general sport competence. This may merge with other important aspects of the physical self to produce a healthy level of physical self-worth and so on. Of course, we must bear in mind that the converse is likely to occur with repeated failure in physical education.

At least two limitations are apparent with structures such as the hierarchical model described here. First, at best they provide simplistic nomographic networks on which to view the 'typical' self-perception content of a particular group of individuals. Each structure is therefore population-specific, representing the pervading cultural or group values. It might be expected, then, that content varies between age, socioeconomic, ethnic and gender groups. Among children, besides

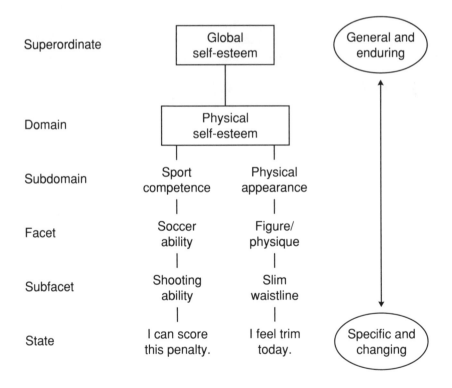

Figure 2.2 Levels of specificity of self-perception within the physical domain.

these cultural factors, there will also be content variation by developmental stage, as cognitive maturation increases the sophistication of children's ability to perceive (Harter, 1990a). Young children will function quite differently in their self-perceptions than adolescents.

Second, these networks are generally limited to explaining the competency/ adequacy base to self-esteem. Content is derived from the individual's perceptions of ability or characteristics in a variety of culturally relevant life settings. In societies that heavily value personal standards of achievement, especially where appearance also becomes a major commodity, these structures become vital to self-esteem explanations. Certainly, this seems to reflect developed societies such as the United States, as combinations of perceived competence in several domains and appearance for most individuals explain a good portion of global self-esteem variance. However, examples exist, such as the Mexican culture, that indicate that more social and less achievement-oriented bases to self-esteem exist, and one might suspect that certain Eastern cultures may be more spiritually founded. Also, other important contributors to self-esteem, such as social support and regard from others that is independent of appearance or abilities, have been identified (Harter, 1990b).

Normative content structures will remain a necessary component of self-esteem research. Without them, there is no foundational basis on which to compare individuals and populations or to confirm patterns of normal self-perception development in children. What is important to physical educators is that self-perceptions concerned with physical abilities and physical-appearance attributes appear to be consistently represented from a very early age and remain present in some form throughout the life span. They offer a possible route for the mediation of self-esteem and also appear to hold the key to achievement-seeking behaviour in the physical environment. Both have important implications for mental well-being and lifetime involvement in sport and exercise.

Personalizing Self-Perception Structures

Normative profiles and structures provide a valuable means of charting individual differences but fall short of identifying mechanisms by which the different elements contribute to self-esteem. An intuitively appealing attempt at increasing the sophistication of the hierarchical model is to introduce measures that assess the importance attached by each individual to areas of content. For example, Tony is a 14-year-old who is quite bright academically and even comes top of his class at maths. He also has high aspirations for sporting success but unfortunately limited ability, and when his attempts to be selected for the school team result in disappointment, the outcome is a lowered sense of sport competence. The high importance he attaches to this domain, combined with a low sense of ability, affects his self-esteem to a greater extent than his perceived and actual prowess in maths. His ability in maths is much less important to him, with a resultant net lowering of self-esteem. Through such use of importance weights, it is probable that youngsters, as they mature intellectually, individualize their self-esteem structures.

The concept of perceived importance has been supported by Harter (1986). Her work has built upon the formulations of James (1892), who described global self-worth in terms of the ratio of successes to aspirations. When pretensions exceed perceived levels of success, the individual would be predicted to have low levels of self-esteem. This notion has been operationalized with children and adults by assessing perceived importance for each domain of self-perception alongside competence. Domains that yield a low importance score are not considered to significantly impact on global self-esteem, but discrepancy scores are calculated by totalling the differences between importance and competence in remaining domains. These scores have been found to be highly correlated to global self-esteem, with small discrepancies associated with high levels of esteem.

An extension to this line of enquiry has been the notion of discounting. It appears that a mechanism for preserving self-esteem and progressing towards mental well-being lies in the ability to discount the importance of those domains that expose one's lack of competence. The converse of this is the low self-esteem of individuals who cannot discount those areas of life in which they feel inadequate. Associated with this mechanism may be an added emphasis, or higher importance, attached to the domains that provide a sense of competence and success. Thus, self-serving selection processes can operate whereby the aspects of life in which incompetence is experienced are eliminated and those that provide a sense of achievement are emphasized in order to maximize the chances of enhancing self-esteem (Rosenberg, 1982). Taken further, this would fit with the belief of Campbell (1984), and competence motivation in general, that situations are avoided that produce failure and that there is an attraction to settings that maximize success. This self-serving process outlines an important link between self-perception and choice of behaviours. For example, physical education programmes oriented to lifetime involvement in sport and exercise have to face the issue of developing a sense of perceived physical competence and success in all youngsters. The threat of discounting hovers for those who emerge from programmes with low perceived physical competence, the natural outcome being to turn their backs to the physical domain and seek self-gratification elsewhere.

We have utilized the notions of discrepancy and discounting in our study of physical self-perceptions (see Fox, 1990), and the link between discounting and avoidance is precisely what we have found. A perceived importance subscale was developed for each of the subdomains shown in Figure 2.1, and discrepancy scores calculated and totalled. A strong, graded relationship existed between total discrepancy in the physical domain and both physical and global self-esteem for young adult males and females. The discounting hypothesis was supported by a congruence between low competency and low importance ratings among high-self-esteem individuals. Females across several samples scored much lower than males on the sport competence subscale. However, discounting appears to operate, as low importance scores are attached to the sport subdomain, preventing a transfer of negative perceptions to more global aspects of worth—the motivational corollary being that by late adolescence most females discount, and rarely participate in, sport. A smaller percentage of males appear to do the same. On the other hand, despite the low perceived attractiveness of many females, the majority do not seem able to assign a low importance to it, so that its effect cannot be offset. It seems that discounting can only take place to the extent that powerful societal pressures allow. It is well-known that females are under greater pressure than males to be concerned about their appearance. They tend to score lower in perceived attractiveness but value it highly, with the result that their physical self-worth and self-esteem suffers.

Put together, the evidence on discrepancy and discounting suggests that the relationship between competence and self-esteem cannot be fully understood in isolation of individual, group, and cultural values. Physical education has traditionally seen its primary role as promoting physical prowess and skill. We should not expect to impact upon self-esteem through the improvement of specific physical competencies if they are neither socially nor individually sought-after commodities. Certainly, following competence motivation theory and the argument of Rosenberg and Campbell for self-serving selection processes mentioned earlier, a sense of personal achievement will draw the youngster further to the physical domain and help prevent the need for discounting and avoidance behaviour. The practical challenge then remains as to how perceptions of competence can be nurtured in students of clearly different potentials. Additionally, we should be aware that group or social values may be sufficiently powerful to overcome the competence or achievement motive. The young adolescent female who is athletically gifted and enjoying considerable success in sport, for example, may be drawn away because of her desire to be accepted as a member of a group whose value for sporting prowess in females is low.

Influencing perceptions of physical appearance offers an additional, and perhaps more powerful, route to self-esteem change. This opens up the can of worms concerned with education and its role in influencing cultural values. The rise of interest in fitness education and health-related exercise has brought increased attention to the body and its physical condition. The health lobby would argue for the need to educate and help students achieve and maintain a body that is healthy. But because appearance is such a dominating construct, particularly for adolescents, it is vital that issues such as weight management, slimness, obesity, muscularity and the cultural, as well as health, connotions they carry are carefully thought out before they are tackled in the PE programme. Calls have been made elsewhere, for example, for PE to examine its role in perpetuating cultural stereotypes (Tinning, 1985, 1990). It may be that physical education, for the sake of the mental welfare of many adolescents, must actively challenge the dominance of some values, such as slenderness, that might potentially be unhealthy for some youngsters. There is an alarming increase in the numbers of adolescents who diet unnecessarily or who are overconcerned with weight loss (Wardle & Beales, 1986), and this may well be associated with the more serious problems of bulimia and anorexia nervosa. Physical education will have to be carefully selective in the values it attempts to promote and those it decides to challenge. It may be necessary to find ways of establishing a sense of importance for aspects of health-related exercise in youngsters, for instance, while downplaying rather than reflecting the powerful media pressures for slimness.

Self-Acceptance

A closely related issue can be found in the literature on self-acceptance (Rogers, 1951; Shepard, 1979). This approach is concerned with the concept of a realistic versus an idealistic sense of self. Self-accepting people are able to work quite happily and successfully within a view of themselves that accurately portrays their weaknesses as well as their competencies. Self-acceptance also suggests that a stable core of self-esteem has been developed that is independent of high levels of achievement. Instead of adopting the escapist mode of the discounter, who is inclined to turn away from his or her inadequacies, the self-accepting individual is more likely to face up to deficiencies or limitations and work within them. A major difference then lies in the motivational consequences. The self-accepting person may continue towards relative self-improvement after failure or disappointment, whereas the discounter will tend to search elsewhere for alternative sources of competence. The notion of self-acceptance implies a move from a reliance on comparison with others as a source of competence information towards self-reference. It also suggests that a sense of competence can arise through the process of doing and accomplishing in the absence of the achievement of high normative performance standards.

Self-acceptance would appear to have important implications for physical education, especially in terms of how children will eventually view and assess their physical competence and appearance. Genetic factors tend to dominate the rate at which individual children learn physical skills and improve fitness. They also largely determine children's potential for high levels of performance in sport and fitness-related activities. Additionally, age and rate of the child's physical maturation and her or his height, weight and body type will also determine the physical capacity of the child as she or he grows into adulthood. Eventually the reality of the physical inequalities in life becomes apparent to us all. It would seem logical that achievement and success cannot be experienced by all children in a system that crystallizes these differences by frequent peer-group cross-comparison and ranking. By definition, most will not achieve high standards or excellence, and it is vital to find ways of motivating these children, especially at a time when they may be judging quite realistically that they are not one of the most able performers. A solution is required that will help teenagers accept their limitations with some degree of forgiveness while leaving the motivational door open for further involvement. This can surely be achieved only if the yardstick for success in the physical domain is self-improvement. Additionally, if physical educators wish to extend their influence to the issue of appearance, planners will have to identify means by which adolescents can be helped to accept the aspects of their bodies that they cannot change. At the same time, education can empower youngsters with expertise to tackle the aspects they might choose to improve. Certainly, self-acceptance in the physical domain appears possible for all. Many physically handicapped youngsters seem to have been successful in accepting their limitations and still manage to take on the challenge of personal improvement.

The Role of Social Support

Harter has worked for some time in the perspective of Cooley's (1902) 'looking glass self', a concept that describes the way we use the reactions and reflections of others to assess our performance and worth. It has been operationalized as the amount of social support provided an individual by classroom peers, close friends, family and significant others such as teachers. This type of support has generally been closely associated with self-esteem for young children and teenagers as well as adults. It seems that for most youngsters it is very important to feel that parents, friends and teachers are concerned with one's welfare and achievements. Often social support is expressed in terms of approval and concern for actions and performance. Words may not be sufficiently salient. For example, parents may verbally express an interest in their youngster's sport involvement, but attendance at a game may be required before a youngster is fully convinced of the parent's concern. In addition, significant others provide an important source of competence information, particularly for younger children who are unable to accurately assess the standard of their own performances. The nature and quality of this type of feedback from coaches and teachers has been shown to be very important to children's subsequent motivation and self-esteem, with positive reinforcement and constructive information being associated with higher self-esteem (Smith, Zane, Smoll, & Coppel, 1983). This has important implications for the types of teaching style adopted in PE and the nature and tone of the interface between student and teacher. It also raises the issue of the degree to which PE should take on board some concern for the type and degree of support provided by parents and peer groups. Demeaning attitudes towards clumsiness, obesity, disfigurations and physical handicaps may be more damaging for children than the physical problem itself. In an environment that is particularly public, it will be the role of the physical educator to establish accepting attitudes so that they may be adopted by others.

Philosophical calls that are related to self-acceptance have been made regarding the nature of social support provided for children. Lockhart (1989) has argued that there is a given and unquestionable value inherent in each life. Actual worth is therefore equal for each human being and cannot be altered. In contrast to the competence base of self-esteem, this unconditional-worth perspective holds that self-worth is independent of behaviour and achievement and cannot be earned, only realized and appreciated. The search for self-esteem is really concerned with recognition of this given value and so may represent that core of self-esteem that appears to underlie self-acceptance. Lockhart argues that this core of self-worth needs to be established by the unconditional regard or love of others. Put simply, youngsters require acceptance as human beings of worth regardless of what they can do or what they look like.

Some empirical support for this notion is in evidence (Harter, 1990b; Harter & Marold, 1990). A finding that depressed adolescents reported levels of social support similar to normal adolescents led Harter to look more closely to its nature. The conditionality of the social support upon meeting high performance standards and parental expectations was closely related to youngsters' feelings of self-worth. Those teenagers who felt that their competencies could not match up to their parents' aspirations had lower self-esteem and were more likely to be depressed. This may be the first empirical information indicating a phenomenon that good teachers have been aware of for some time. The quality of their relationships with children lies in their ability to convey a real concern for children's welfare, regardless of physical prowess or limitations. The early signs are that this may provide an important alternative or additional route to self-esteem promotion, particularly in youngsters who have been denied this type of support elsewhere (see Figure 2.3). Physical education teachers might have influence over children's self-esteem at several points in this diagram. They will have some command over the nature of children's exposure to physical achievement situations, which can be designed to maximize positive experiences. They will also be in a position to act as an important source of positive competence feedback. Additionally, through the quality of their relationships with children, they may be able to provide unconditional support so that children come to accept their worth, regardless of what their physical achievements or potential might be.

Developmental Changes in Self-Perceptions

Although several developmental issues have been indicated so far in this chapter, it may be helpful, before going on to discuss specific curricular implications, to outline in more detail some of the main self-perception changes that take place as children mature, particularly as they occur in the physical domain.

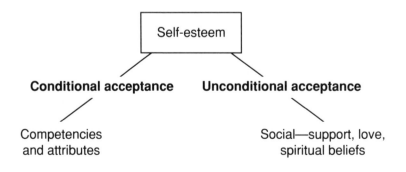

Figure 2.3 Conditional and unconditional sources of self-esteem.

For young children (5 to 8 years), the concept of self-esteem does not exist. Children of this age are capable of describing single attributes such as 'I have long hair' or behaviours such as 'I can run fast' but lack the cognitive ability to construct a single conglomeration of their diverse abilities. Children will respond with pleasantly overoptimistic estimates of their abilities, which Harter explains as a closer approximation to their *fantasied* self as opposed to their real self. It may be, as Corbin (1989) has argued, that children who have experienced a supportive upbringing have developed a core of unquestioned self-worth that, because children of this age do not yet have a concept of it, has not yet been open to challenge. Children of this age are well motivated, so this is a profitable time to expand their repertoire of physical skills. It is a time when they should be given the opportunity to establish a dynamic foundation to their physical selves, so that they feel they are equipped to take up the physical challenges of more formal sports and activities that lie ahead. Provision of positive reinforcement from parents and teachers will not only enhance children's commitment but also convey their value for particular skills and activities. Children's inability to accurately compare themselves with other children should not necessarily be compensated by realistic performance-related feedback from the teacher, parent or coach. They should be allowed to dream a little longer, so that when a youngster declares that he is much stronger than his father, then so be it. This phrase of innocent mastery involvement should be allowed to continue. What is important is the doing of the activity and the associated improvement and fun.

By middle childhood, abilities become more differentiated and classified into categories, so that the beginnings of self-esteem hierarchies are detectable. Children can provide self-ratings of reasonable accuracy, on a wide range of physical skills and sports that will depend on their exposure to physical activities, both formal and informal. A general construct of sport competence seems to exist. We are currently investigating the concept that British children of this age have of fitness attributes such as strength and stamina, as we are concerned to see at what age these are conceptualized. To date it seems that at the age of 10, they have an unsophisticated view, with fitness described by single physical competencies such as being able to run fast.

There is an increased capacity for social comparison at this age, and children quickly learn how they stand in relation to their peers. Peers themselves become important sources of competence information, but parental input also remains significant. Children begin to understand the relationships between effort and ability in assessing their physical abilities. Towards the end of this phase, for example, many will be able to determine that performance can be enhanced by effort (an unstable attribute) but is ultimately limited by ability (a more stable attribute).

By early adolescence (11 or 12 years), most children not only are reasonably familiar with their present level of competence compared to age-group norms in a wide range of physical activities, but will also have some idea of their future potential. Although at this stage, children can express a sense of esteem, they show little interest in their global selves and do not appear to understand the links among the components. It is a task of the early adolescent to begin to integrate abilities and social roles into a single identity, a feature that often results in confusion and frustration. The focus becomes introspective and there is an overconcern for the reflections of others, particularly peers. This is the time when youngsters, through a type of cost-benefit analysis of self, begin to weigh up domains of involvement against each other. Those that produce limited potential for success or a high expectancy of failure, or that involve achievement that is not highly valued by their peers, are placed under threat of being discounted. For instance, at the ages of 12 and 13, given the choice, many females decide that sport participation is unfulfilling. This could be explained by their perceived lack of competence, their perceptions that physical education interferes with their attempts to maintain an attractive appearance, or an increasing pressure to conform to other group values. Bodies and appearance are changing drastically at this time, often leading to awkwardness. Alongside a changing mental self that is becoming increasingly concerned with sexuality, this encourages further confusion. It is hardly surprising that many teenagers give their teachers conflicting identity messages. During adolescence, however, there is often still an optimistic search for opportunities to experience success and competence, and this would appear to be an appropriate time to begin to tackle the more abstract and self-relevant issues of health-related exercise and lifestyle change.

This description of developmental change has been brief and oversimplistic. However, it is clear that from a self-esteem and self-perception perspective, physical educators are faced with different priorities at different stages. Stage 1 represents a period of magic when children are unburdened by the pressures of social comparison. Programmes should utilize children's intrinsic mastery and fantasy to develop an array of physical skills and nurture creativity. Middle childhood appears to be a critical period that requires particularly thoughtful planning of curricular material and teaching methodology. It is a time when children begin to assign general labels to themselves. If they are to label themselves as physically 'OK', and the physical domain is to remain attractive to most youngsters of this age, there will be a need to establish a sense of hopefulness rather than helplessness. Towards the end of this phase, many children will come to realize their physical limitations and, unless there is appropriate intervention, will begin to look elsewhere for self-gratification.

Adolescence is a time of mental and physical turmoil requiring understanding and sensitivity from parents and teachers, particularly regarding the physical changes that are occurring. Strategies designed to help adolescents be more comfortable with their bodies are required alongside further opportunities to display competence and improvement. Because of the inward-looking nature of adolescence, this may be an ideal time to draw serious attention to the opportunities provided by sport and exercise participation for promoting their mental and physical well-being.

Conclusion

This chapter has outlined several general concepts regarding the content and mechanisms of change involved in the development of self-esteem, several of which have important implications for curricular policy in physical education:

1. Multidimensionality alerts us to the existence of the physical self as one component in the psychological makeup of children and adults. It draws attention to the full array of achievement settings and reminds us that physical education does not have sole rights to self-esteem promotion. It would be a political mistake for physical education to build its case on self-esteem promotion, because this fails to identify its unique contribution. Physical education has a primary curricular responsibility for the physical self, and physical competence, fitness and physical appearance self-attitudes have emerged as targets for intervention.

2. The hierarchical model provides us with a process by which our regular interactions with youngsters can influence more global aspects of self-esteem over time. The quality and nature of these encounters will ultimately determine whether self-perception outcomes are positive or negative.

3. The notions of perceived importance, discrepancy and discounting bring our attention to the fruitlessness of promoting physical competence without addressing youngsters' pervading value systems. This, in turn, raises important issues regarding which values physical education seeks to influence and the way it seeks to influence them.

4. The concepts of self-acceptance and unconditional social support raise our awareness that a 'marketplace' sense of self that is based solely on achievement or appearance is fraught with dangers. They identify a need for physical education to contribute by finding ways of helping children to develop an inner, stable core of self-esteem that is independent of their talents and inadequacies.

5. It is also clear that developmental changes in cognitive sophistication and self-esteem style and content have to be appreciated in order to design age-appropriate curricula in physical education.

It is hoped that this discussion has established that self-esteem promotion through physical education is a complex affair. The National Curriculum is committed to provision for the full range of abilities in children, and the promotion of mental well-being has emerged as an underlying objective. Some important issues in physical education must therefore be reconciled.

In a world where physical inequalities are a fact of life, serious thought must be given to finding the best ways to allow all children to experience continued success in the physical domain. The concepts put forward by Nicholls (1984) in the academic domain and developed in the sport domain by Duda (1989) must have considerable significance. Different goal orientations have been identified in children. By the time youngsters are in their early teens, they have the ability to utilize different sources of information for judging their competencies. An ego orientation focuses heavily on social comparison and performing better than peers. A mastery orientation is introspective and assesses personal improvement or the ability to complete increasingly demanding tasks. The ego-oriented child who has a high level of talent will tend to do well as long as comparisons remain favourable but will be discouraged after failure. The consequences for the ego-involved child who has limited ability are obvious. A strong leaning towards a mastery orientation appears to be the most effective alternative. One suspects that it is the dominant information mode for physically handicapped children who often display great courage and confidence in the physical domain. It must also have motivational significance for lifetime participation, even for those with a great deal of sport talent, as sooner or later age diminishes one's ability to compete with younger counterparts.

The development of a climate of mastery orientation in PE will require constant reinforcement for personal effort and improvement (a self-reference mode) and a downplaying of young children's tendency towards social comparison (an external-reference mode). Formalized comparisons and ranking need to be limited, at least until a mastery orientation has been internalized by children. A mastery-oriented child will eventually be empowered to take public rankings, norms, and competitive situations and translate the available information into a predominately self-referenced mode. A list of cross-country times, for example, will be interpreted in terms of past and future performances rather than current ability in relation to others. It is possible that a truly mastery-oriented child will come to judge participation itself as an important achievement, a requirement for successful maintenance of lifetime exercise patterns.

A National Curriculum should consider the style and content of outcome measures in terms of achievement theory, as these will influence teaching mode. The dangers of focusing on standards of skill or fitness attainment in the absence of sufficient time for establishing a mastery orientation are clear. Instead of attainment targets being used to form the basis of a personal goal-setting plan, they will be interpreted by children as normative statements of competence or incompetence. It seems logical, also, that programmes designed to improve psychological welfare should begin to assess outcomes involving affect, attitudes, predominant values, and self-perceptions.

A new look, in the light of this discussion, at curriculum content might reveal that different types of physical activities have greater appeal for most youngsters. Although the physical-self-perception content of British children has not been fully identified, single physical abilities, such as running fast, and sport competence seem to be represented. This will be in part a result of PE programmes. The predominance of competitive team sport in the curriculum makes it unnecessarily difficult for teachers to help many youngsters experience a sense of personal improvement and fulfillment. Activities that require a lower level of physical skill or do not require a particular physique or shape, but that are also valued by youngsters, are likely to increase the quality of the PE experience for many. Fitness-related activities such as aerobic dance, weight training and swimming for fitness provide excellent opportunities for a personal improvement orientation and also bring the added physical benefits of improved fitness.

Finally, the implications of this discussion are for a wider call for a more sensitive understanding of the mental complexities involved in children's public participation in physical activity. It emphasizes that although the identification of the most appropriate curricular content is important, ultimately teaching style and method of delivery hold the key to success. The information presented in this chapter indicates that for the sake of the mental and physical welfare of children of all physical potentials, an approach that emphasizes a mastery orientation to competence and that also encourages self-acceptance of worth is most likely to succeed.

References

Bandura, A. (1982). Self-efficacy mechanism in human agency. *American Psychologist*, **37**, 122-147.

British Council of Physical Education. (1990). *Physical Education in the National Curriculum* (Interim report). London: Physical Education Association of Great Britain and Northern Ireland.

Campbell, R.N. (1984). *The new science: Self-esteem psychology*. Lanham, MD: University Press of America.

Combs, A., & Snygg, D. (1959). *Individual behavior* (2nd ed.). New York: Harper.

Cooley, C.H. (1902). *Human nature and the social order*. New York: Scribner's.

Coopersmith, S. (1967). *The antecedents of self-esteem*. San Francisco: W.H. Freeman.

Corbin, C.B. (1989, April). *Educational perspective on self-esteem: Putting it all together for kids*. Paper presented at the Annual Convention of the American Alliance for Health, Physical Education, Recreation & Dance, Boston, MA.

Department of Education and Science. (1989a). *Physical education from 5 to 16*. London: Her Majesty's Stationery Office.

Department of Education and Science. (1989b). *Health education from 5 to 16*. London: Her Majesty's Stationery Office.

Department of Education and Science. (1989c). *Personal and social education from 5 to 16*. London: Her Majesty's Stationery Office.

Diener, E. (1984). Subjective well-being. *Psychological Bulletin*, **95**, 542-575.

Duda, J.L. (1989). Goal perspectives and behavior in sport and exercise settings. In C. Ames and M. Maehr (Eds.) *Advances in motivation and achievement* (Vol. VI) (pp. 81-115). Greenwich, CT: JAI.

Epstein, S. (1973). The self-concept revisited, or a theory of a theory. *American Psychologist*, **28**, 405-416.

Erikson, E. (1968). *Identity, youth, and crisis*. New York: Norton.

Fox, K.R. (1990). *The physical self-perception profile manual*. De Kalb, IL: Office for Health Promotion, Northern Illinois University.

Fox, K.R., & Corbin, C.B. (1989). The physical self-perception profile: Development and preliminary validation. *Journal of Sport and Exercise Psychology*, **11**, 408-430.

Griffin, N.S., & Crawford, M.E. (1989). Measurement of movement confidence with a stunt movement confidence inventory. *Journal of Sport and Exercise Psychology*, **11**, 26-40.

Gruber, J.J. (1986). Physical activity and self-esteem development in children: A meta-analysis. *American Academy of Physical Education Papers*, **19**, 30-48.

Harter, S. (1978). Effectance motivation reconsidered: Toward a developmental model. *Human Development*, **1**, 34-64.

Harter, S. (1985a). *Manual for the self-perception profile for children*. Colorado: University of Denver.

Harter, S. (1985b). Competence as a dimension of self-evaluation: Toward a comprehensive model of self-worth. In R. Leahy (Ed.), *The development of the self* (pp. 55-121). New York: Academic Press.

Harter, S. (1986). Processes underlying the construction, maintenance, and enhancement of the self-concept of children. In J. Suls & A.G. Greenwald (Eds.), *Psychological perspectives on the self: Volume 3* (pp. 137-181). Hillsdale, NJ: Erlbaum.

Harter, S. (1990a). Causes, correlates and the functional role of global self-worth: A lifespan perspective. In J. Kolligian and R. Sternberg (Eds.), *Perceptions of competence and incompetence across the lifespan* (pp. 67-98). New Haven, CT: Yale University.

Harter, S. (1990b). Developmental differences in the nature of self-representations: Implications for the understanding, assessment, and treatment of maladaptive behavior. *Cognitive Therapy and Research*, **14**, 113-142.

Harter, S., & Marold, D. (1990). A model of the determinants and mediational role of self-worth: Implications for adolescent depression and suicidal ideation. In G. Goethals & J. Strauss (Eds.), *The self: An interdisciplinary approach*. New York: Springer-Verlag.

Harter, S., & Pike, R. (1984). The pictorial scale of perceived competence and social acceptance for young children. *Child Development*, **55**, 1969-1982.

James, W. (1963). *Psychology*. New York: Fawcett. (Originally published in 1892).

Lockhart, B.D. (1989, April). *Unconditional worth: A philosophical perspective*. Paper presented at the Annual Convention of the American Alliance for Health, Physical Education, Recreation & Dance, Boston, MA.

Marsh, H.W. (1987). The hierarchical structure of self-concept and the application of hierarchical confirmatory factor analysis. *Journal of Educational Measurement*, **24**, 17-39.

Marsh, H.W., & O'Neill, R. (1984). Self-Description Questionnaire 3 (SDQ 3): The construct validity of multidimensional self-concept ratings by late adolescents. *Journal of Educational Measurement*, **21**, 153-174.

Marsh, H.W., & Shavelson, R. (1985). Self-concept: Its multi-faceted hierarchical structure. *Educational Psychologist*, **20**, 107-123.

Maslow, A. (1954). *Motivation and personality*. New York: Harper & Row.

Mead, G.H. (1934). *Mind, self, and society*. Chicago: University of Chicago.

Nicholls, J.G. (1984). Achievement motivation: Conceptions of ability, subjective experience, task choice, and performance. *Psychological Review*, **91**, 328-346.

Physical Education Association of Great Britain and Northern Ireland. (1987). *Physical education in schools*. London: Author.

Piaget, J. (1969). *Science of education and the psychology of the child*. (D. Coltman, Trans.) New York: Viking.

Piers, E. (1969). *Manual for the Piers-Harris Children's Self-Concept Scale.* Nashville: Counselor Recordings and Tests.

Rogers, C.R. (1951). *Client-centered therapy.* Boston: Houghton Mifflin.

Rosenberg, M. (1965). *Society and the adolescent self-image.* Princeton, NJ: Princeton University.

Rosenberg, M. (1979). *Conceiving the self.* New York: Basic Books.

Rosenberg, M. (1982). Psychological selectivity in self-esteem formation. In M. Rosenberg & H.B. Kaplan (Eds.), *Social psychology of the self-concept* (pp. 535-546). Arlington Heights, IL: Harlan Davidson.

Secord, P.F., & Jourard, S.M. (1953). The appraisal of body cathexis: Body cathexis and the self. *Journal of Consultant Psychology,* **17,** 343-347.

Shavelson, R.J., Hubner, J.J., & Stanton, G.C. (1976). Self-concept: Validation of construct interpretations. *Review of Educational Research,* **46,** 407-441.

Shepard, L.A. (1979). Self-acceptance: The evaluative component of the self-concept construct. *American Educational Research Journal,* **16,** 139-160.

Smith, D.E., Zane, N.W.S., Smoll, F.L., & Coppel, D.B. (1983). Behavioral assessment in youth sports: Coaching behaviors and children's attitudes. *Medicine and Science in Sports and Exercise,* **15,** 208-214.

Sonstroem, R.J. (1976). The validity of self-perceptions regarding physical and athletic ability. *Medicine and Science in Sports,* **8,** 126-132.

Sonstroem, R.J. (1984). Exercise and self-esteem. *Exercise and Sport Sciences Reviews,* **12,** 123-155.

Sonstroem, R.J., & Morgan, W.P. (1989). Exercise and self-esteem: Rationale and model. *Medicine and Science in Sports and Exercise,* **21,** 329-337.

Soule, J.C., Drummond, J., & McIntire, W.G. (1981). Dimensions of self-concept for children in kindergarten and grades 1 and 2. *Psychological Reports,* **48,** 83-88.

Tinning, R. (1985). Physical education and the cult of slenderness. *Australian Journal of Physical Education,* **107,** 10-13.

Tinning, R. (1990). *Idealogy and physical education: Opening Pandora's box.* Deakin: Deakin University Press.

Vealey, R. (1986). Conceptualization of sport confidence and competitive orientation: Preliminary investigation and instrument development. *Journal of Sport Psychology,* **8,** 221-246.

Wardle, J., & Beales, S. (1986). Restraint, body image, and food attitudes in children from 12 to 18 years. *Appetite,* **7,** 209-217.

Weiss, M. (1987). Self-esteem and achievement in children's sport and physical activity. In D. Gould & M.R. Weiss (Eds.), *Advances in pediatric sport sciences. Volume 2. Behavioral issues* (pp. 87-120). Champaign, IL: Human Kinetics.

White, R.W. (1959). Motivation reconsidered: The concept of competence. *Psychological Review,* **66,** 297-333.

Wylie, R. (1979). *The self-concept, Volume 2: Theory and research on selected topics.* Lincoln: University of Nebraska.

Chapter 3

Information Technology and Physical Education in the National Curriculum

David A. Brodie
Michael Skinsley

Information Technology

Information technology is the broad term used to describe the many ways in which modern technology, usually in the form of computers, may be used today in schools and elsewhere. It relates to a wide variety of possible operations and tasks these machines perform, such as receiving, manipulating or reproducing information and data, with a speed and accuracy only dreamed about a few years ago.

Computers can provide many benefits throughout education for both the teacher as well as the student. In a consideration of the overall potential use and development of information technology as part of the National Curriculum, the value and benefits for students must be considered alongside applications more appropriate for teachers. If teachers can become more efficient in carrying out administrative duties by using a computer, then hopefully they will be more effective in their teaching role.

The National Curriculum has recognized the value and importance of technological developments within education. Information technology has been included as part of the wider curriculum area of Technology in the new legislation. Whilst information technology undoubtedly falls within that category, there can be many links with other curriculum areas, and physical education is no exception.

Microcomputers

Not that long ago there was no 'technology' or 'computer studies' as part of the school curriculum. This relatively new initiative in education has come about with the rapid development of computers, which earlier were expensive and large, had small memories, were slow to process data and therefore were inappropriate for widespread school use. With the introduction of the microcomputer, their true value and potential in education was explored and exploited more fully.

Computers are now compact and very powerful machines. They are versatile, flexible and reliable, yet portable and robust enough to be used just as effectively in the gymnasium as in the classroom or the physical education office. Using a computer successfully and regularly no longer requires a degree in computing, knowledge of the inner workings of the computer, or the ability to write software. Any student or teacher should now be able to load and run any good software program quickly and easily.

Using a computer has been made much easier by a myriad of recent innovations—including the mouse, touch-sensitive boards (e.g. the concept keyboard), light pens, optical scanners that read text and pictures directly into the computer, floppy discs, window icon graphics, large-memory hard drives, a variety of highly versatile printers, extremely sophisticated yet user-friendly (easy-to-use) software programs, and so on. But what brought computer technology within reach of most people for the first time was the microcomputer's small size and relatively low price. These also brought computers within the reach of education. A deliberate promotion by the government to provide every school with a computer in the early 1980s started the move towards today's information technology.

Computers in Physical Education— Some Frustrations and Advantages

In addition to the standard frustrations any microcomputer user can expect to encounter—such as coveted software that's incompatible with one's brand of computer, huge chunks of data lost because of a power failure or hitting the wrong key, days of downtime while waiting for repairs to be made—some PE computer users also have the somewhat unique frustration of the fact that damp air in offices near the swimming pool can cause electrical disturbances that make the computer unusable.

These frustrations have to be weighed against the advantages of introducing and regularly using computers for physical education purposes. Considerable savings in time can be achieved once a system is established, particularly for the administration aspects of running physical education.

PE teaching can be enhanced through a range of programs to provide variety in our teaching styles. Colourful graphics, diagrams, text, sound and movement maintain students' attention. Storing and analysing student information on computer is more effective than keeping such data on record cards or in mark books. Reasonably inexpensive sensors that collect data for direct input and analysis have opened up new possibilities within our curriculum area in conjunction with other subjects such as science. There is no end to the possibilities of incorporating information technology into physical education, and teachers should be encouraged to be innovative in their approach and not close their minds to any new ideas.

Information Technology in the National Curriculum

Serious progress in the use of information technology within physical education, especially in schools, is quite recent. However, computer programs were being used regularly and successfully in physical education long before the introduction of the National Curriculum, and many of these applications are now able to contribute directly to the attainment target (AT) and programmes of study for information technology.

The AT for Information Technology in the National Curriculum requires that students should be able to '(a) communicate and handle information; (b) design, develop, explore and evaluate models of real or imaginary situations; (c) measure and control physical variables and movement. They should be able to make informed judgements about the application and importance of information technology, and its effect on the quality of life' (Department of Education and Science [DES] 1990).

There are 10 levels of attainment that apply to all pupils from the age of 5 to 16 years of age. They range from a simple ability to work with a computer, at level 1, to a discussion of the environmental, ethical, moral and social issues raised by information technology, at level 10.

The programmes of study associated with the attainment target are designed to develop in a student elements of confidence, satisfaction, flexibility, perseverance, and a broader understanding of the use and effect of information technology. In addition, it should enable students to become familiar with the keyboard and be more responsible for their own learning.

Only two specific examples of work are quoted in the AT that relate directly to physical education: a data-handling program for processing the results of sport day (level 6) and a program to trace the trajectory of a tennis ball (level 9). However, examples of work associated with PE could be incorporated throughout the programmes of study to help in the achievement of the levels of attainment at each of the Key Stages. For example, when using word processors to input, store and retrieve information, students could write an article about their experiences in a sporting activity or in a PE lesson. Individual performance achievements in the gym, or the track, and so on could be collected, entered and integrated through an appropriate computer database.

The use of word processors and databases appears at several levels, becoming more complex as the students get older. Even by the age of 7 years most pupils will be expected to have experienced both of these applications in a simple form. Many examples of how physical education data can be used for these two applications are described in a later section of this chapter.

As students get older they will be expected to know and understand more about sensors, data-logging devices, computer-aided design and simulation. These can all be illustrated through examples in physical education. A cross-curricular project could involve making a device using an interrupted light beam to record the time taken for a student to complete a run. Body sensors detecting heart and breathing rates can be used as examples of data-logging equipment. Computer-aided design programs could be used to design sport facilities, a fitness or weights room, or the layout of gymnastic equipment for a movement sequence. Simulation can provide experience with alternative situations that might otherwise be dangerous or expensive. Some of the newer games programs (for example, for playing golf) can provide a realistic background for discussion (e.g. on the type of approach shot, club selection, or tactics to employ). They will not replace the actual physical experience (e.g. of hitting a ball), but they can provide some learning about the game in the space of a lesson without the student leaving the school.

Teachers will need to continually reappraise their teaching styles and their curriculum content as new technology becomes available or as new software is developed. Information technology in education is here to stay, and a rapid expansion of suitable hardware and software can be expected in schools in the future. Each teacher must consider the extent to which information technology can best fit into her or his way of teaching and organizing physical education. Not every application that follows will be appropriate to each teacher or school, but all teachers and students will benefit by the introduction of some of them.

Current Applications of Information Technology in Physical Education

All of the applications listed here have a physical education potential, although only some are suitable for use by students as part of the National Curriculum. Some guidance is given where particular programs could form a part of the programmes of study and at what level. Some of the software described is particularly relevant only for administration, some for teaching and learning purposes. It is left to the readers to judge which may be the most appropriate for them in their school situations. Where a program is described, it does not follow that it is available for every computer (one of those frustrations). Further information concerning individual software is being updated regularly and may be obtained from the second author of this chapter.

Word Processing

When teachers start to use a computer, a word processor is the application they are most likely to use. It helps to develop typing skills and provides an awareness of the position of keys. Any teacher, with a little practice, can soon become familiar with the word processor and learn to write, store, print and reproduce a variety of printed material. Which computer is being used, or which word processor, does not matter. The outcome will be the same—a well-presented, neat looking, clear piece of information.

A physical education department generates a great deal of printed work throughout the school year. This could range from an information sheet for a specific activity, such as a swimming gala, to a handbook containing the principles and practices of running the physical education department. Letters to parents, minutes of meetings, work sheets, team sheets, recording sheets, event programmes and so on, can all be easily produced and stored. The format of the annual swimming gala may not change from year to year, and so the information sheet will remain the same the next time it is needed. When this work is stored on a disc, it takes only minutes to retrieve it, change the date, print it out and photocopy it, without having to type it out once more.

Once one is familiar with the workings of a word processor, one can prepare many other items, such as letter headings ready to load and commence typing. For those who might be a secretary of a school sport association and need to circulate information regularly, a great deal of time will be saved by keyboarding in, and storing on disc, a series of school address labels.

By attainment level 2 for information technology, students must be able to store and retrieve information using a word processor package. It is a target that all children by the age of 11 should have achieved, although some will achieve it much earlier. By level 9, students would be expected to not only use a desktop publishing package, which integrates word-processed text, numerical data and graphics, but also to evaluate the package and assess its efficiency, ease of implementation and appropriateness.

Throughout all these stages students will be producing word-processed material in different forms, such as poems, essays, class newsletters, newspaper articles and contributions to class books. Those taking the General Certificate of Secondary Education (GCSE) examination courses should consider submitting their coursework word processed. Wherever possible, students should be encouraged to prepare on the word processor information related to their experiences and knowledge of physical education.

Database

In physical education we can become overwhelmed by vast quantities of data that are recorded but seldom analysed fully. A computer database offers the potential to manipulate and study these data more effectively. A general database will be available for all makes of computer, and although there will be slight differences in the way they operate, the principles will be the same. The user initially has to set up the program according to his or her needs.

If we wish to enter the names of a class of students and their times to run 100 metres, we would set up two fields (items of information) and name them ('name' and 'time'). The database will allow us to sort, select and in some cases statistically analyse the material before reproducing it in a numerical, alphabetical or graphical format. From our class data we could print out a list according to time taken or an alphabetical list of names with times or compare times through a variety of charts and graphs. Some databases are already programmed with an ability to perform certain basic statistical analyses of numerical data in the form of the mean, standard deviation, variance, maximum and minimum value, range and coefficient of variation. Others allow you to write your own program of more advanced statistics if you have the programming expertise and ability.

'The organiser of a cross country event received 500 entries for the senior men's race. He allocated each runner a number and wrote out by hand the list of names in numerical order. When the runners came to collect their numbers, he would need the names in alphabetical order. It took the organiser a whole day to reorganise the 500 names into alphabetical order and re-write the list. When entered into a database the computer took 53 seconds to sort out the names and a further five minutes to print out the list!'

This ability to sort and analyse within seconds is of value to students as well as teachers. Using the above example, the teacher could enter the information to find the mean time for her or his class or to assess whether there is a normal distribution within the group by viewing a bar chart of the performances. Similarly, a student engaged in producing a piece of coursework for a GCSE Physical Education examination could collect some performance data, enter them into a database, produce a detailed analysis and write the script using a word processor.

The first mention of a database in the National Curriculum is at level 3, where it is suggested that the structure is prepared in advance. Data about the number of gold medals different countries were collecting at a Games event could be entered, retrieved and compared. By levels 7 and 8, students should be accessing as well as evaluating the ease of analysis of large databases. Here a large library or careers database could be used to search for sport-related information.

Spreadsheet

With the introduction of Local Management of Schools (LMS), all teachers have to be more financially accountable for their spending and maintenance of their departmental stock. A spreadsheet can assist considerably with this administrative task. The spreadsheet can be set up like a database, according to the needs of the user. Items of equipment can be recorded along with the quantity held, new items purchased and the cost of each item. A series of mathematical formulae can be inserted to multiply the number of items with their cost and insert that figure into a new column. Similarly, calculations can be made down columns or along rows so that overall totals can be automatically processed by the computer.

Students are not likely to investigate the use of spreadsheets until key stage 3, after the age of 11. This is partly because of the more complex operations that can be built into a spreadsheet, where students would have to define or change the way information is grouped into columns.

A teacher who has volunteered her or his services as treasurer for a school sport association would find the spreadsheet, or the similar bank account computer programs, of assistance in maintaining the accounts.

Electronic Mail and Viewdata Systems

A computer can be connected to a modem, which is an electronic device that enables communication between computers through the telephone lines. This capability enables both teachers and students to exchange information, around the world if necessary, more quickly than by traditional communication methods. The system can be used effectively as either an electronic mailing facility or a resource base.

A message may be sent by electronic mail from one school to another, perhaps arranging or confirming fixtures. A printed copy of that message can be produced, and an immediate reply can be returned. Through the same system, access can be made into various resource databases. For instance, the Campus 2000 system has a sport database, called SPORTNET, that holds details about various organizations, including the Physical Education Association. Access can be gained into other even larger databases to obtain information on teaching, coaching, facilities, equipment, and so on.

It has to be remembered that using these systems costs money because they use the telephone, although many are charged at only local rates. The use of electronic mail is not a requirement of the National Curriculum, although there could be many reasons students might wish to communicate with students from other schools or countries as part of the overall information technology education.

Another form of communication can be achieved through the use of a viewdata system, which is similar in appearance and function to the CEEFAX and ORACLE system on television, where up-to-date information is displayed on a number of pages that can be controlled by the user. The operation of this system begins with a number of pages being prepared and stored on disc. These pages can be sent out to a number of terminals to display that information. These terminals can operate under remote control and be there just for display, like the traffic information screens at the motorway services. Or they could be controlled by the public to retrieve only the information they wanted to see. The terminals could be sited within one building or, as in Coventry, they could be situated in all the community schools to inform students and adults of the sporting activities that are available and operating. A simple numerical keypad would be all that is required to allow the public to select information from a menu of choices.

It is suggested that students could select and use viewdata software to provide information about local amenities, which could include all the sport facilities. This appears at level 8 as an example of capturing and storing data.

Analysis Programs

Teachers and students can use a wide variety of analysis programs that have been written specifically for physical education and sporting activities, particularly to produce neatly printed results faster and more accurately. Events such as cross-country, athletics, swimming, knock-out or league competitions, whether at local, county or even national level, all benefit from a computerized results service.

Preparation before the event is essential when there is ample time to enter into the computer names or details of teams and events. The less there is to process on the day, the better. Programs are now available to receive entries, sort according to age group and event, and print out recording/results sheets with competitors named and ordered in lanes where appropriate. When heats or semifinals are required, the computer will select those who qualify and reissue new recording sheets. In timed events, those with the fastest times will be allocated lanes 4 and 5 if there are eight lanes, with the slowest being given lanes 1 and 8. What occurs in the Olympics can also apply at a school event.

A different form of analysis can occur when computers are set up in the gymnasium during fitness testing. As soon as students complete a fitness test, they can enter their own data into a computer and have it analysed and printed out immediately. This releases the teacher from often complex and lengthy calculations either during or after the lesson. Programs are used regularly by pupils to analyse the JCR test or the 20-metre shuttle-run test. A more comprehensive computerized fitness test, which has been especially designed to appeal to children (see Figure 3.1), has been produced at Texas Christian and Northern Illinois Universities and marketed by the American Alliance for Health, Physical Education, Recreation and Dance.

Health fitness profile   **Age: 14**

	Distance run	Skinfold	Sit-ups	Sit-and-reach
Terrific!				★
Getting there!				
Work harder!	★			
Need lots of work!		★	★	
Test score	7:30	45.0	34	45
percentile	39	3	7	86

Figure 3.1   AAHPERD Health Related Physical Fitness Test computer output.

Another health-related application, produced by Griffin and George, Ltd., allows the input of up to four physiological variables to a 'black box' unit worn on the belt. The accompanying software uses animated graphics to present the data in a form of interest to students. Similarly, the heart's electrical signal is transmitted to a watch-size recorder strapped to the wrist in the Sport Tester unit. The heart rate can be recorded for several hours and then either replayed in beats per minute on the watch face or downloaded into a computer to show heart rates over time in graphical format, as shown in Figure 3.2.

Physical education teachers can reduce their time spent on administration by using analysis programs to process student information. These data can be ordered into any grouping, saved on disc and printed out for purposes such as the registration of teaching groups or for team selection. The stored data can also be used in some of the other event-analysis programs already mentioned, thereby avoiding the necessity to keep writing out student names. Such a system is used, for example, when running an options in physical education analysis program. Here choices made by pupils are fed into the computer, which produces a swift and accurate numerical analysis. If too many or too few students have opted for certain activities, changes can be made before printing the final selection in the form of a named group for each activity and a list of student choices.

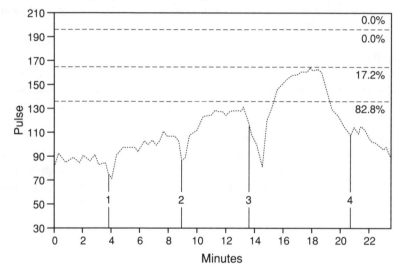

Figure 3.2   Graphical printout of heart rate against time from a Sport Tester recording.

Assessment and Evaluation

All educational establishments have become more deeply involved with the evaluation and recording of student achievement. The assessment and recording of levels of attainment achieved in the National Curriculum are now an additional feature of that process. Many different computer-based systems have been developed to try to provide a better system for preparing and producing the final document. Some programs operate on the word processing principle, whilst others use a system of selecting appropriate phrases from a prepared bank of predetermined written comments.

The advantage of computer-prepared assessment is that the data can be quickly recalled, unlike most of the traditional handwritten school reports, which are often left in office filing cabinets. When such data are stored over a number of years, the computer can produce an overall profile of achievement.

Some of these programs can be adapted to produce a 5-year fitness profile for secondary pupils based upon data collected from a health-related fitness programme.

Computer-Assisted Learning

Computer-assisted learning (CAL) has been demonstrated to enhance the learning capabilities of children within physical education lessons. A recent study (Skinsley & Brodie, 1990) using CAL was found to be particularly effective when teaching badminton to low-achieving students. They made more progress in relative terms than other children of the same age. The program was enhanced considerably by using three-dimensional graphics as opposed to the more easily programmed two-dimensional version.

The use of the reaction-test programs can open a discussion and study on the importance of the nature and type of responses vital to successful performance in different sports. Testing girls on a simple visual and then audio reaction test produced a better response to the visual stimulus by the netball players, whilst the swimmers responded better to the sound. For that GCSE group it provided a debate based upon experience and factual information that would have been difficult to provide as effectively in any other way.

The teaching of aspects of anatomy and physiology can be improved by using the most appropriate sections of the many science-based computer programs now available on the human body. They contain graphical representation and factual information about such matters as the skeleton, heart and lungs, and digestive system.

Future Applications of Information Technology in Physical Education

Information technology in physical education has in many cases been initiated within higher education and subsequently has been taken up in schools. However, some teachers of physical education have been increasingly generating their own 'designer' software to suit specific applications. It has been shown (Skinsley, 1991) that the level of computer awareness and experience amongst teachers of physical education is very low (13.6%). As teachers become more confident and competent in using the technology, the demand will grow for good quality software.

National Governing Sporting Bodies have appreciated that commissioning information technology material is one way of keeping schools abreast of developments in their sport. Computer-assisted learning is recognized by organizations such as the Badminton Association of England as an effective method of enhancing teaching. The National Coaching Foundation is supporting and encouraging the development of computer software to assist in event and game analysis. Although the research is at national level at present, there is no reason why such techniques should not be available for schools in the future.

There have been such quantum leaps in technology that hardware is now both more powerful and smaller in size. It must be expected that further advancements will lead to even smaller yet more powerful computers with an ability to communicate with a whole range of other technological devices. This means that such equipment will be in regular use in the gymnasium, on the games field, attached to the person, or even sewn under the skin!

The leading-edge technology of a few years ago, which saw individual heart beats being recorded onto cassette tape and played back at 60 times real speed, is now outmoded. Current electronic circuitry allows a 24-hour heart record to be placed on a credit-card-size piece of plastic and scanned automatically for arrhythmias.

For predictions of future applications of information technology in schools, it is necessary to examine some of the current applications in higher education. Whilst some of the following possible applications may seem well removed from the current school situation, it must be remembered that it is not long ago that the idea of a physical education teacher using a computer would have been laughed at.

Interactive Videodisc

On a special hard disc, the size of a long-playing record, it is now possible to hold a combination of text, graphics, pictures and active video material—whole encyclopaedias are available in interactive videodisc format. The interactive capability means that it is possible within seconds to obtain written, diagrammatic, pictorial and photographic information on any chosen subject. The Doomsday project involved children across the country in providing information about their local environment. Using two videodiscs, it is now possible to access a wide range of information, from health statistics to street maps, from sporting organizations to details of churches.

Future projects could include the development of a range of teaching and coaching videodiscs for every sport. They could provide an enhanced version of the current CAL programs; the best video material could be studied in real time, slow motion, or frame by frame. Such discs would incorporate the latest ideas in teaching and coaching techniques.

The potential of interactive videodiscs for sport and physical education is vast; instructional and educational materials are the obvious application. To develop any CAL or videodisc material, one needs an individual who is intimately aware of the teaching process to work in conjunction with a computer programmer. Interactive videodisc applications are limited not by the technology but by the initiation cost of the disc.

Smartcards

Cards of credit-card size on which information can be stored will become increasingly used in future. Information about sport club membership can be stored electronically and read at points of entry or sale. Charges or fees can be deducted from a bank balance following the current 'Switch' card principle, thus reducing the need to carry as much money and reducing the prospect of theft. Entry to a sport centre can be controlled using a Smartcard, giving access only to authorized users. Squash courts can be booked and paid for using the same card, usage surveys can be undertaken at the same time, and it could even be used to record and modify training procedures on a range of fitness equipment.

Students attending schools in the future may be issued these cards to register themselves on classroom terminals as well as to gain access to certain specialist timetabled facilities, including sport facilities. They may even hold personal best performances in a number of skills or activities as well as personal medical and family details in the event of an accident or emergency.

Televised Sport

Information technology has enhanced spectator interest in televised sport with computer-generated scorecards in cricket, player profiles at the touch of a director's button, computer graphics used to illustrate territorial play in rugby or the lie of a ball in golf. Miniature cameras placed in the helmet of a racing driver, on the cap of the cox of a rowing eight or attached to the stumps at a test match all improve interest in the game.

The availability of data on television with CEEFAX or ORACLE is now commonplace, and a similar remote-control handset is used in Canada to provide a range of options for certain sports: Four buttons control the alternatives of

1. the normal camera position,
2. a camera on one specific player at all times,
3. a camera tracking another specified player, and
4. a 10-second delay.

This means that a spectator watching the game on television can observe an ice hockey game, note a player who has been involved in a specific incident and produce a personal 'action replay' of the incident by pressing the appropriate button on the remote control. Although this style of television viewing is still in its infancy, the prospect of coaches, managers, players, teachers, students and the general public able to obtain detailed analysis of play is fascinating.

Kinematics

The study of the mechanics of movement using high-speed film or video is enhanced considerably if computers are used to analyse the motion in more detail. KINEMAN software produced by Williams and Davis (1990) provides information on joint positions, angles, velocity, acceleration, loci of anatomical landmarks and centres of gravity. The physical activity is often videoed and replayed through a large monitor so that a specific anatomical landmark (e.g. the hip) or a joint complex (e.g. wrist, elbow, shoulder) can be identified clearly. These positions are digitized using either a sonic digitizer or a mouse-driven cursor, and the coordinates are stored in the computer. Subsequent analysis can produce single-frame or multiple-frame reconstructions of the human body, usually in the form of stick figures. Further computations then generate graphs of the various parameters over time, which can be used to understand more about the activity with subsequent improvement in technique.

An example of the application of KINEMAN is provided by Williams and Riley (1990) showing the effects of relationship play on movement control for children with severe learning difficulties.

Most of the work to date has been using two-dimensional images, but with additional cameras and processing ability in microcomputers, three-dimensional analyses are becoming more common. Now that these computer techniques have been redesigned around low-cost microcomputers of the type one would commonly find in schools (e.g. BBC Archimedes), the potential for sporting applications increases dramatically.

Kinetics

Kinetics involves direct or indirect measurement of energy in movement (e.g. in human movement), a good example being the ground reaction forces measured during gait. As a foot is placed on some type of force sensor, such as a force plate or pedobarograph, the transducers produce electronic signals that are stored in the computer's memory. These can then be displayed as graphs over time to demonstrate different aspects of gait, as shown in Figure 3.3.

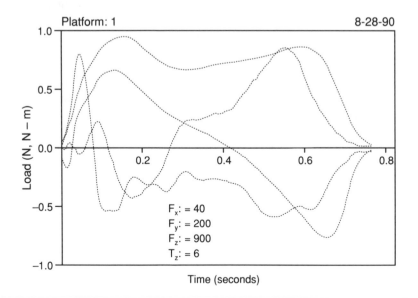

Figure 3.3 Graphical output of forces and torque against time taken from a force plate.

The metabolic measurements in ergometric tests, such as exercise on a treadmill, can also use computers to generate the data in tabular form. Many high-priced metabolic analysers will produce graphs of such things as oxygen consumption against fraction of carbon dioxide in expired air, or heart rate against time. Although these will be outside the price range of most schools, the basic principle applies. Any biological measure that can be made to generate an analog electrical signal via a transducer can be displayed in digital format. For example, a sensitive thermister placed on the upper lip will detect the change in temperature caused by heated air passing from the nose. The thermister will be capable of producing a changing electrical signal responding to the breathing frequency, and this could be faithfully recorded via an analog-to-digital converter as a breathing rate. This technology could be the basis of a school project combining Craft, Design, and Technology (CDT) and computer studies and exemplifies cross-curricular involvement.

Timing and Notation

Timing is the essence of many aspects of sport and becomes increasingly important not just for athletic records but also for pace judgement in training. Computers will be used to present work/recovery periods in interval training, to show lap times and to optimize training conditions. Some training pools are fitted with underwater lights at metre intervals that can be preset to come on at exactly the required swimming pace.

The in-built clock of the microcomputer would be used in conjunction with methods of notation so that game analysis can be undertaken. One effective method is to use a touch-sensitive, or 'concept', keyboard. For example, part of a concept keyboard could represent areas of a soccer pitch. Other parts of the board would represent incidents in the game, such as the player in possession, a foul or a shot at goal. The appropriate area of the keyboard is touched as the geography and the style of the game dictates, and all the data is stored for later processing. The sequence of play can then be established in an objective manner, and the perceptions of the players and manager can either be supported or disproved by the evidence provided by the computer.

As voice recognition units become more common, simple terms as in a television commentary could be used to provide computerized details of a soccer match. Detailed playing patterns of teams could be built up to provide an invaluable resource for team management and opposition alike.

Energy Control

Most sport centres and gymnasia are costly in terms of running, maintenance and general recurrent costs, especially heating and lighting. Computer technology can be used with advantage to monitor heating, lighting, water dosages, air-flow rates, humidity, and so on, and would identify wastage, peak and off-peak usages and misfit between ambient conditions and client comfort. A feedback loop that enables management to control optimum conditions will most probably reduce wastage and repay the original investment in the capital equipment.

Sport Discus

In many levels of education, the ability to search for information rapidly and with authority is a boon. As the style of the National Curriculum becomes more investigative and project based, it is helpful to be able to have an overview of a field of study. This can be achieved most succinctly by reviewing the literature using a CD ROM database. Silver Platter is one of the companies manufacturing these, and as the name suggests, the data are stored on disc similar to a compact disc. The data, with many thousands of references per disc, are accessed by using key words recognized by the system's thesaurus. For medical information, the MEDLINE Silver Platter uses the *Index Medicus* thesaurus, but for sporting applications the Sports Discus database is the most useful. This is based on the Coaching Association of Canada's holding of journals and is very comprehensive. So, using the FIND command (see Figure 3.4), one would input key words such as 'games' and 'curriculum' and 'children' to obtain articles relating to games activities within the National Curriculum.

The key words can be adjusted until a reasonable number of references are indicated, and the user can then read details on the terminal or have a permanent record of the full reference title and abstract from the printer. With practice the whole process takes little longer than 30 minutes and, after the initial capital

SilverPlatter		MEDLINE <R> 1989	F10=Commands F1=Help
No.	Records	Request	
#1	89	Dyslexia	
#2	1730	Learning	
#3	247	Disabilities	
#4	93	Learning disabilities	
#5	89	Dyslexia	
#6	1730	Learning	
#7	247	Disabilities	
#8	167	Dyslexia or (learning disabilities)	
#9	167	#1 or #4	
#10	17173	Adolescen*	
#11	50	#9 and Adolescen*	
#12	187006	LA=English	
#13	48	#11 and LA=English	

FIND: __

Type search then Enter (↵).   To see records use Show (F4).   To print use (F6)

Figure 3.4 A typical FIND screen using a CD ROM system of literature retrieval. *Note.* From *Getting Started* by Seif/Mann Associates, Inc. Copyright 1988 by Silver Platter International. Reprinted by permission.

costs, saves considerably on the telephone charges that were a feature of previous computer retrieval systems.

Conclusion

Advanced technology, especially when sale volumes are low, can be very costly. This can reduce the opportunities for involvement from public-sector institutions such as schools. The future will therefore require a compromise between developing information technology and cost, particularly if school-aged students are to experience the opportunities that will soon become available.

Almost every day new applications of information technology are seen. Just as the military and space exploration requirements have benefitted health and other aspects of science, physical education can gain from general computing developments. Environmental control, finances, information retrieval, measurement accuracy, training methodology, maintenance of student interest and immediate knowledge of results are all examples of how the computer can interface with physical education. Computers are now part of our culture, and even if taking them into the gymnasium is still uncommon, their potential use in many spheres of physical activity presents an exciting challenge for future directions in physical education.

References

Department of Education and Science. (1990). *Technology in the National Curriculum*. London: Her Majesty's Stationery Office.

Skinsley, M. (1991). *Information technology and physical education: An empirical study for teachers and children*. Unpublished Master's Thesis, University of Liverpool.

Skinsley, M., & Brodie, D.A. (1990). A study of the effectiveness of computer-assisted learning in physical education. *British Journal of Physical Education Research Supplement*, 7, 14-16.

Williams, J.G., & Davis, M.J. (1990). KINEMAN: A microcomputer-based video digitising system for movement analysis. *Physiotherapy*, 76, 353-356.

Williams, J.G., & Riley, S. (1990). Video motion analysis of the effects of 'relationship-play' on gross motor control in children with severe learning difficulties. *Physical Education Review*, 13, 151-155.

Chapter 4

Health-Related Physical Activity in the National Curriculum

Neil Armstrong
Stuart Biddle

Failure to protect the physical, mental and emotional development of children is the principal means by which humanity's difficulties are compounded and its problems perpetuated. (Grant, 1990, p. 7)

This may seem to be a rather dramatic quotation with which to open a paper on the physical activity and health of children in Western society, particularly as Grant (1990) was referring specifically to children from the third world. Nevertheless, the changing trends of human mortality and morbidity in the 20th century necessitate a close look at the way adults involve themselves in physical activities and whether there are lessons to be learned, at least from a health perspective, for children's education and lifestyles.

It is now well documented that the major public health problems of our society are degenerative, or lifestyle, problems rather than infectious diseases (Powell, 1988). If this is the case, it has important implications for the process of educating children about lifestyle and health habits. Recent evidence, to be reviewed later in this chapter, shows that physical activity can be an important part of this process.

Given the evidence on physical activity and health from epidemiology, medicine and public health (Powell, 1988), has the wider community sought to bring about a greater emphasis on preventive medicine? If so, has the physical education profession changed to accommodate this?

National and International Statements

The importance of placing greater emphasis on preventive health measures and policies can be highlighted with reference to several major statements. For example, the World Health Organization (WHO, 1986) has 'set out the fundamental requirements for people to be healthy, to define the improvements in health that can be achieved by the year 2000 for the peoples of the European Region of WHO, and to propose action to secure these improvements' (p. 1). More specific targets identified by WHO that are most relevant to this paper are listed in Table 4.1.

Table 4.1   Selected WHO 'Health for All' Targets up to the Year 2000 That Are Particularly Relevant to Exercise Science

Target number	Target
9	*Disease of the Circulation:* by the year 2000, mortality in the Region[1] from diseases of the circulatory system in people under 65 should be reduced by at least 15%.
13	*Healthy Public Policy:* by 1990, national policies in all Member States[2] should ensure that legislative, administrative and economic mechanisms provide broad intersectoral support and resources for the promotion of the people at all levels of such policy-making.
15	*Knowledge and Motivation for Healthy Behaviour:* by 1990, educational programmes in all Member States should enhance the knowledge, motivation and skills of people to acquire and maintain health.
16	*Positive Health Behaviour:* by 1995, in all Member States, there should be significant increases in positive health behaviour, such as balanced nutrition, non-smoking, appropriate physical activity and good stress management.
32	*Research Strategies:* before 1990, all Member States should have formulated research strategies to stimulate investigations which improve the application and expansion of knowledge needed to support their 'health for all' developments.

Note: Compiled from various World Health Organization sources.
[1]Region: Europe.
[2]Member States: the 33 European countries who are members of WHO.

The U.S. Department of Health and Human Services (DHHS, 1980) set 223 'health objectives for the nation', 11 of which were specifically related to physical fitness and exercise. Of these, 3 were specific to children. These are listed in Table 4.2.

Impetus has also been given to health-related physical activity (HRPA) in children by several organizations. The American College of Sports Medicine (ACSM, 1988) has produced an opinion statement on physical fitness and children, and a joint position statement from the Sports Council and Health Education Authority (1988) also lists recommendations for action, including the need for more research into effective strategies for promoting exercise habits in children.

In summary, there is plenty of support and guidance for the promotion of HRPA in children. However, despite this apparent support, British literature on

Table 4.2   Health 'Objectives for the Nation' Set by DHHS (1980) That Are Related to Children, Exercise and Fitness

"By 1990, the proportion of children and adolescents ages 10 to 17 participating regularly in appropriate physical activities, particularly cardiorespiratory fitness programmes which can be carried into adulthood, should be greater than 90 percent."

"By 1990, the proportion of children and adolescents ages 10 to 17 participating in daily school physical education programmes should be greater than 60 percent."

"By 1990, a methodology for systematically assessing the physical fitness of children should be established with at least 70 percent of children and adolescents 10 to 17 participating in such an assessment."

Note: Adapted from *Exercise Adherence: It's Impact on Public Health* (pp. 431 and 433) by R. Dishman (Ed.), 1988, Champaign, IL: Human Kinetics. Copyright 1988 by R.Dishman. Adapted by permission.

the topic has been diffuse and largely atheoretical. This chapter, therefore, attempts to draw together contemporary research findings in paediatric exercise science to produce a review of children, health and physical activity with specific reference to the British physical educator.

What's in a Name? Clarification of Terms

Physical education (PE) has adopted many terms for its work in physical fitness and health. *Health-related fitness* (HRF) has been the most prominent because this is the term most often used in the United States (see Corbin and Lindsey, 1988). However, it could be argued that *health-related exercise* (HRE) or *health-related physical activity* are better terms. The operational definitions of health, physical fitness, physical activity, exercise, and sport that have been adopted for this discussion are summarized in Table 4.3.

In respect of the content of Table 4.3, we are advocating a greater emphasis on physical activity and exercise, with a view to promoting health and wellness. This is illustrated in Figure 4.1 on page 75, where a distinction between fitness and wellness is shown. Movement from the right side of the fitness continuum does not necessarily equate with better health or wellness.

Physiological Outcomes of Health-Related Physical Activity

The physiological outcomes of HRPA are dependent upon the mode, intensity, duration and frequency of physical activity. In this section we consider the health-related aspects of fitness and discuss the mode of physical activity, and the exercise prescription, required for the optimum development of each of the components of health-related fitness (Caspersen, Powell, & Christenson, 1985;

Table 4.3   Operational Definitions of Key Terms

Term	Definition
Health	This refers to disease prevention and avoidance, as well as risk reduction, and also considers mental and physical 'well-being'. *Wellness* might be a better word for describing the goal of 'healthy' physical movement.
Physical fitness	This is the overarching term used to describe the individual's capability for physical movement. Usually, two major types of fitness are described: 'health-related' (HRF) and 'skill-related' (SRF). Components of HRF include cardiopulmonary fitness, muscular strength and endurance, flexibility and body composition (Corbin & Lindsey, 1988). SRF components of fitness comprise agility, balance, coordination, power, reaction time and speed (Corbin & Lindsey, 1988) and refer to 'athletic ability'. HRF components are known to have implications for risk reduction of chronic disease.
Physical activity	Any musculoskeletal movement resulting in energy expenditure (Caspersen, Powell, & Christenson, 1985). Physical activity known to have a beneficial health outcome is known as 'health-related physical activity' (HRPA).
Exercise	A subcategory of physical activity that is more structured and planned and usually designed to maintain or improve fitness. Exercise known to have a beneficial health outcome is known as 'health-related exercise' (HRE).
Sport	A subcategory of physical activity that includes activities that are structured, organized, rule governed, competitive, and involve gross motor actions.

Note: Readers are also referred to Bouchard, Shephard, Stephens, Sutton and McPherson (1990).

Corbin & Lindsey, 1988). We have discussed elsewhere (Armstrong, 1987a) the principles of training (see Table 4.4), the value of warming up and cooling down, and the importance of taking appropriate safety precautions.

Cardiopulmonary Fitness

Cardiopulmonary fitness may be defined as the ability of the circulatory and pulmonary systems to supply fuel and eliminate waste products during physical activity. Much more is known about children's cardiopulmonary fitness than about other health-related aspects of their fitness, but very few data are available from samples of British children.

Any physical activity that is rhythmic and aerobic in nature, uses large muscle groups and can be sustained continuously for a reasonable length of time can

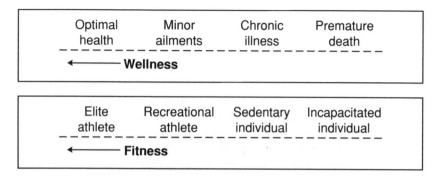

Figure 4.1 A comparison of wellness and fitness continua.

Table 4.4 The Principles of Exercise Training

Exercise principle	Definition
Overload	Exercising against a resistance greater than that which is normally encountered. Progressively overloading a system will cause it to respond and adapt.
Progression	The frequency, duration and intensity of exercise should be gradually increased over a period of time.
Specificity	Exercise-induced changes are stimulus specific. A particular activity may induce a change in one tissue or organ but not in another.
Reversibility	Exercise effects are reversible. If exercise training is infrequent or not sufficiently intensive, the effects of a previous exercise programme will decay.

improve cardiopulmonary fitness. Typical activities include running, swimming, cycling, skipping, skating, some types of dancing and cross-country skiing. On the other hand, in the context of developing cardiopulmonary fitness, physical activities that involve the predominant use of small muscle groups or isometric contractions should be avoided because of the enhanced blood pressure response. Although a consensus exists concerning the mode of exercise in which children should engage to improve cardiopulmonary fitness, the minimum and optimum levels for intensity, frequency and duration of exercise have not been unequivocally identified. Recommendations for frequency of exercise range from 3 days per week (e.g. Riopel, Boerth, Coates, Hennekens, and Miller, 1986) to every day (e.g. Haskell, Montoye, and Orenstein, 1985). Recommendations for the duration of each exercise session range from 20 to 30 minutes (Simons-Morton, Parcel, O'Hara, Blair, & Pate, 1988). It is, however, important to consider children's attention spans, when determining the length of exercise sessions, and other commitments, when prescribing the number of exercise sessions. We therefore feel that three 20-minute periods per week is probably the optimum for children.

Some researchers have reported higher training thresholds for children than for adults (Massicotte & MacNab, 1974). This is supported by Yates and Grana (1981) and in line with the application of Karvonen's formula to children (Borms, 1986). It appears that an exercise intensity that maintains the heart rate at about 80% of maximum (160 beats/min [BPM]) produces the best results (Armstrong & Bray, 1987). With children, jogging at about 8 km/h will raise the heart rate to about 160 BPM. When this type of programme is followed, children can expect changes in cardiorespiratory fitness very similar to those documented for adults (Armstrong & Davies, 1984).

Maximal oxygen uptake ($\dot{V}O_2$max), 'the highest rate of oxygen consumed by the body in a given period of time during exercise involving a significant portion of the muscle mass' (Krahenbuhl, Skinner, & Kohrt, 1985, p. 503), is widely recognized as the best single index of cardiopulmonary fitness (Åstrand & Rodahl, 1986). For reasons discussed elsewhere (Armstrong & Davies, 1984), the correct term to use with children is *peak oxygen uptake* (peak $\dot{V}O_2$), the highest oxygen consumption elicited during an exercise test to exhaustion. But for ease of exposition, the two terms will be used interchangeably in this chapter. Until the recent report by Armstrong, Balding, Gentle, Williams, and Kirby (1990), data on the peak $\dot{V}O_2$ of British children were sparse, derived mainly from cycle ergometry and based on small sample sizes. Armstrong and his colleagues determined the peak $\dot{V}O_2$ of 420 children, aged 11 to 16 years, and their results refuted the well publicized views that British children's cardiopulmonary fitness is deteriorating or inferior to children from other countries. Armstrong pointed out that the first laboratory-based scientific studies of children's cardiopulmonary fitness were carried out by Robinson (1938) and Morse, Schultz, and Cassels (1949) in the United States, and their results almost exactly reflect the current levels of cardiopulmonary fitness of British children. The relative stability of the cardiopulmonary fitness of North American children over several decades has also been noted (Simons-Morton, O'Hara, Simons-Morton, & Parcel, 1987). The cardiopulmonary fitness (peak $\dot{V}O_2$) levels of British children were shown to be comparable to those of children from elsewhere, and when the children's scores were compared with the available United Kingdom data on other age groups, it was concluded that, in terms of peak $\dot{V}O_2$, children are probably the fittest section of society (Armstrong, 1989a).

Muscular Fitness

Muscular fitness has two components, *muscular strength* (the ability of a muscle group to exert force against a resistance in one maximal effort) and *muscular endurance* (the ability of a muscle group to perform contractions against a light load for an extended period of time). Adults' muscular fitness and its improvement are well documented, but children, particularly prepubertal children, have been the subject of few studies. Nevertheless, our understanding of children's muscular fitness and the physiological outcomes of appropriate training programmes is gradually increasing, and several excellent reviews of the literature are available to the interested reader (e.g. Sale, 1989).

Muscular fitness training involves repeatedly overcoming increasing resistances, and appropriate programmes can be structured around each type of muscular contraction (see Table 4.5). However, because of the disadvantages of isometric exercises (e.g. enhanced blood pressure response), eccentric exercises (e.g. increased muscle soreness) and isokinetic exercises (e.g. expensive apparatus required), we will concentrate upon isotonic exercises that use apparatus normally available in a school. To develop an isotonic muscular fitness programme, the principles of training (e.g. overload, progression and specificity) must be thoroughly understood, and in addition it is necessary to be fully cognizant of the concept of a repetition maximum (RM). A RM is the maximal load that a muscle group can lift over a given number of repetitions before fatiguing. Although individual overload recommendations in the literature differ slightly, it is generally agreed that training with heavy weights (e.g. 1 RM) should be avoided and the principle of progression (see Table 4.4) strictly adhered to with young children (Sale, 1989). Specific optimal development of muscular strength would involve the use of heavier resistances than those necessary for optimal development of muscular endurance, but we believe that with children a reasonable compromise that would develop both muscular strength and muscular endurance is preferable to two distinct training programmes. For optimal physiological development we recommend that children perform about 8 to 12 repetitions to contraction failure (i.e. 8 to 12 RM). In practice this requires the 8 RM to be determined for each exercise, and when the child can do 12 repetitions with the initial 8-RM resistance (now the 12 RM), a small (5% to 10%) increase in resistance can be made to bring the maximal repetitions back down to 8 (the 'new' 8 RM).

Table 4.5   Types of Muscular Contraction

Contraction	Definition
Isometric (static) contractions	Tension develops, but there is no change in the length of the muscle.
Eccentric contractions	The muscle returns to habitual length while developing tension.
Isokinetic contractions	The tension developed by the muscle while shortening at constant speed.
Isotonic (dynamic or concentric) contractions	The muscle shortens with varying tension while lifting a a constant load.

For a balanced development, each session of exercises should consist of one exercise for each major muscle group. It is advisable to start each session with large muscle groups and work down to smaller muscle groups. Upper legs and hips, chest, back and posterior aspects of legs, lower legs, shoulders and posterior aspects of upper arms, abdomen and then anterior aspects of upper arms would be a suitable rotation of exercises. We recommend one, gradually progressing to three, sets of each exercise per session, with not more than three training sessions per week, with at leasts 1 day's rest between sessions.

Early studies of prepubescent children failed to show a significant increase in muscular strength following training programmes, and these results, combined with young children's low levels of androgens and immature nervous systems, caused many researchers to question whether prepubescent children were trainable (Sale, 1989). However, more recent research has indicated that prepubescent children are quite capable of increasing voluntary strength in response to resistance training, even though they experience more difficulty in increasing skeletal muscle mass (Sale, 1989). It is problematic to compare relative increases in training-induced muscular fitness between prepubescent and pubescent children and adults, as it is difficult to resolve the issue of using absolute or percentage gains in muscular fitness as the criterion measure. Nevertheless, children and adolescents who follow our recommended programme can expect significant gains in muscular fitness, although substantial increases in muscle mass may be experienced only by adolescent boys.

In the United Kingdom over 88,000 adults are unable to work each day because of back pain. Twenty-six million working days are lost through backache every year at a cost to the nation of £1,000 million in medical care, sickness benefit and lost production. Improved muscular fitness will help to prevent or alleviate back pain and other postural problems. In addition, gains in muscular endurance, brought about through an enhanced microcirculation and positive effects on energy-generating enzyme systems, will promote resistance to fatigue during everyday tasks. There is also evidence to support the view that weight training may reduce the blood pressure of hypertensive adolescents (Hagberg et al., 1984), but this remains to be substantiated.

Flexibility

Flexibility may be defined as the range of motion about a joint. Less is known about children's flexibility than about any other component of HRF. Flexibility is joint specific, and there is no single indicator of body flexibility. It is a popular belief that young children are very flexible and then gradually lose this flexibility as they grow older. The scientific evidence for this premise is extremely limited, and 'flexibility' seems to vary with the test administered. Leighton (1956) reported a steady downward trend with age (10- to 18-year-old boys) in the range of motion of a majority of the joint movements he measured with his flexometer. On the other hand, Renson, Beunen, and Van Gerven (1972), studying 12- to 19-year-old boys, found a progressive increase in flexibility with age, as indicated by the sit-and-reach test, but this was not confirmed with either a trunk twist or an ankle flexibility test. Huprich and Sigerseth (1950) reported no significant differences among girls, aged 9 to 15 years, on six flexibility test items. Although the research evidence on changes in flexibility with growth is equivocal, it does appear that it is beneficial to initiate exercises for increased joint flexibility before puberty, as long as they are carried out with a concern to avoid damage to the joints and vertebral column.

Flexibility may be increased by either ballistic or static stretching exercises. *Ballistic stretching* uses momentum to produce the stretch. The momentum is generated by a bouncing, bobbing or jerking movement, and because this produces a sudden and sometimes excessive stretch on the muscle, there is a potential for injury. *Static stretching* involves slowly stretching a muscle longer than its normal length and holding the stretch for a period of time. There is much less chance of tearing the soft tissue and less likelihood of causing muscle soreness. We therefore recommend static stretching for the development of flexibility and for including in warm-up routines. The muscle should be slowly stretched beyond its normal length and the stretch held for a minimum of 6 to 10 seconds. Each major muscle group should be stretched in this manner per set of flexibility exercises, and each session should consist of three sets of exercises. The exercise sessions should be repeated daily or not less often than every other day. More advanced techniques of improving flexibility (e.g. proprioceptive neuromuscular facilitation), the problems of 'overflexibility' and contraindicated exercises are considered in detail by Alter (1988).

Although unequivocal research evidence is not available, it appears that optimal flexibility is associated with the prevention of back pain and postural defects. It helps to prevent muscle, joint and connective tissue injuries, and it may reduce dysmenorrhea (Corbin & Lindsey, 1984). In addition, reasonable flexibility is required for the performance of many recreational and sporting activities.

Body Composition

Changes in body composition are a function of energy intake and energy expenditure. Energy intake should be based upon sound nutritional principles, and several expert committees (British Cardiac Society, 1986; Committee on Medical Aspects of Food Policy, 1984; National Advisory Committee on Nutrition Education, 1983) have recently made recommendations concerning diet. The principal recommendations are, in summary, to reduce fat, sucrose, salt and alcohol intake, increase fibre-rich carbohydrate intake and maintain protein intake.

Energy intake must be defined in relation to maintenance of optimal body weight (see Royal College of Physicians [RCP], 1983) and level of physical activity. It must be recognized that adolescents who choose to severely limit their energy intakes might not obtain all the nutrients they require, and they should be particularly encouraged to adhere to the expert recommendations above. On the other hand, many adolescents have large appetites and high energy intakes, particularly from foods and snacks with a high energy content. Because adolescents seem to prefer to eat more of their food as snacks rather than as meals, they need to have access to snacks that are low in sugar, fat and salt.

The accumulation of body fat is normally a result of long-term energy imbalance (i.e. energy intake is greater than energy expenditure) and should be addressed through a small reduction in energy intake (in line with the recommendations above) and an increase in energy expenditure. Energy expenditure can be subdivided into basal metabolism, thermic effect of food (during digestion etc.), adaptive thermogenesis (during body temperature regulation) and physical activity. The greatest potential for increasing an individual's energy expenditure lies with his or her level of physical activity. This increase in energy expenditure comes about not just from the direct effect of physical activity on metabolic rate but also from the persistent elevation of metabolism following physical activity (Thompson, Jarvie, Lahey, & Cureton, 1982). In a research study, Ward and Bar-Or (1986) estimated that a 30-kilogram child with an energy expenditure of 7,500 kJ/day can increase her or his daily energy expenditure by 20% to 25% through 40 to 50 minutes of jogging or swimming. Such an increase in daily energy expenditure, without an increase in energy intake, would result in a 1-kilogram fat loss within 23 days. Although the definitive study of the effect of physical activity and exercise intervention on energy intake has yet to be carried out, the weight of available evidence (reviewed by Thompson et al., 1982) suggests that only very small changes in energy intake accompany exercise training.

The mode and volume of physical activity described in the cardiopulmonary fitness section can also be recommended in this context. When we are concerned with body composition, and in particular body fat content, not exceeding the recommended maximum level of intensity of physical activity is important. Exercising at intensities that elicit heart rates higher than 80% of maximum may be counterproductive. Such high-intensity exercise is significantly supported by anaerobic metabolism with a buildup of lactic acid in the muscles. The high anaerobic content will probably restrict the duration of the exercise and, in addition, because fat cannot be metabolized anaerobically, there will be an increased reliance on glycogen stores (carbohydrate) as the major source of energy. To increase lean body mass (fat-free mass) in line with a reduction in body fat, it is advisable to supplement any aerobic exercise programme with a muscular fitness programme such as that described in the muscle fitness section.

The assessment of children's body composition is problematic (Lohman, 1986), and although there is some evidence to suggest that North American children are getting fatter (Ross & Gilbert, 1985), data on British children are sparse. Armstrong and colleagues (Armstrong, Balding, Gentle, & Kirby, 1990a) assessed 357 boys and 350 girls, aged 11 to 16 years, and according to the criteria of the RCP (1983), 13% of the boys and 10% of the girls could be classified as 'overweight'. The magnitude of the problem of children's overfatness can be put into perspective when one realizes that obesity acquired in childhood is highly predictive of obesity in adult life (Johnson et al., 1975; Weil, 1977). It appears that the later into adolescence the individual remains obese, the greater the persistence of obesity into adulthood. Abraham and Nordsieck (1960) concluded that the risk of an obese adolescent becoming an obese adult is 63% to 72%.

Psychological Outcomes of Health-Related Physical Activity

The identification of the psychological outcomes of involvement in sport, exercise and physical activity has proved to be a difficult problem for researchers over many years. Although ancient civilizations recognized the potential of the therapeutic benefits of exercise from a psychological point of view (Ryan, 1984), and emotional development was discussed in the early sport psychology literature (Layman, 1970), it has not been until quite recently that researchers have been able to pursue a consistent line of research. Unfortunately, from a paediatric perspective, little is known about the effects of physical activity on children, whereas considerably more research has been conducted on adults in both clinical and nonclinical settings (see Biddle and Mutrie, 1991).

Psychiatric and Psychological Epidemiology

Vikan (1985) reported on the psychiatric epidemiology of 1,500 children in Norway aged 10 years. The prevalence rate for 'psychological problems' was 5%. More transitory mood swings were probably not included in this figure. However, this suggests that children are not immune from psychological problems, although the source of such problems will likely be different from that for adults, in many cases, and change across the life cycle through childhood and adolescence. In addition to negative emotions, positive psychological aspects, such as self-esteem, 'character' development and cognitive functioning, have also been addressed in the context of physical activity.

From an epidemiological perspective, the data provided by Stephens (1988) are important in identifying the possible links between exercise and mental health. Stephens analysed data from four large population surveys from North America. These included over 56,000 people, and data were available on measures of physical activity and mental health. Thirty-two analyses were conducted, and in 25 of these the results showed a positive association between physical activity levels and mental health. These results were obtained using different measures of both activity and mental health, with the latter being defined as 'positive mood, general well-being, and relatively infrequent symptoms of anxiety and depression' (p. 41). Unfortunately, the results by age only referred to those under and over 40 years, thus it is not possible to detect any trends for children. Overall, the effects were more positive for older subjects and for women.

Such data do not allow clear statements to be made about the direction of the relationship. Are persons with positive mental health more likely to be active, or does activity 'cause' good mental health? Other evidence from biochemical, physiological and psychological sources supports the latter position. However, it is likely that some people with particularly poor mental health, such as those suffering depression, will have low activity and fitness levels (see Martinsen, Strand, Paulsson, and Kaggestad, 1989). In short, mental health can be both an antecedent and a consequence variable in exercise and physical activity.

Consensus statements on exercise and mental health include the following (Morgan & Goldston, 1987):

1. Exercise is associated with reduced state anxiety.
2. Exercise has been associated with a decreased level of mild to moderate depression.
3. Long-term exercise is usually associated with reductions in traits such as neuroticism and anxiety.
4. Exercise may be an adjunct to the professional treatment of severe depression.
5. Exercise results in the reduction of various stress indices.
6. Exercise has beneficial emotional effects across all ages and in both sexes.

Although evidence can be produced to suppport most of these statements, the research is not always without problems or conflicts. For example, there is very little evidence to support statement 6 in terms of 'all ages'. Indeed, Morgan and Goldston (1987) later acknowledge that the effects of exercise on the mental health of children need investigation. In short, we have very little evidence on children, although there is no indication, as far as we know, that the benefits reported for adults will elude children or youths.

Negative Affect

Much of the research on the mental health outcomes of exercise and physical activity has focused on negative emotion/affect and, in particular, anxiety and depression. Although adult data do suggest that positive changes in these factors can occur with activity, few data are available on children (Brown, 1982). Similarly, the reduced physiological response to psychosocial stressors thought to occur in subjects with higher levels of physical fitness (Crews & Landers, 1987) has not been studied in children.

North, McCullagh, and Tran (1990) conducted a meta-analysis of the literature on exercise and depression. A meta-analysis is a quantitative summary of research findings across a number of studies and produces an 'effect size' (ES), or index of magnitude, for a particular intervention. In this case, the ES shows the strength of the effect of exercise on the change in depression scores across studies. The ES is expressed in standard deviation units, and therefore an ES of 0.5 shows that the subjects receiving the treatment scored, on the average, one half of a standard deviation above subjects in a control condition.

North et al. (1990) located five studies with subjects under 18 years old, although three of these were unpublished dissertations. These studies yielded 17 effect sizes, the strength of which can be compared for those of college students and middle-aged subjects in Figure 4.2. Also included in Figure 4.2 is the ES for high school students, which is the mean score of 12 ESs from three studies. This shows that depression decreased after exercise across all these age categories, with the most positive effect occurring for the oldest group of subjects. The mean effect size for all groups was significantly different from zero, although caution should be expressed about the result for those under 18 years and the high school subjects, as the numbers of effect sizes used in the analyses (17 and 12 respectively) were much smaller than for the college (55) and middle-aged (161) groups. Nevertheless, this is the first meta-analytic study showing an effect for exercise on depression in younger people.

The underlying reasons or mechanisms for the effects of exercise on mental health are unclear, although a number of possibilities exist (see Biddle and Mutrie, 1991). Biochemical mechanisms provide an intriguing possibility for explaining the effects of acute exercise. For example, some have suggested that exercise produces elevations in plasma endorphin ('endogenous morphine') levels and that this has been implicated in mood elevation. Similarly, physiological explanations can be offered, such as reductions in muscle tension after exercise, thus producing the postexercise relaxation effect. Finally, psychological factors have been suggested, such as increased self-esteem, mastery and competence from participation in an activity deemed worthwhile or where some success is perceived.

In summary, it is quite likely that negative affect can be changed through physical activity and exercise, but the research on children is virtually nonexistent, and the mechanisms of such effects are still not clearly understood.

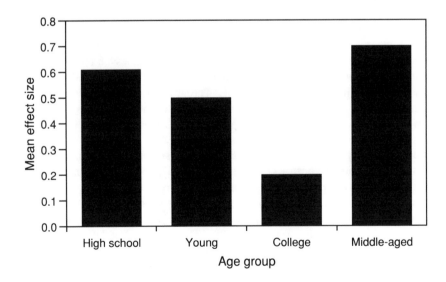

Figure 4.2 Magnitude of the effect of exercise on reducing depression across age groups. Middle-aged = 25-64 years; college = 18-24 years; high school = 12-18 years. *Note.* Data compiled from North, McCullagh, and Tran (1990).

Positive Affect and Cognitive Functioning

How many school PE programmes in the past have been justified based on 'character' and moral development? This argument supports the notion that participation in particular activities (usually competitive team sports and outdoor education activities) can produce positive changes in the individual's personality and moral behaviour. Regrettably, this assumption is largely untested and naive as far as character is concerned. In short, there is little evidence, that has scientific rigour, to support such assumptions or to delineate which children benefit under which circumstances. There is little doubt that positive changes can be brought about by professional, skilful leadership in most activities, but equally, character can be damaged through inappropriate strategies (Sage, 1986).

Weiss and Bredemeier (1990), however, state that 'when structured purposefully and guided by sound educational principles, sport can build character and develop a sound mind in a sound body' (p. 331). They go on to say that 'we strongly believe that physical education and sport settings provide children, adolescents and adults with ideal opportunities for realising optimal moral growth. . . . The few studies that have been designed to effect changes in moral reasoning and behaviours through sport-related experiences have been optimistic' (p. 368). Further discussion of the role of sport and physical activity in moral development can be found in Weiss and Bredemeier (1990).

Another important issue in the study of psychological outcomes from physical activity and exercise is the development of self-esteem in children. Although this topic is dealt with in more detail elsewhere in this volume, a summary statement will be made here.

The effect that physical activity might have on self-esteem (SE) has interested teachers and researchers for some time. Although evidence supports a link, it is far from clear under what circumstances SE is affected or what the underlying mechanisms might be that produce such changes. Nevertheless, a meta-analysis of studies on physical activity and SE in children (Gruber, 1986) did find evidence for a positive influence of activity on SE. The greatest effects were found for children with disabilities and for children in aerobic fitness activities, although all of the types of activities studied (creative, fitness, sport skills and other motor skills) demonstrated a positive relationship with SE.

Recent developments in the study of SE suggest that SE is a hierarchical and multidimensional construct. In other words, SE consists of a number of subdomains, such as perceptions of competence in sport, as well as such domains as physical self-worth, in addition to 'global self-esteem'. Physical self-worth is also one of many domains (e.g. academic, social) of SE, hence it has a multidimensional structure (see Fox, 1988). The influence of HRPA on self-esteem, therefore, might be seen in this light. HRPA may affect some subdomains of the hierarchy (e.g. perceptions of body attractiveness) and, over time, physical self-worth and global self-esteem. However, the complexities of such an approach are not yet understood fully (Fox, 1988).

An issue currently arousing the interest of physical educators, and one associated with the physiological outcomes of physical activity, is that of 'enjoyment'.

It is recognized that activities that are enjoyable are more likely to be intrinsically motivating and therefore approached through free choice. However, from a research perspective, the concept of enjoyment has remained elusive.

Perhaps the most comprehensive analysis of enjoyment has been made by Csikszentmihalyi (1975), who studied activities that were participated in for purely intrinsic reasons. He suggested that enjoyment, or a state of 'flow', was optimized when the demands of the activity were matched by the individual's abilities. A mismatch produced either anxiety or boredom.

Scanlan and Lewthwaite (1986) studied the factor of enjoyment in 9- to 16-year-old male sport participants. They suggested that enjoyment from physical activity was best described in terms of intrinsic/extrinsic and achievement/ nonachievement dimensions. This is illustrated in Figure 4.3

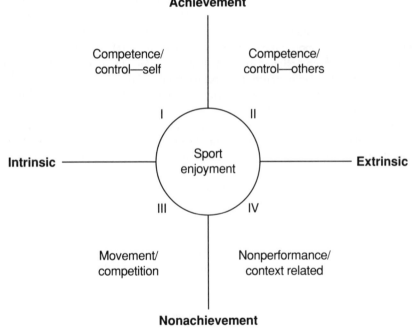

Figure 4.3   Proposed model of sport enjoyment. *Note.* From 'Social Psychological Aspects of Competition for Male Youth Sport Participants: IV. Predictors of Enjoyment' by T.K. Scanlan & R. Lewthwaite, 1986, *Journal of Sport Psychology*, **8**, p. 33. Reprinted by permission of Human Kinetics Publishers.

The four quadrants identified in Figure 4.3 were explained by Scanlan and Lewthwaite (1986, p. 33) as follows:

    I—Achievement-Intrinsic: 'predictors related to personal perceptions of competence and control, such as the attainment of mastery goals and perceived ability'

II—Achievement-Extrinsic: 'predictors related to personal perceptions of competence and control that are derived from other people'

III—Nonachievement-Intrinsic: 'predictors related to (a) physical activity and movement such as sensations, tension release . . . , and (b) competition such as excitement'

IV—Nonachievement-Extrinsic: 'predictors related to nonperformance aspects of sport such as affiliating with peers'

Finally, physical educators have shown an interest in the potential effects of physical activity on cognitive functioning. Indeed, arguments for increasing the amount of time devoted to physical education, as through daily PE programmes, usually suggest that cognitive functioning will improve as a result of increased involvement in physical activity. The evidence is not convincing for older school students, however, as many potentially extraneous variables are rarely controlled for, such as teacher expectancy effects. However, research in perceptual-motor development has suggested that early development of neuromuscular control and psychomotor function could assist academic learning in young children. One of the mechanisms for this could be the increase in cerebral blood flow that has been documented after physical activity and, in particular, the increase in blood flow in the prefrontal somatosensory and primary motor cortices of the brain (see Williams, 1986).

So far, the discussion has centred on the possible outcomes of physical activity and exercise. However, an important issue here is that of children's actual physical activity patterns.

Children's Physical Activity Patterns

The evidence linking an active lifestyle with a reduced risk of some diseases is well documented for both adults (Bouchard, Shephard, Stephens, Sutton, & McPherson, 1990; Fentem, Bassey, & Turnbull, 1988) and children (Bar-Or, 1983; Rowland, 1990). Regular weight-bearing physical activity is known to be essential for the normal growth and development of the skeleton (Office of Health Economics, 1990). Most studies of physical activity as a preventative modality have, however, been carried out in relation to coronary heart disease (CHD). There is no clear understanding of the mechanisms involved, but it is generally agreed that physical activity has positive effects on other coronary risk factors (e.g. serum cholesterol, blood pressure and body fatness), and other plausible theories include physical-activity-induced changes in blood coagulability, platelet function, fibrinolytic activity, myocardial vascularity and coronary artery size (Leon & Blackburn, 1983; Fentem et al., 1988). Very few prospective studies have been carried out, the available evidence is equivocal, and several of these beneficial adaptations have yet to be convincingly demonstrated in human subjects (Bourey & Santoro, 1988; Pearl, 1987; Sinzinger & Virgolini, 1988). The well-documented improvement in cardiorespiratory efficiency, at rest and during submaximal exercise, brought about by appropriate physical activity may also offer some protection against CHD (Åstrand & Rodahl, 1986). Nevertheless, the circumstantial evidence amassed by epidemiological studies associating an active lifestyle with a low incidence of CHD is incontrovertible (reviewed by Armstrong, 1990). A recent analysis of all published papers in the English language that provide sufficient data to calculate a relative risk ratio for CHD at different levels of physical activity concluded that

> the inverse association between physical activity and incidence of CHD is consistently observed, especially in the better designed studies; this association is appropriately sequenced, biologically graded, plausible, and coherent with existing knowledge. Therefore, the observations reported in the literature support the inference that physical activity is inversely and causally related to the incidence of CHD. (Powell, Thompson, Casperson, & Kendrick, 1987, p. 283)

The form of physical activity that is consistently and substantially associated with a lower incidence of CHD involves large muscle groups for sustained periods of time. Heartbeat Wales (1987) summarized the current research:

> in practical terms a minimum of 20/30 minutes of exercise (of at least brisk walking intensity) three times a week is recommended as a contribution towards the prevention of coronary heart disease. (p. 3)

The hypothesis that participation in HRPA in childhood increases the likelihood of such participation as an adult is compelling. Although research data are sparse and results equivocal (Powell & Dysinger, 1987), evidence to support the view that children's physical activity patterns persist into adulthood is accumulating (Sofranko & Nolan, 1972; Yoesting & Burkhead, 1973). Engstrom (1986) appears to have carried out the only published prospective longitudinal study of physical activity through to adulthood. He interviewed 2,464 randomly selected 15-year-olds about their sport activities during leisure time and followed the same group through mailed questionnaires 5, 10 and 15 years later. He obtained a full set of data on 2,072 subjects, and his results indicated that 'early experiences of physical activity are important for psychological readiness to participate in keep-fit activities in later life' (p. 89). These findings reinforce the importance of adopting an active lifestyle during childhood.

Simons-Morton et al. (1988) reviewed the published 'physical activity recommendations for children' and concluded that appropriate (i.e. health-related) physical activity involves large muscle groups in dynamic movement for periods of 20 minutes or longer. They emphasized that this type of physical activity should occur at least three times per week and that it should be of sufficient intensity to elicit heart rates equal to or in excess of 140 BPM. We have shown that for children, brisk walking on the treadmill at 6 km/h equates with steady-state heart rates of about 140 BPM (Armstrong, Balding, Gentle, & Kirby, 1990b). It appears, therefore, that there is a close agreement between the volume (frequency, duration and intensity) of physical activity recommended as health-related for children and the volume that is coronary preventive for adults.

The assessment of adults' physical activity is one of the most difficult tasks in epidemiological research (Andersen, Masironi, Rutenfranz, & Seliger, 1978), and the estimation of the daily physical activity patterns of children is even more problematic. The technique used must be socially acceptable, it should not burden the child with cumbersome equipment, and it should minimally influence the child's normal physical activity pattern. Ideally the relative intensity and duration of activities should be monitored, and if a true picture of habitual activity is required, some account of day-to-day variation must be taken. Bar-Or (1983) suggested that with children a minimum follow-up of 3 days, including 1 weekend day, should be employed.

A range of methods for assessing the level of adults' physical activity has been developed, and several of these methods have been used with children without due consideration being taken of the differences between children and adults. The vast majority of studies have used self-report techniques, and it is well documented that these techniques are particularly problematic with children as subjects (Bar-Or, 1983). Few studies of children's physical activity patterns have satisfied the criteria outlined above, and it is only very recently that objective evidence of British children's level of HRPA has become available.

Armstrong et al. (1990a) carried out the first study to unobtrusively monitor heart rates of British children for extended periods of time. They estimated the volume of physical activity of 266 children, aged 11 to 16 years, using a self-contained, computerized telemetry system (Sport Tester 3000). The Sport Tester system is capable of storing and replaying minute-by-minute heart rates for up to 16 hours; when it is interfaced with a microcomputer, sustained periods with heart rates above 139 BPM (70% of maximum—Armstrong et al., 1990a) can be readily identified and recorded. This methodology does not give a direct measure of physical activity, but, more importantly in this context, it measures the stress placed on the cardiopulmonary system. Armstrong et al. (1990a) monitored each child from about 0900 to 2100 during a normal schoolday. The receivers were retrieved, replaced and refitted the next morning, and the process was repeated over 3 days. In addition, 212 of the children were monitored from 0900 to 2100 on a Saturday.

Seventy-seven percent of the boys and 88% of the girls failed to elicit a single 20-minute period with their heart rate equal to or above 70% of maximum over the 3-weekday monitoring period. Only four boys and one girl averaged a daily 20-minute period of HRPA. Thirty-six percent of the boys and 52% of the girls did not even experience a single 10-minute period of HRPA during the 3 weekdays of monitoring. During Saturday monitoring, 88% of the boys and 97% of the girls failed to exhibit a 20-minute period of HRPA, and 71% of the boys and 94% of the girls did not even experience a 10-minute period of physical activity equivalent to brisk walking. These data demonstrated for the first time that British children exhibit very low levels of habitual HRPA. When the data were analysed by sex, it was shown that boys were significantly more physically active than girls. Furthermore the girls' level of HRPA significantly decreased with age.

These results provoked the research group to recruit a group of 42 primary school children, aged 10 years, from the same catchment area as some of the secondary school children (mean age 13 years) already surveyed (Armstrong, Balding, Bray, Gentle, & Kirby, 1990). The physical activity patterns of the younger children were monitored using the same techniques, and a comparison of HRPA levels revealed that although there was no difference in the level of physical activity of primary and secondary school boys, the primary school girls were significantly more physically active than their secondary school counterparts. The research team concluded that children have generally low levels of physical activity but that teenage girls appear to be particularly inactive.

More detailed analysis of the primary school data revealed that there was no difference between the physical activity patterns of 10-year-old boys and 10-year-old girls. Armstrong and Bray (1991) confirmed this finding in a further study of 67 boys and 65 girls, but their results illustrated the relatively low levels of physical activity of even 10-year-old children. Sixty-one percent of the boys and 66% of the girls failed to experience a single 20-minute period of HRPA during 3 days of heart rate monitoring. Nineteen percent of the boys and 25% of the girls failed to elicit even a 10-minute period with their heart rate about 139 BPM. During Saturday monitoring the children appeared to be even more sedentary, with 75% of the boys and 65% of the girls failing to experience a 10-minute period of HRPA.

The results of these studies clearly demonstrate that British children currently exhibit sedentary physical activity patterns and that many children seldom experience the intensity and duration of physical activity associated with health-related outcomes. This suggests that a great deal more emphasis needs to be placed on the underlying reasons for such patterns of behaviour. Strategies and interventions designed to promote increased participation in HRPA will now be discussed.

Promoting Health-Related Physical Activity

Motivating Participation

The issue of motivation is a complex one. Sallis and Hovell (1990), in a review of the determinants of exercise, suggest that a 'natural history' model is useful. This model is shown in Figure 4.4 and depicts the various stages that may occur in the adoption and maintenance of exercise. The model shows the move from a sedentary situation to the adoption of exercise. This can be followed either by immediate dropout or by a period of maintenance. The maintenance period may also end in dropout, although ceasing exercise may not be permanent, and the resumption of activity may take place.

Four major phases of the natural history of exercise

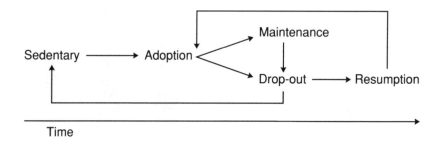

Figure 4.4   A natural-history model of exercise. *Note.* From Sallis & Hovell (1990, p. 309). Reprinted by permission of the publisher.

This model is probably more applicable to adults, because children will be more sporadic and informal in their activity patterns. Nevertheless, the Sallis and Hovell (1990) model provides a useful base from which to consider the psychological correlates of HRPA in children. This section will focus on the processes of maintenance and dropout; little is known about the adoption of exercise in children.

Motives for Participation and Reasons for Dropout

Several papers have reported data on why children participate in or drop out of sport (Fox & Biddle, 1988). The motives most commonly identified by children are to have fun, to learn or improve skills, to be with their friends, to have excitement, to win, to be successful, and for health and fitness. The Canada Fitness Survey (1983) showed that youth aged 10 to 18 years rated a mix of physical and psychological health factors as 'very important' reasons for being active. These are shown in Figure 4.5.

Reasons cited for giving up sport include a lack of playing time (this is more usual for children in North America, where the use of substitutes is more prevalent), a lack of improvement, not having fun, or an overemphasis on winning, parental pressure, and dislike of the coach.

A study by White and Coakley (1986), on school leavers in South East England, revealed a number of influences on why older teenagers did not take part in community sport programmes. Such decisions were influenced by negative perceptions of competence, constraints such as lack of money, lack of support from significant others, and past negative experiences in school PE. Negative memories of PE included boredom, perceived lack of choice, feelings of incompetence, and negative peer evaluation. Girls reported feelings of discomfort and embarrassment, dissatisfaction with the physical environment in school PE, as well as the rules relating to kit and showers.

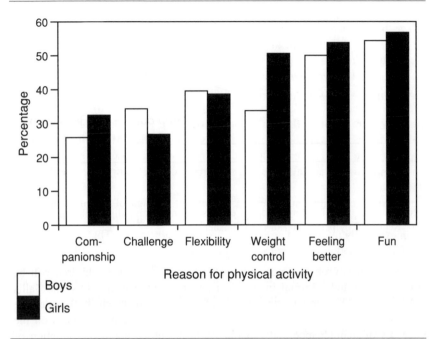

Figure 4.5 Major reasons rated as 'very important for being active' by Canadian youth aged 10 to 18 years. *Note.* Data from Canada Fitness Survey (1983).

The reasons cited by children for participating in sport and exercise do not, of course, necessarily reflect the initial influences or determinants of their involvement. For example, a child may start playing badminton at the local sport centre simply because his or her friends are there. However, once the child is involved, the reasons for continuing playing may change to, say, skill development. Teachers are encouraged to ask children why they do or do not participate in certain activities and use such information to their advantage in motivating and planning participation. Where a matching of activities with motives occurs, participation is more likely to be sustained. Similarly, despite the emphasis on competitive activities, not all children are motivated by competition. Telema and Silvennoinen (1979) found that motivation toward competition and performance declined across the teen years, whereas recreation and relaxation motives became more important.

Intrinsic Motivation

Intrinsic motivation (IM) is motivation related to participation for its own sake rather than for external rewards such as badges or money. Intrinsic motivation has been conceptualized in a number of different ways, but Deci and Ryan (1985) say that it is concerned with self-determination and competence and with feelings of enjoyment and interest.

The belief that IM is important for participation in HRPA in children is probably correct, although the relationship between IM, other influences, and behaviour is far from simple. For example, the use of external rewards or other external events have been shown, under some circumstances, to reduce IM.

Whitehead and Corbin (1991) investigated the effects on IM of giving norm-referenced feedback to children after a fitness test (agility run). Children were told they were in either the top or the bottom 20% for students of their age. In reality, the scores were bogus. The results showed that IM declined for those told they were in the lower group, and IM increased for those in the upper group. Analyses showed that this was due to perceptions of competence held by the children.

Intrinsic motivation, and the accompanying feelings of self-determination, interest, and enjoyment, are not likely to accrue to large numbers of children when externally referenced criteria are used for judgements. This was supported by Vallerand and colleagues (Vallerand, Gauvin, and Halliwell, 1986a, 1986b) for children in competitive situations. From a health-related perspective, an important aim is to have as many people participating as possible. A reorientation of the way some activities are presented may therefore be required.

Perceptions of Success and Goal Orientations

A number of researchers in both the United States (Duda, 1989) and Britain (Whitehead, 1986) have highlighted the importance of recognizing that children may differ from each other in terms of the goals that they may have in achievement situations. Two of the most commonly found goals are those labelled 'mastery-oriented' goals and 'ego-oriented' goals. The former refer to children who measure their success in terms of the extent to which they improve or master the activity, and this is independent of the success of other people. Ego-oriented goals are held by children who judge their success by winning and losing. Social comparison then becomes the important factor.

Some researchers have suggested that these goals will focus children on either effort or ability judgements. Ego goals will create a situation whereby the child considers others and her or his ability to do better, and therefore ability is the main attribution used to explain success or failure. Under failure conditions this can be debilitating (see Dweck and Leggett, 1988). For mastery goals, because the motivation is to improve or master a task, personal effort becomes more salient. This is a controllable attribution that allows the child a possibility of success after a failure situation. This would suggest that a mastery orientation to HRPA will predict higher participation levels. These notions have support in the education literature (Dweck & Leggett, 1988) but require support in health and physical activity contexts (see Biddle and Fox, 1988).

Exercise Motivation: Support

Motivation is a complex topic, and space does not allow justice to be done to some of the issues raised. Nevertheless, educators need to be aware of various approaches to motivation and sport and exercise in children. These include recognizing children's motives for participation, the possible reasons predicting dropout, the nature of intrinsic motivation, children's various goal orientations and the possible consequences of these for participation.

Intervention Strategies

Attempts at increasing children's involvement in HRPA can be made at both the individual and the institutional level. Both of these will be addressed briefly here.

Institutions

Parcel et al. (1987) suggest that schools should use social learning theory and organizational change if the impact of a health programme is to be felt. Interventions based on social learning theory would include modelling (role models), behaviour reinforcement, and cognitive change. In addition, organizational changes in the school may be required. Parcel et al. suggest four major stages in this: institutional commitment, structured alterations in school policies and practices, changes in the role and actions of staff, and the implementation of learning activities for students. These interventions, as applied to the promotion of aerobic exercise, are illustrated in Figure 4.6

One intervention frequently cited as a possible remedy for low activity levels in children is the introduction of daily periods of physical activity (PA) or physical education, particularly in primary schools (School Sport Forum, 1988). However, it is not clear whether this would simply be a daily 'training' session or constitute a more educational use of time by teaching physical education. More time is not necessarily the answer, and studies evaluating the physical fitness outcomes of daily PE programmes (e.g. Pollatschek and O'Hagan, 1989) have been relatively unsuccessful in demonstrating major changes, probably due to the current lack of valid and reliable field tests and the problems of assessing children's fitness in the field (see later in this chapter).

Similarly, daily PE/PA studies have attempted to demonstrate that academic performance is at least unaffected, and probably improved, as a result of the extra physical activity (Dwyer, Coonan, Leitch, Hetzel, & Baghurst, 1983; Pollatschek & O'Hagan, 1989). Regrettably, the methodological problems inherent in these studies precludes firm conclusions being drawn.

In short, we believe that daily vigorous PA is not the answer. What is required is a quality teaching programme emphasizing the processes and benefits of HRPA across the life span and how such activity can be accommodated in an individual's lifestyle.

One of the problems of approaches such as daily PE/PA is obtaining a balance between short- and long-term objectives. If such an institutional intervention is applied because children have low activity levels, is it the role of the school to promote physical activity, exercise and fitness in the short term or to encourage

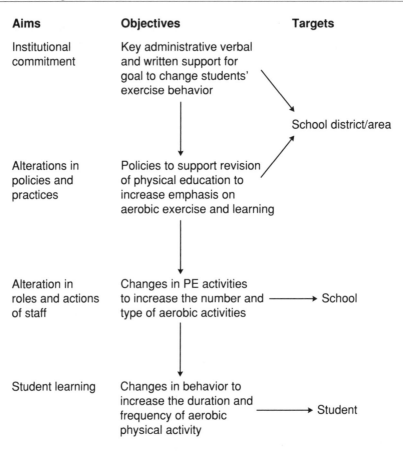

Aims   **Objectives**   **Targets**

Institutional   Key administrative verbal
commitment   and written support for
goal to change students'
exercise behavior

School district/area

Alterations in   Policies to support revision
policies and   of physical education to
practices   increase emphasis on
aerobic exercise and learning

Alteration in   Changes in PE activities
roles and actions   to increase the number and ⟶ School
of staff   type of aerobic activities

Student learning   Changes in behavior to
increase the duration and
frequency of aerobic ⟶ Student
physical activity

Figure 4.6   A school health-promotion model applied to aerobic exercise. *Note*. Adapted with permission. Parcel, G.S., Simons-Morton, B.G., O'Hara, N.M., Baranowski, T., Kolbe, L.J., Bee, D.E. School Promotion of Healthful Diet and Exercise Behavior: An Integration of Organizational Change and Social Learning Theory Interventions. *Journal of School Health,* **57**, p. 4, April 1987, p. 154. Copyright, 1987. American School Health Association, P.O Box 708, Kent, OH 44240.

and develop long-term behaviour-change strategies that will be used by the students once they have left school? Current pleas for extra time in PE are often based on the assumption that PE teachers require this time to 'get children fit'. Such an approach could lead to negative experiences for many pupils. The goals must be reoriented towards the achievement of longer-term aims and objectives, such as behaviour change. This is not to say that children should not experience exercise appropriate for fitness development, but teachers will realize that time does not permit genuine long-term fitness development in curriculum time. Physical education teachers may wish to consider the use of homework assignments (for knowledge, practical learning exercises etc.) to make up for the erosion of PE time in the schools in the last 2 decades (Physical Education Association [PEA], 1987).

Individuals

There are a number of strategies for individual-behaviour change that can be implemented in schools to help children learn about long-term involvement in HRPA. Space here permits brief discussion only.

Teaching children 'self-regulatory' skills holds an important key to future participation in HRPA. One of the main elements of this is the ability to understand and set personal goals. The goal-setting process (see Wraith and Biddle, 1986) can be complex, but the following guidelines should be taught to children:

1. Set short-, medium- and long-term goals. See goal setting as a stairway, with long-term goals at the top of the stairs.
2. Set goals that relate to the *process* of exercise rather than just the product. In other words, focus on goals that encourage participation over and above fitness or performance outcomes. This is particularly important for those less fit or willing. Indeed, some have advocated that for the initial stage in an exercise programme, fitness improvement should be discouraged so that time is allowed for gradual and comfortable changes in behaviour to be made (Rejeski & Kenney, 1988). We concur with such an approach for children.
3. Set goals that are specific, realistic and reasonably challenging. Goals must act as a stimulus—not too hard and not too easy.
4. Goals must be accepted by the participant, and he or she must be committed to achieving them. This can be enhanced by having the participant set the goals or at least be involved in the goal-setting process. Goals set externally, by the teacher for example, often have less impact.
5. Monitor the goals by writing them down, and obtain feedback on progress.

In addition to goal setting, children should be taught how to programme exercise into their lives. This should include programme-planning exercises where children are introduced to the following ideas and topics:

• Why people exercise
• Why people may quit exercise, and the barriers that can inhibit participation
• How to construct an exercise timetable
• Which activities may be appropriate from the point of view of individual motives and interests, convenience and likely adherence, and health/fitness requirements
• How to set appropriate goals

Other self-regulatory skills might include positive self-talk, where negative thoughts about physical activity are modified to be more positive; planning and understanding the process of temporary dropout (due to illness for example) so that exercise can restart again; and self-reinforcement. Further discussion on these and other techniques can be found in Knapp (1988).

Health-Related Fitness Testing and Monitoring in Schools

The availability of cheap equipment and elementary computer software packages seem to have restimulated interest in performance tests of health-related fitness. A number of PE departments are administering their own fitness test batteries and developing norm tables or percentile charts against which to compare their students. Some departments are including scores in student profiles, and others are using them as a means of evaluating the effectiveness of their teaching programmes. The Council of Europe Committee of Ministers has recommended that member states adopt the Eurofit tests of physical fitness for the purpose of measuring and assessing the physical fitness of school-age children in the range 6 to 18 years old (Recommendation No. R(87)9, 1987). The Inner London Education Authority (ILEA, 1988) Working Party on Physical Education and School Sport recommended that all pupils from 10 to 18 years old should be tested for fitness at regular intervals and parents informed of their children's fitness rating assessed against accepted norms. A nationwide survey of Northern Ireland children's physical fitness has recently been published (Riddoch, 1990), yet there has been little informed debate about the validity of using HRF tests with children (Armstrong, 1987b, 1989b). This section will evaluate the role of HRF testing and monitoring procedures within the school PE curriculum.

The quantitative assessment of children's HRF is one of the most complex problems in exercise science, and HRF tests suitable for use in the school environment that provide valid and objective measures of HRF are currently not available. All fitness test scores are influenced by a number of factors, and these are illustrated in Figure 4.7. Fox and Biddle (1986, 1987) have discussed these at length, and interested readers are referred to these papers. In short, only part of the score obtained from performance tests (e.g. shuttle runs, sit-ups, flexed arm hangs) is related to HRF. The dependence of test scores upon the subject's motivation to do well, for example, was vividly illustrated by Schwab's 1953 study (cited in Welford, 1968, p. 245). Schwab required subjects to hang from a horizontal bar (flexed arm hang) in a manner similar to the test recommended to assess local muscular endurance in the *Handbook for the Assessment of Physical Fitness* (PEA, 1978). He found that with instructions to hold on 'as long as possible', the average length of time before letting go was less than 1 minute. With a $5 reward promised for beating their previous records, subjects managed to hang on for an average of nearly 2 minutes. So their 'local muscular endurance' was doubled with a financial inducement!

Several advocates of HRF testing emphasize the use of norm tables, but norm tables confound rather than clarify the issue of relative fitness. Norms are based

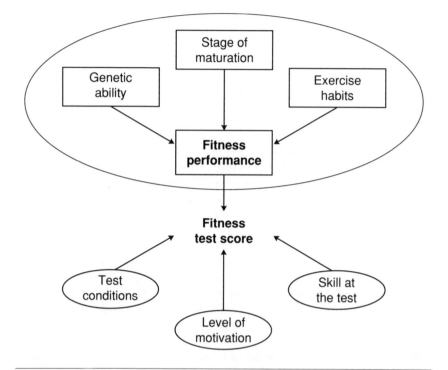

Figure 4.7 Factors affecting HRF test scores. *Note*. This article is reprinted with permission from the *Journal of Physical Education, Recreation & Dance*, February, 1988, p. 49. The *Journal* is a publication of the American Alliance for Health, Physical Education, Recreation and Dance, 1900 Association Drive, Reston, VA 22091.

on performance rather than capabilities, and, for example, if teachers accept lower norms for girls as reflecting acceptable performance, then girls will tend to meet these lower expectations (see Thomas and Thomas, 1988). The constant comparison of children on the basis of test scores is likely to negatively affect those who score low. Furthermore, how can tables constructed on the basis of chronological age provide worthwhile information about children at different levels of skeletal and biological maturation? With 13-year-old boys, a teacher may be testing a group in which 10% are prepubertal, 10% are in pubertal stage 5 (fully mature) and the remainder are somewhere in between. The effects of growth and maturation on performance and children's responses to exercise training are well documented, and for further clarification interested readers are directed to more detailed analyses (e.g. Armstrong and Davies, 1984).

Each of the components of HRF could be used to illustrate the futility of HRF testing from a physiological viewpoint (see Armstrong, 1987b), but as cardiopulmonary fitness is arguably the most important component, we will, for the purpose of this chapter, concentrate upon the testing of children's cardiopulmonary fitness.

No one parameter can fully describe cardiopulmonary fitness, but it is widely recognized (e.g. Åstrand and Rodahl, 1986) that the best single physiological indicator is the maximal rate at which oxygen can be consumed ($\dot{V}O_2$max or peak $\dot{V}O_2$). The results of any test claiming to measure children's cardiopulmonary fitness must be correlated strongly with peak $\dot{V}O_2$ if the test is to be judged valid. The determination of peak $\dot{V}O_2$ requires sophisticated apparatus and expertise usually only available in a well-equipped exercise physiology laboratory. However, several performance tests designed to predict cardiopulmonary fitness using cheap and simple apparatus have been developed and are currently in use in schools. The most commonly used procedure is to predict peak $\dot{V}O_2$ from a single submaximal heart rate measurement and the corresponding oxygen consumption or power output on a step bench or cycle ergometer, using the Åstrand nomogram (Åstrand & Rodahl, 1986), which is often supplied as a computer program. The nomogram was, however, derived from data on an adult population, and several incorrect assumptions are made when it is applied to children. The cardiopulmonary responses of children to submaximal exercise do not parallel those of adults, and children's maximal heart rates are often much higher than those of adults, with a much greater range (Armstrong & Davies, 1984). Realizing the obvious problems involved, the Åstrands have never seriously tested their nomogram with individuals below the age of 20 years (P.O. Åstrand, personal communication), but others persist in doing so.

Wilmore and Sigerseth (1967) found the prediction of $\dot{V}O_2$max to be 'questionable' with girls aged 7 to 13 years. Hermansen and Oseid (1971) concluded that an indirect method of estimating $\dot{V}O_2$max should be used only when accurate individual values are not required. Washburn and Montoye (1984) commented that the prediction of an individual's $\dot{V}O_2$max from submaximal data was subject to large errors. Woynarowska (1980) tested 80 boys and 43 girls and reported that the Åstrand nomogram underestimated the measured $\dot{V}O_2$max in boys by an average of 26% and in girls by an average of 23%. Buono and colleagues (Buono, Roby, Micale, & Sallis, 1989) reported similar results and suggested that 'use of the Åstrand nomogram to predict $\dot{V}O_2$max in children and adolescents is not warranted at this time' (p. 281). Koch, Karlegard, and Fransson (1989) obtained extensive cardiovascular and lung function data annually on a group of 10 boys from the age of 12 to 17 years. They investigated the accuracy of predicting $\dot{V}O_2$max from data obtained at submaximal exercise, including the Åstrands' methodology, and concluded that 'in the age group of 12 to 17 years, true $\dot{V}O_2$max cannot be properly evaluated from submaximal measurements but has to be directly determined' (p. 175). (Binkhorst, Saris, Noordeloos, Van't Hoff, and de Haan (1986) summed up their studies with the recommendation that 'it is therefore strongly advised not to use prediction formulas for an accurate individual $\dot{V}O_2$max determination' (p. 232). In our laboratory the standard error of prediction using either the Åstrand nomogram or the similar Margaria, Aghemo, and Rovelli (1965) procedure with young boys has proved to be 10% to 12% (Armstrong & Davies, 1984).

A substantial volume of data concerned with children's PWC170 has also been accumulated, and most published 'fitness' surveys from the United Kingdom and

Ireland have relied on this measure (e.g. Paliczka, Boreham and Kerr 1986; Watson and O'Donovan, 1976). The PWC170, first promoted by Wahlund (1948), is a measure of 'physical work capacity' (more correctly, power output) at a heart rate of 170 BPM during cycle ergometry. There are, however, many problems with the use of the PWC170 test, and it is of limited value as a measure of cardiopulmonary fitness in children. The fundamental assumption of a constant mechanical efficiency during cycling is not valid. In adults the mechanical efficiency of cycling is assumed to be 22% to 23%, but with children it has been shown to vary from 14.5% to 34.4% (Mellorwicz [1967], cited in Shephard, 1982, p. 7; Seliger, 1970, cited in Shephard, 1982, p. 71; Taylor, Bal, Lamb, & Macloed, 1950). This variation is probably due to the facts that most children are not accustomed to pedalling at a slow and constant speed against a heavy resistance and that the posture required on a cycle ergometer differs from that adopted on most modern bicycles. Mechanical efficiency improves with practice, and familiarization with the test has been demonstrated to increase scores by as much as 10% (Shephard, 1982). Furthermore, in our experience (e.g. Armstrong and Davies, 1981) the coefficient of variation of children's maximal heart rate during cycle ergometry is about 5%, which makes the PWC170 data very difficult to interpret in terms of children's peak $\dot{V}O_2$.

Some investigators have used maximal performance tests, such as the 12-minute run (Cooper, 1968), to predict $\dot{V}O_2$max (Cumming, cited in Shephard, 1971, p. 336; Shephard, 1978), but this type of test is more a reflection of the environment, the child's pace judgement and the potency of the motivational conditions under which the test takes place than of $\dot{V}O_2$max. Kemper and Verschuur (1985) studied the relationship between $\dot{V}O_2$max and the 12-minute run on a longitudinal basis and discovered that in boys, 12-minute-run performance increased with age, whereas $\dot{V}O_2$max in relation to body weight remained constant, and in girls the decrease in $\dot{V}O_2$max in relation to body weight was not accompanied by a fall in 12-minute-run performance. They concluded that the 12-minute run and $\dot{V}O_2$max in relation to body weight were measuring different fitness (performance) factors. Following his review of the literature, Cunningham (1980) concluded that performance tests such as running for 12 minutes were relatively weak predictors of $\dot{V}O_2$max.

Leger (Leger & Lambert, 1982) recently introduced a performance test, the 20-metre progressive shuttle run, that has been enthusiastically adopted by the National Coaching Foundation (1988) and the Health Education Authority (HEA)/ PEA Health and Physical Education Project (1988, pp. 12-15). The validity of the test with children is not well documented, but initial results with small groups of boys and girls were initially encouraging (Boreham, Paliczka, & Nichols, 1987; van Mechelen, Hlobil, & Kemper, 1986). However, we (Armstrong, Williams, & Ringham, 1988) examined the relationship of directly determined peak $\dot{V}O_2$ to peak $\dot{V}O_2$ predicted from progressive shuttle-run performance in 77 boys, aged 11 to 14 years, and found that the common variance between the two scores was only 29%. This is not better than can be achieved from other simple field tests, and it was concluded that the use of the 20-metre progressive shuttle run as a valid substitute for a direct determination of an individual's $\dot{V}O_2$max cannot be supported.

Cumming (1971) stated that in normal children the prediction of $\dot{V}O_2$max is little better than can be obtained from height, weight and skinfold measurements. He felt that performance tests distinguish the obvious and can tell the athlete from the nonathlete but are of limited value in the evaluation of physiological functions in the average population. Shephard (1982) commented that performance tests are a complicated way of identifying tall or fat pupils.

Recent research results are therefore unequivocal and confirm that with children there is no valid substitute for a direct determination of peak $\dot{V}O_2$ (cardiopulmonary fitness).

In earlier sections of this chapter we described the analysis by Armstrong et al. (1990a) of children's physical activity patterns through continuous heart rate monitoring. They also examined the same children's cardiopulmonary fitness (peak $\dot{V}O_2$) determined during either treadmill or cycle ergometry (Armstrong, Balding, Gentle, Williams, and Kirby, 1990). When these researchers compared peak $\dot{V}O_2$ with heart rate indicators of habitual physical activity, they failed to detect any significant relationship between the two. This, they argued, was not an unexpected finding when one considers the presence of an as yet unquantified genetic component of peak $\dot{V}O_2$ (Bouchard & Lortie, 1984) and the influence of the body size/maturation interaction on the development of peak $\dot{V}O_2$ (Cunningham, Paterson, & Blimkie, 1984). However, it does put the use of fitness testing, whether the tests are valid or not, into perspective. If one is interested in physical activity as a means of preventing degenerative diseases, numerous epidemiological studies (reviewed by Armstrong, 1990) have demonstrated that it is current physical activity, more than cardiopulmonary fitness, that should be emphasized. The simple fact is that few children experience the recommended volume of physical activity, and even fewer children exhibit the levels of physical activity associated with the improvement of peak $\dot{V}O_2$ (cardiopulmonary fitness).

Pedagogical Issues

The discussion so far has centred on the problems inherent in *measuring* children's fitness. Our conclusion is that valid and reliable measures in the field are not available and that tests currently in use are too reliant on factors *unrelated to current exercise habits*. This renders fitness tests obsolete in the curriculum unless other objectives can be stated and justified. One objective proposed by Fox and Biddle (1986) and Whitehead, Pemberton, and Corbin (1990) is the *educational* development of the child. In other words, if performance (or other) tests can be justified from an educational perspective, then the problems associated with measurement become less of an issue.

It is our belief that if the performance of some kind of HRF test takes place in PE sessions, such as running the 20-metre progressive shuttle, and can be justified on the grounds that it helps children to learn about exercise and health and assists in the promotion of HRPA, then that HRF test is an acceptable use of time. It is likely, however, that the value of such HRF tests will lie not in any scoring or classifying procedure but in the feedback provided by the teacher. PE often emphasizes performance, but a different philosophy is required to properly use HRF tests, where the emphasis should be on learning, self-improvement and motivation. Regrettably, certain types of feedback are as likely to demotivate as to motivate.

Teachers and students must be aware of the severe limitations of HRF tests in the complex analysis and assessment of children's fitness. Teachers must ask themselves why they are 'testing' children's fitness, and if the answer is 'to classify children', then perhaps they would be better employed seriously addressing the problem of children's sedentary physical activity patterns.

Towards the National Curriculum

In earlier sections of this chapter we argued the case for HRPA and described the psychological and physiological outcomes associated with an active lifestyle. On the surface it appears that physical educators have taken on board the issues we have raised, and the 1980s saw a reemergence of emphasis upon health-related fitness within the physical education programme (Armstrong, 1987c; Armstrong and Davies, 1980; Biddle, 1981, 1987). A survey by the Physical Education Association (1987) illustrated that heads of department rated the promotion of physical development (HRF) the 2nd most important objective of physical education. A previous survey (Kane, 1974) had ranked physical development 7th in order of importance. The PEA (1987) commented that 'this major shift represents accurately the recent and positive encouragement being given to the movement for health-related fitness in the physical education programme' (p. 25).

The following year the Inner London Education Authority (ILEA) School Sport Working Party concluded, 'Enthusing and informing the young about physical activity to be the top priority for teachers of physical education' (ILEA, 1988, p. 1).

By the end of the decade Her Majesty's Inspectorate (Department of Education and Science, 1989) had endorsed the view that 'to develop an understanding of the importance of exercise in maintaining a healthy life' is a fundamental aim of physical education.

In the previous volume of this series, however, one of us (Armstrong, 1990) pointed out that although heads of PE departments may perceive the importance of promoting HRF/PA, their curricula may not be geared to this objective. Recent attempts (reviewed earlier) to promote active lifestyles through the PE programme or supplements to it have generally been unsuccessful. In this chapter we have documented unequivocal evidence, from studies in the PEA Research Centre, that despite 10 years of a supposed emphasis on the promotion of active lifestyles, both primary and secondary British schoolchildren exhibit very low levels of habitual HRPA.

We have therefore reaffirmed our view that physical educators must promote active lifestyles more explicitly and that HRPA must be a central issue in physical education. HRPA should underpin the physical education programme, and we endorse the view of the British Association of Sports Sciences (BASS)/HEA/ PEA Working Group that children need to experience

> a wide variety of individual, partner and team activities, with the emphasis placed upon developing a sound foundation of motor skills, which can contribute to successful and enjoyable physical activity experiences both in the present and the future. (Armstrong, Bellew, et al., 1990, p. 225)

These experiences need to be supported by a theoretical framework, and pupils should develop understanding of HRPA's beneficial effects and the ways these benefits can be achieved and sustained through adult life.

We opened this chapter with a quotation from Grant (1990): 'Failure to protect the physical, mental and emotional development of children is the principal means by which humanity's difficulties are compounded and its problems perpetuated' (p. 7). We have shown that physical educators are well placed to address major aspects of this problem. They must meet this challenge, and we look to the National Curriculum to recommend appropriate programmes of study.

References

Abraham, S., & Nordsieck, M. (1960). Relationship of excess weight in children and adults. *Public Health Reports*, **75**, 263-273.

Alter, M.J. (1988). *Science of stretching*. Champaign, IL: Human Kinetics.

American College of Sports Medicine. (1988). Opinion statement on physical fitness in children and youth. *Medicine and Science in Sports and Exercise,* **20**, 422-423.

Andersen, K.L., Masironi, R., Rutenfranz, J., & Seliger, V. (1978). *Habitual physical activity and health* (World Health Organization Regional Publications, European Series, No. 6). Copenhagen: World Health Organization.

Armstrong, N. (1987a). The physiological foundations of health-related fitness. In N. Armstrong (Ed.), *Health and fitness in the curriculum* (Perspectives 31, pp. 35-48). Exeter: University of Exeter.

Armstrong, N. (1987b). A critique of fitness testing. In S. Biddle (Ed.), *Foundations of health-related fitness in physical education* (pp. 136-138). London: Ling.

Armstrong, N. (Ed.) (1987c). *Health and fitness in the curriculum* (Perspectives 31, pp. 1-109). Exeter: University of Exeter.

Armstrong, N. (1989a). Children are fit but not active. *Education and Health*, **7**, 28-32.

Armstrong, N. (1989b). Is fitness testing in schools either valid or useful? *British Journal of Physical Education*, **20**, 66-67.

Armstrong, N. (1990). Children's physical activity patterns: The implications for physical education. In N. Armstrong (Ed.), *New directions in physical education Volume 1*, (pp. 1-15). Champaign, IL: Human Kinetics.

Armstrong, N., Balding, J., Bray, S., Gentle, P., & Kirby, B. (1990). The physical activity patterns of 10 and 13 year old children. In G. Beunen, J. Ghesquiere, R. Reybrouck, & A.L. Claessens (Eds.), *Children and exercise 14* (pp. 152-157). Hamburg: Schriftenreihe der Hamburg-Munnheimer-Stiftung für Informationsmedizin.

Armstrong, N., Balding, J., Gentle, P., & Kirby, B. (1990a). Patterns of physical activity among 11 to 16 year old children. *British Medical Journal, 301*, 203-205.

Armstrong, N., Balding, J., Gentle, P., & Kirby, B. (1990b). The estimation of coronary risk factors in British school children—a preliminary report. *British Journal of Sports Medicine, 24*, 61-66.

Armstrong, N., Balding, J., Gentle, P., Williams, J., & Kirby, B. (1990). Peak oxygen uptake and habitual physical activity in 11 to 16 year olds. *Pediatric Exercise Science, 2*, 349-358.

Armstrong, N., Bellew, B., Biddle, S., Bray, S., Gardonyi, P., & Winter, E. (1990). Health-related physical activity in the National Curriculum. *British Journal of Physical Education, 21*, 225.

Armstrong, N., & Bray, S. (1987). Foundations of health-related activity. *British Journal of Physical Education, 18*, 171-172.

Armstrong, N., & Bray, S. (1991). Physical activity patterns determined by continuous heart rate monitoring. *Archives of Disease in Childhood, 66*, 245-247.

Armstrong, N., & Davies, B. (1980). Coronary risk factors in children—the role of the physical educator. *Bulletin of Physical Education, 16*, 5-11.

Armstrong, N., & Davies, B. (1981). An ergometric analysis of age group swimmers. *British Journal of Sports Medicine, 15*, 20-26.

Armstrong, N., & Davies, B. (1984). The metabolic and physiological responses of children to exercise and training. *Physical Education Review, 7*, 90-105.

Armstrong, N., Williams, J., Balding, J., Gentle, P., and Kirby, B. (1991). Peak oxygen uptake of British children with reference to chronological age, sex and sexual maturity. *European Journal of Applied Physiology, 62*, 369-375.

Armstrong, N., Williams, J., & Ringham, D. (1988). Peak oxygen uptake and progressive shuttle run performance in boys aged 11-14 years. *British Journal of Physical Education Research Supplement, 4*, 10-11.

Åstrand, P.O., & Rodahl, K. (1986). *Textbook of work physiology*. New York: McGraw-Hill.

Bar-Or, O. (1983). *Paediatric sports medicine for the practitioner*. New York: Springer-Verlag.

Biddle, S.J.H. (1981). The "why" of health-related fitness. *Bulletin of Physical Education, 17*, 28-31.

Biddle, S.J.H. (Ed.) (1987). *Foundations of health-related fitness in physical education*. London: Ling.

Biddle, S.J.H.,& Fox, K.R. (1988). The child's perspective in physical education: 4. Achievement psychology. *British Journal of Physical Education, 19*, 182-185.

Biddle, S.J.H., & Mutrie, N. (1991). *Psychology of physical activity and exercise: A health-related perspective.* London: Springer-Verlag.

Binkhorst, R.A., Saris, W.H.M., Noordeloos, A.M., Van't Hoff, M.A., & de Haan, A.F.J. (1986). Maximal oxygen consumption of children (6 to 18 years) predicted from maximal and submaximal values in treadmill and bicycle tests. In J. Rutenfranz, R. Mocellin, & I. Klimt (Eds.), *Children and exercise 12* (pp. 227-232). Champaign, IL: Human Kinetics.

Boreham, C.A.G., Paliczka, V.J., & Nichols, A.K. (1987). *A comparison of two field tests of aerobic capacity in schoolchildren.* Paper presented at the British Association of Sports Sciences Annual Conference, West London Institute of Higher Education, London.

Borms, J. (1986). The child and exercise: An overview. *Journal of Sports Sciences, 4*, 3-20.

Bouchard, C., & Lortie, G. (1984). Heredity and endurance performance. *Sports Medicine, 1*, 38-64.

Bouchard, C., Shephard, R.J., Stephens, T., Sutton, J.R., & McPherson, B.D. (Eds.) (1990). *Exercise, fitness, and health: A consensus of current knowledge.* Champaign, IL: Human Kinetics.

Bourey, R.E., & Santoro, S.A. (1988). Interactions of exercise, coagulation, platelets and fibronolysis—a brief review. *Medicine and Science in Sports and Exercise, 20*, 439-446.

British Cardiac Society. (1986). *Report of the British Cardiac Society Working Group on Coronary Disease Prevention.* London: Author.

Brown, R.W. (1982). Exercise and mental health in the pediatric population. *Clinics in Sports Medicine, 1*, 515-527.

Buono, M.J., Roby, J.J., Micale, F.G., & Sallis, J.F. (1989). Predicting maximal oxygen uptake in children: Modification of the Åstrand-Ryhming test. *Pediatric Exercise Science, 1*, 278-283.

Canada Fitness Survey. (1983). *Canadian youth and physical activity.* Ottawa: Canada Fitness Survey.

Caspersen, C.J., Powell, K., & Christenson, G. (1985). Physical activity, exercise and physical fitness: Definitions and distinctions for health-related research. *Public Health Reports, 100*, 126-131.

Committee on Medical Aspects of Food Policy. (1984). *Diet and cardiovascular disease.* London: Department of Health and Social Security.

Cooper, K.H. (1968). A means of assessing maximal oxygen uptake. *Journal of the American Medical Association, 203*, 135-138.

Corbin, C.B., & Lindsey, R. (1984). *The ultimate fitness book.* Champaign, IL: Leisure Press.

Corbin, C.B., & Lindsey, R. (1988). *Concepts of physical fitness* (5th ed.). Dubuque, IA: Brown.

Crews, D., & Landers, D.M. (1987). A meta-analytic review of aerobic fitness and reactivity to psychosocial stressors. *Medicine and Science in Sports and Exercise,* **19**, S114-S120.

Csikszentmihalyi, M. (1975). *Beyond boredom and anxiety.* San Francisco: Jossey-Bass.

Cunningham, D.A. (1980). Physical working capacity of children and adolescents. In G.A. Stull (Ed.), *Encyclopedia of physical education, fitness and sports* (pp. 481-494). Salt Lake City: Brighton Publishing.

Cunningham, D.A., Paterson, D.H., & Blimkie, C.J.R. (1984). The development of the cardiorespiratory system with growth and physical activity. In R.A. Boileau (Ed.), *Advances in pediatric sport sciences* (Vol. 1, pp. 85-116). Champaign, IL: Human Kinetics.

Deci, E.L., & Ryan, R.M. (1985). *Intrinsic motivation and self-determination of human behaviour.* New York: Plenum.

Department of Education and Science. (1989). *Physical education from 5 to 16.* London: Her Majesty's Stationery Office.

Department of Health and Human Services. (1980). *Promoting health/preventing disease: Objectives for the nation.* Washington, DC: U.S. Government Printing Office.

Duda, J. (1989). Goal perspectives and behaviour in sport and exercise settings. In C. Ames & M. Maehr (Eds.), *Advances in motivation and achievement: 6. Motivation enhancing environments.* Greenwich, CT: JAI Press.

Dweck, C.S., & Leggett, E.L. (1988). A social-cognitive approach to motivation and personality. *Psychological Review,* **95**, 256-273.

Dwyer, T., Coonan, W.E., Leitch, D.R., Hetzel, B.S., & Baghurst, R.A. (1983). An investigation of the effects of daily physical activity on the health of primary school students in South Australia. *International Journal of Epidemiology,* **12**, 308-313.

Engstrom, L.-M. (1986). The process of socialisation into keep-fit activities. *Scandinavian Journal of Sports Science,* **8**, 89-97.

Fentem, P.H., Bassey, E.J., & Turnbull, N.B. (1988). *The new case for exercise.* London: Sports Council and Health Education Authority.

Fox, K.R. (1988). The self-esteem complex and youth fitness. *Quest,* **40**, 230-246.

Fox, K.R., & Biddle, S.J.H. (1986). Health-related fitness testing in schools: 1. Introduction and problems of interpretation. *Bulletin of Physical Education,* **22**, 54-64.

Fox, K.R., & Biddle, S.J.H. (1987). Health-related fitness testing in schools: 2. Philosophical and psychological implications. *Bulletin of Physical Education,* **23**, 28-39.

Fox, K.R., & Biddle, S.J.H. (1988). The child's perspective in physical education: 2. Children's participation motives. *British Journal of Physical Education,* **19**, 79-82.

Grant, J.P. (1990). *The state of the world's children 1990.* Oxford: Oxford University Press and UNICEF.

Gruber, J.J. (1986). Physical activity and self-esteem development in children: A meta-analysis. In G. Stull & H. Eckhert (Eds.), *Effects of physical activity on children* (pp. 30-48). Champaign, IL: Human Kinetics.

Hagberg, J.M., Ehsani, A.A., Goldring, D., Hernandez, A., Sinacore, D.R., & Holloszy, J.O. (1984). Effect of weight training on blood pressure and hemodynamics in hypertensive adolescents. *Journal of Pediatrics, 104*, 147-151.

Haskell, W.L., Montoye, H.J., & Orenstein, D. (1985). Physical activity and exercise to achieve health-related physical fitness components. *Public Health Reports, 100*, 202-212.

Health Education Authority/Physical Education Association Health and Physical Education Project. (1988). *The exercise challenge.* Loughborough: Loughborough University.

Heartbeat Wales. (1987). *Exercise for health* (Heartbeat Report No. 23). Cardiff: Author.

Hermansen, L., & Oseid, S. (1971). Direct and indirect estimation of maximal oxygen uptake in pre-pubertal boys. *Acta Paediatrica Scandinavica, 217*, 18-25.

Huprich, F.L., & Sigerseth, P.O. (1950). Specificity of flexibility in girls. *Research Quarterly, 21*, 25-33.

Inner London Education Authority. (1988) *My Favourite Subject.* London: Author.

Johnson, A.L., Cornoni, J.C., Cassel, J.C., Tyroler, H.A., Heyden, S., & Hames, C.G. (1975). Influence of race, sex and weight on blood pressure behaviour in young adults. *American Journal of Cardiology, 35*, 523-530.

Kane, J.E. (1974). *Physical education in secondary schools.* London: Macmillan.

Kemper, H.C.G., & Verschuur, R. (1985). Maximal aerobic power. *Medicine and Sport Science, 20*, 107-126.

Knapp, D.N. (1988). Behavioural management techniques and exercise promotion. In R.K. Dishman (Ed.), *Exercise adherence: Its impact on public health* (pp. 203-235). Champaign, IL: Human Kinetics.

Koch, G., Karlegard, L., & Fransson, L. (1989). How precisely can true maximal oxygen uptake be evaluated from measurements at submaximal exercise? *Pediatric Exercise Science, 1*, 175.

Krahenbuhl, G.S., Skinner, J.S., & Kohrt, W.M. (1985). Developmental aspects of maximal aerobic power in children. *Exercise and Sport Sciences Reviews, 13*, 503-538.

Layman, E.M. (1970). The role of play and sport in healthy emotional development: A reappraisal. In G.S. Kenyon (Ed.), *Contemporary psychology of sport* (pp. 249-257). Chicago: Athletic Institute.

Leger, L.S., & Lambert, J. (1982). A maximal multistage shuttle run test to predict $\dot{V}O_2$max. *European Journal of Applied Physiology, 49*, 1-5.

Leighton, J.R. (1956). Flexibility characteristics of males 10 to 18 years of age. *Archives of Physical Medicine and Rehabilitation, 37*, 494-499.

Leon, A.S., & Blackburn, H. (1983). Physical inactivity. In N.M. Kaplan & J. Stamler (Eds.), *Prevention of coronary heart disease* (pp. 86-97). Philadelphia: Saunders.

Lohman, T.G. (1986). Applicability of body composition techniques and constants for children and youths. *Exercise and Sport Sciences Reviews*, **14**, 325-358.

Margaria, R., Aghemo, P., & Rovelli, E. (1965). Indirect determination of maximal oxygen consumption in man. *Journal of Applied Physiology*, **20**, 1070-1073.

Martinsen, E.W., Strand, J., Paullson, G., and Kaggestad, J. (1989). Physical fitness level in patients with anxiety and depressive disorders. *International Journal of Sports Medicine*, **10**, 58-61.

Masicotte, D.R., & MacNab, R.B.J. (1974). Cardiorespiratory adaptations to training at specified intensities in children. *Medicine and Science in Sports*, **6**, 242-246.

Morgan, W.P., & Goldston, S.E. (Eds.) (1987). *Exercise and mental health.* Washington: Hemisphere.

Morse, M., Schlutz, F.W., & Cassels, D.E. (1949). Relation of age to physiological responses of the older boy to exercise. *Journal of Applied Physiology*, **1**, 683-709.

National Advisory Committee on Nutrition Education. (1983). *Proposals for nutritional guidelines for health education in Britain.* London: Health Education Council.

National Coaching Foundation. (1988). *Multistage fitness test.* Leeds: Author.

North, T.C., McCullagh, P., & Tran, Z.V. (1990). Effect of exercise on depression. *Exercise and Sport Sciences Reviews*, **18**, 379-415.

Office of Health Economics. (1990). *Osteoporosis and the risk of fracture.* London: Author.

Paliczka, V.J., Boreham, C.A.G., & Kerr, M.J. (1986). The physical fitness of Belfast schoolchildren. In T. Riley, J. Williams, & J. Borms (Eds.), *Kinanthropometry 3. Proceedings of the 8th Commonwealth and International Conference in Sport, Physical Education, Dance, Recreation and Health* (pp. 165-171). London: Spon.

Parcel, G.S., Simons-Morton, B.G., O'Hara, N.M., Baranowski, T., Kolbe, L.J., & Bee, D.E. (1987). School promotion of healthful diet and exercise behaviour: An integration of organisational change and social learning theory interventions. *Journal of School Health*, **57**, 150-156.

Pearl, P.M. (1987). The effects of exercise on the development and function of the coronary collateral circulation. *Sports Medicine*, **4**, 86-94.

Physical Education Association. (1978). *Handbook for the assessment of physical fitness.* London: Author.

Physical Education Association. (1987). *Report of a commission of enquiry: Physical education in schools.* London: Author.

Pollatschek, J.L., & O'Hagan, F.J. (1989). An investigation of the psychophysical influences of a quality daily physical education programme. *Health Education Research: Theory and Practice*, **4**, 341-350.

Powell, K.E. (1988). Habitual exercise and public health: An epidemiological view. In R.W. Dishman (Ed.), *Exercise adherence: Its impact on public health* (pp. 15-39). Champaign, IL: Human Kinetics.

Powell, K.E., & Dysinger, W. (1987). Childhood participation in organised school sports and physical education as precursors of adult physical activity. *American Journal of Preventive Medicine, 3*, 276-281.

Powell, K.E., Thompson, P.D., Caspersen, C.J., & Kendrick, J.S. (1987). Physical activity and the incidence of coronary heart disease. *Annual Reviews of Public Health, 8*, 253-287.

Rejeski, W.J., & Kenney, E.A. (1988). *Fitness motivation: Preventing participant dropout.* Champaign, IL: Life Enhancement Publications.

Renson, R., Beunen, G., & Van Gerven, D. (1972). Relation entre des mesures somatiques et les fesultats de certain tests de souplesse. *Kenanthropologie, 4*, 131-145.

Riddoch, C. (1990). *Northern Ireland fitness survey—1989.* Belfast: Queen's University.

Riopel, D.A., Boerth, R.C., Coates, T.J., Hennekens, C.H., & Miller, W.W. (1986). Coronary risk factor modification in children: Exercise. *Circulation, 74*, 1189A-1191A.

Robinson, S. (1938). Experimental studies of physical fitness in relation to age. *Arbeitsphysiologie, 10*, 251-323.

Ross, J.G., & Gilbert, G.G. (1985). The national children and youth fitness study. A summary of findings. *Journal of Physical Education, Recreation and Dance, 56*, 45-50.

Rowland, T.W. (1990). *Exercise and children's health.* Champaign, IL: Human Kinetics.

Royal College of Physicians. (1983). Obesity. *Journal of the Royal College of Physicians, 17*, 3-58.

Ryan, A.J. (1984). Exercise and health: Lessons from the past. In H.M. Eckert & H.J. Montoye (Eds.), *Exercise and health* (pp. 3-13). Champaign, IL: Human Kinetics/American Academy of Physical Education.

Sage, G.H. (1986). Social development. In V. Seefeldt (Ed.), *Physical activity and well-being* (pp. 343-371). Reston, VA: American Alliance for Health, Physical Education, Recreation and Dance.

Sale, D.G. (1989). Strength training in children. In C.V. Gisolfi & D.R. Lamb (Eds.), *Perspectives in exercise science and sports medicine. Volume 2: Youth, exercise and sport* (pp. 165-222). Indianapolis: Benchmark Press.

Sallis, J.F., & Hovell, M.F. (1990). 'Determinants of exercise behaviour.' In *Exercise and Sport Sciences Reviews* (Vol. 18, pp. 307-330). Baltimore: Williams & Wilkins.

Scanlan, T.K., & Lewthwaite, R. (1986). Social psychological aspects of competition for male youth sport participants: 4. Predictors of enjoyment. *Journal of Sport Psychology, 8*, 25-35.

School Sport Forum. (1988). *Sport and young people: Partnership and action.* London: Sports Council.

Shephard, R.J. (Ed.) (1971). *Frontiers of fitness.* Springfield, IL: Thomas.

Shephard, R.J. (1978). The prediction of athletic performance by laboratory and field tests—an overview. In R.J. Shephard & H. Lavallee (Eds.), *Physical fitness assessment—principles, practice and application* (pp. 113-141). Springfield, IL: Thomas.

Shephard, R.J. (1982). *Physical activity and growth*. London: Year Book Medical.

Simons-Morton, B.G., O'Hara, N.M., Simons-Morton, D.G., & Parcel, G.D. (1987). Children and fitness: A public health perspective. *Research Quarterly for Exercise and Sport*, **58**, 295-302.

Simons-Morton, B.G., Parcel, G.S., O'Hara, N.M., Blair, S.N., & Pate, R.R. (1988). Health-related physical fitness in childhood. *Annual Reviews of Public Health*, **9**, 403-425.

Sinzinger, H., & Virgolini, I. (1988). Effects of exercise on parameters of blood coagulation, platelet function and the prostaglandin system. *Sports Medicine*, **6**, 238-245.

Sofranko, A.J., & Nolan, M.F. (1972). Early life experiences and adult sports participation. *Journal of Leisure Research*, **4**, 6-18.

Sports Council and Health Education Authority. (1988). *Children's exercise, health and fitness: Fact sheet*. London: Sports Council and Health Education Authority.

Stephens, T. (1988). Physical activity and mental health in the United States and Canada: Evidence from four population surveys. *Preventive Medicine*, **17**, 35-47.

Taylor, C.M., Bal, M.E.R., Lamb, M.W., & Macleod, G. (1950). Mechanical efficiency of cycling of boys seven to fifteen years of age. *Journal of Applied Physiology*, **2**, 563-570.

Telema, R., & Silvennoinen, M. (1979). Structure and development of 11 to 19 year olds' motivation for physical activity. *Scandanavian Journal of Sports Sciences*, **1**, 23-31.

Thomas, J.R., & Thomas, K.T. (1988). Development of gender differences in physical activity. *Quest*, **40**, 219-229.

Thompson, J.K., Jarvie, G.J., Lahey, B.B., & Cureton, K.J. (1982). Exercise and obesity: Etiology, physiology and intervention. *Psychological Bulletin*, **91**, 55-79.

Vallerand, R.J., Gauvin, L.I., & Halliwell, W.R. (1986a). Effects of zero-sum competition on children's intrinsic motivation and perceived competence. *Journal of Social Psychology*, **126**, 465-472.

Vallerand, R.J., Gauvin, L.I., & Halliwell, W.R. (1986b). Negative effects of competition on children's intrinsic motivation. *Journal of Social Psychology*, **126**, 649-657.

van Mechelen, W., Hlobil, H., & Kemper, H.C.G. (1986). Validation of two running tests as estimates of maximal aerobic power in children. *European Journal of Applied Physiology*, **55**, 503-506.

Vikan, A. (1985). Psychiatric epidemiology in a sample of 1,510 ten-year-old children: 1. Prevalence. *Journal of Child Psychology and Psychiatry*, **26**, 55-75.

Wahlund, H. (1948). Determination of the physical working capacity. Physiological and clinical study with special reference to standardization of cardiopulmonary functional tests. *Acta Medica Scandinavica*, **215**, 1-78.

Ward, D.S., & Bar-Or, O. (1986). Role of the physician and the physical education teacher in the treatment of obesity at school. *Pediatrician*, **13**, 44-51.

Washburn, R.A., & Montoye, H.J. (1984). The validity of predicting $\dot{V}O_2$max in males age 10-39. *Journal of Sports Medicine and Physical Fitness,* **24,** 41-48.

Watson, A.W.S., & O'Donovan, D.J. (1976). The physical working capacity of male adolescents in Ireland. *Irish Journal of Medical Science,* **145,** 383-391.

Weil, W. (1977). Current controversies in childhood obesity. *Journal of Pediatrics,* **91,** 175-187.

Weiss, M.R., & Bredemeier, B.J. (1990). Moral development in sport. *Exercise and Sport Sciences Reviews,* **18,** 331-378.

Welford, A.T. (1968). *Fundamentals of skill.* London: Methuen.

White, A., & Coakley, J.J. (1986). *Making decisions: The response of young people in the Medway towns to the 'Ever Thought of Sport?' Campaign.* London: Greater London and South East Regional Sports Council.

Whitehead, J. (1986). A cross-national comparison of attributions underlying achievement orientations in adolescent sport. In J. Watkins, T. Reilly, & L. Burwitz (Eds.), *Sports science* (pp. 297-302). London: Spon.

Whitehead, J.R., & Corbin, C.B. (1991). Youth fitness testing: The effect of percentile-based evaluative feedback on intrinsic motivation. *Research Quarterly for Exercise and Sport,* **62,** 225-231.

Whitehead, J.R., Pemberton, C.L., & Corbin, C.B. (1990). Perspectives on the physical fitness testing of children: The case for a realistic educational approach. *Pediatric Exercise Science, 2,* 111-113.

Williams, H.G. (1986). The development of sensory-motor function in young children. In V. Seefeldt (Ed.), *Physical activity and well-being* (pp. 105-122). Reston, VA: American Alliance for Health, Physical Education, Recreation and Dance.

Wilmore, J.H., & Sigerseth, P.O. (1967). Physical work capacity of young girls, 7-13 years of age. *Journal of Applied Physiology,* **22,** 923-928.

World Health Organization. (1986). *Targets for health for all.* Copenhagen: Author.

Woynarowska, B. (1980). The validity of different estimations of maximal oxygen uptake in children 11-12 years of age. *European Journal of Applied Physiology,* **43,** 19-23.

Wraith, S., & Biddle, S.J.H. (1986). Goal-setting in sport and exercise. *British Journal of Physical Education,* **17,** 208-210.

Yates, C., & Grana, W.A. (1981). Adapatations of prepubertal children to exercise. *Journal of Oklahoma State Medical Association,* **74,** 173-177.

Yoesting, D.R., & Burkhead, D.L. (1973). Significance of childhood recreation experience on adult leisure behaviour. An exploratory analysis. *Journal of Leisure Research,* **5,** 25-36.

Chapter 5

Track-and-Field Athletics in the National Curriculum

Richard J. Fisher

Within the general precepts of the National Curriculum is the notion of providing a broad and balanced educational experience for all pupils, which must also 'be fully taken up by each individual pupil'. The Education Reform Act (1988) defines this as a curriculum that 'promotes the spiritual, moral, cultural, mental and physical development of pupils at the school and of society'.

Physical education has a clear and important part to play in this process and should also, therefore, provide pupils with as broad and balanced a range of suitable movement opportunities as they are capable of absorbing. Track-and-field athletics have been identified as an essential element in this package and are fortunate in encompassing a wide variety of movement possibilities that can make an outstanding contribution to the achievement of balance and breadth in PE. However, it is necessary to ensure that a reasonable sample of the full range of work in athletics is presented, in order to ensure that these principles are supported. Often, for example, throwing receives far less attention than running and jumping, and so a whole set of relevant experiences is lost. It is worth mentioning here that within the context of the curriculum from 5 to 16, the notion of track-and-field athletics undergoes quite a transformation, from elements in guided play to a full-blown sport form. It is relevant, therefore, that teachers of Key Stages 1 and 2 appreciate the crucial contribution they make to future developments, even though they may not consider them in such a formal way while working with young children.

However, if athletics is to be an effective medium through which the National Curriculum is delivered, the current content and process of teaching athletics will need rethinking along the lines suggested in a number of publications over the last couple of years (e.g. Almond, 1987; Fisher, 1990). A number of exciting developments in the teaching of athletics are under way around the country, and these offer a good basis for development. On the whole, there is a need for more effective, experiential modes of teaching in order that pupils achieve a better understanding of athletics and of their own development within this area, including how and why their learning is progressing. In this way it should be possible to provide a valuable learning experience, within the National Curriculum for physical education, that can be utilized by all pupils and enable them to pursue track-and-field athletics at a level relevant to their own individual needs and interests.

This chapter draws on the best of current practice and ideas to examine the possibilities for track-and-field athletics in the National Curriculum.

Principles and Practice

Fundamental to any discussion of track-and-field athletics in the National Curriculum is the process of learning envisaged within the context outlined above. In the debate so far, the essence of this process would seem to revolve around the concepts of performing, knowing, understanding, planning and appraising. These embrace the development of physical competence, an evolving sense of knowledge and understanding of the principles central to performance, the promotion of an ability to plan and organize physical activities and the capacity to evaluate the consequences of one's actions. Transcending these essential elements are the eduction of positive attitudes to the activity in question and an appreciation of its cultural significance, as well as the promotion of a whole range of personal and social qualities considered to be of value within our society.

There would appear to be three practical ramifications of adopting these principles in athletics in the National Curriculum.

Developing an Understanding of Basic Skills

The fundamental orientation in teaching track and field should be towards developing a sound understanding of the principles central to the three groups of track-and-field events: running, jumping and throwing. In this way pupils should be able to build a good repertoire of increasingly more complex skills in the various events from a sound base in the 'roots' of the particular groups (see Dick, 1987). They should also be able to develop a better understanding of their own development and performance.

Running is a skill that is rarely taught effectively in schools or clubs and yet is a significant element in a host of sporting activities. Its 'roots' are in the functions of legs, trunk, arms and head. The efficient use of these major elements can be extracted in a number of ways, and pupils can be helped to understand such essential factors as posture, balance and rhythm.

Jumping in all its forms is concerned with approach, takeoff, flight and landing. Through various introductory jumping activities, pupils can come to understand how these elements combine in different situations, depending on whether they are jumping for height or for length.

Throwing, the most neglected and yet potentially one of the most enjoyable aspects of athletics in schools, has been encapsulated in four main principles by

Dick (1987). These are (a) starting from a bent rear leg, (b) rotating the trunk towards the front, (c) transferring body weight from the rear to the front and (d) bracing the front side of the body. The training exercise developed by Schwanbeck can be utilized to put these principles into practice, and as far as the pupils are concerned, it is not so far removed from a soccer-style throw-in and probably within their experience. (See Figure 5.1).

Figure 5.1   The Schwanbeck exercise. *Note.* From *Throwing* (p. 77) by M. Jones, 1987, Ramsbury, Wiltshire: Crowood Press. Reprinted by permission of the British Amateur Athletic Board.

From this base the teacher can develop such throwing essentials as applying force over as great a range as possible and the angle and height of release. Jones (1987, pp. 9-12) has outlined further useful principles to help in throwing better:

1. Slow to fast—building up to a fast release
2. Summation of forces—the sequential application of force from the larger to the smaller and faster muscles
3. Low to high—starting in a low position and finishing high
4. Legs dominant—the legs dictating and dominating the throw
5. Balance—essential throughout the throw
6. Rhythm—developing the tempo of the throw

Ensuring Children's Involvement

The teaching modes most likely to promote effective pupil learning in this context ensure that the pupil has an immediate and active involvement in the process. Exploration methods make possible this instant immersion into a base of experience from which effective movement patterns can be extracted and utilized. Moreover, the pupils should then understand how and why the phrasing of particular skills has developed. It is essential, of course, that teachers must have a good understanding of athletics to teach effectively in this way. Primary teachers will already be versed in such modes of teaching, and provided a suitable supply of essential information continues to be produced, they should be reasonably well equipped to cope. Secondary teachers may need to be prepared to adopt different ways of working if they are to realize the sorts of objectives that appear to be envisaged for the National Curriculum.

For work on running skills, pupils can be set any number of tasks, such as running backwards, sideways or in personally developed odd styles (which can be referred to in the teaching situation as 'silly' runs). In this way they can experience inefficient and restrictive patterns in an enjoyable way, and so it should be easier to underscore what is involved in running properly.

In the initial stages of jumping, pupils can start immediately on tackling a variety of tasks such as clearing low obstacles with one- or two-footed takeoffs and landings. They can also extend this into simple competitions in small groups, using a cane balanced across two cones with adjustable heights. Conditions such as holding the arms by the sides while jumping can be introduced and the effect discussed. In this way the most efficient methods of jumping in relation to achieving height or length, and the effect of a short approach, can be explored and should lead to a grasp of fundamental principles. This should in turn give the teacher a better base from which to tackle formal events.

Throwing appears to have a natural attraction for most pupils, and it is best to capitalize on this advantage by engaging them immediately in a variety of throwing situations utilizing such things as beanbags, 'wellies', balls, cones, canes, quoits etc. Pupils can then experiment with various foot placements and arm actions, which should enable the teacher to lead them to the notion of a stable base for throwing and other important principles. It can also help pupils appreciate the importance of the implement's shape to finding the most effective way of throwing it. This experience can be developed by focusing on throwing for height, accuracy or length, all of which can provide a sound basis for particular throws. By using the many fundamental throwing practices, such as those outlined in Dick (1987), the teacher can get larger numbers of pupils throwing at the same time while working on core elements of particular throwing events. The exercise shown in Figure 5.2 is but one example of such an activity, and 10 or 12 pupils can throw at the same time. Another useful exercise is throwing footballs or netballs in pairs from a kneeling position to emphasize key principles in hip, trunk, and arm movements.

Using adapted implements has many advantages when teaching throwing (e.g. using quoits for discus) but this is well known and needs no elaboration here. In summary, the process of teaching envisaged here (see Figure 5.3) would appear to sit well with developments in the process of teaching games.

Demonstrating Development Through the Four Key Stages

Commensurate with the intentions outlined in the National Curriculum and developed for physical education in the report of the Interim Working Group (British Council of Physical Education [BCPE], 1990), athletics should also

Figure 5.2 Throwing exercise. *Note.* From *Throwing* (p. 77) by M. Jones, 1987, Ramsbury, Wiltshire: Crowood Press. Reprinted by permission of the British Amateur Athletic Board.

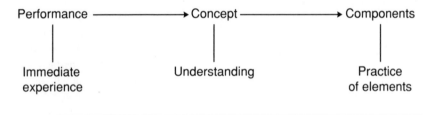

Figure 5.3 The process of teaching in athletics.

demonstrate development and progression through the four key stages. This should be sensitive to pupils' natural development, progress from a broad general base to increased specialization and encourage an increasing responsibility for self-directed learning. Attention should also be paid to fostering school-to-community links, most notably with athletic clubs, providing for personal and social education and the concept of safety. In addition there should be an awareness of, and contribution to, cross-curricular links and themes that are viewed as the cement into which the various bricks of the National Curriculum will rest. In this regard athletics has an excellent reservoir of technical and personal performance parameters to offer as well as the many physical aspects of response to exercise.

Towards the National Curriculum

Discussion in physical education so far has concentrated on profile components that revolve around the notions of performing, planning/composing and appraising—although this may change, and the relative emphasis placed on each one has yet to be established. However, there is a strong feeling in the profession at large that the major emphasis should be placed on performance, particularly given the constraints of such factors as the time available for physical education, although one should not deny the value of the other two components, which can each contribute meaningfully to the process. At present the most fruitful contribution would appear to be to identify appropriate programmes of study relevant to the respective key stages with these thoughts in mind. What follows, then, is an elaboration of the ideas just outlined, in the shape of suggested programmes of study that are relevant to each key stage and capable of reflecting the processes of performing, planning/composing and appraising. The central elements have been elaborated in many examples that illustrate how the programmes could work.

Key Stage 1: Ages 5 to 7

This is a prime time, of course, for the futher development of the essential movement repertoire that will form the basis of more complex skills in later years. Work related to athletics is to be found in the overall pattern of experiences provided for children in this phase and centred on the concept of play. This will inevitably contain many aspects of running, jumping and throwing, which can then be emphasized to a certain extent. Our knowledge of schema theory (Schmidt, 1988) informs us that the more varied the environment in which these fundamental skills are developed, the richer the schema that are generated and the greater the potential for future skill development. Consequently, children should be encouraged to run, jump and throw in as many playful situations as possible, to generate a broad base of personal experience from which the more complex skills of the formal events can later be developed. However, it is a common mistake to underestimate the capabilities of this age range, and the tasks set for the pupils should not be at too low a level.

Running

- Simple activities to start to open up an awareness of what it is to run properly (e.g. running first with knees high and then with straight legs, and experimenting with other arm and leg actions to find the best and most comfortable method)
- Games that involve as wide a variety of walking and running movements as possible
- Running activities that call for changes of direction and balance, including the need to follow a set course (e.g. a diamond or heart shape, or a small slalom course)
- Simple relays, touching hands or passing small objects such as tennis balls
- Running over light and small obstacles (e.g. low canes) in as natural a fashion as possible

Jumping

- Games that involve and encourage jumping and hopping
- Activities emphasizing changes of feet through skipping, hopping and jumping (e.g. simple combinations of two feet to one, or one to two, or two hops on one leg to two on the other)
- Landing under control from various jumping activities and from various heights
- Elementary jumping tasks over low canes: taking off or landing from one or two feet, first from a standing start, then from a short approach run

Throwing

- Throwing a wide variety of small equipment in prescribed directions
- Throwing underarm and overarm to a partner and alone
- Throwing for accuracy and height (length, if all goes well)—for instance, throwing at targets on a wall or over a rope or string, or using beanbags to throw into hoops set on the floor at various distances from the pupils

In general, setting challenges requires pupils to plan suitable strategies and evaluate their success rates. The recording of personal point totals according to schemes established by the teacher can be helpful in this process. Observing and analysing other children's movement patterns is not easy for children at this stage; they can really do this only in a restricted way with specific emphases, such as watching an arm action. In organizational terms, it can be a great help, for children at the top end of the age range, to use a simple athletic circuit where different athletics-related activities can be experienced in sequence by children working in small groups.

Key Stage 2: Ages 7 to 11

The age span for Key Stage 2 (7 to 11 years) is a wonderful period in which to teach athletics. The pupils' ability to cope with more sophisticated concepts, allied to their better agility and strength, allows the teacher great scope for development. In particular there is the opportunity to set a wide range of tasks and challenges and to use questions about the nature of the experience to promote a deeper understanding of the principles of the three groups of athletic events and to develop the basis of good performance. This will enable pupils to develop their ability to plan responses by reacting to the tasks set for them and, in reacting to questioning, to evaluate their relative success. The pupils' ability to observe and appraise increases, and they will be able to spot the bigger errors in performance and to articulate their reasons for selecting a performance as good. As in Key Stage 1, it is easy in this 2nd stage to underestimate pupils' ability, and care is needed to present tasks in ways that challenge all pupils at levels appropriate to their capabilities. Of great importance in this stage is the need to focus on how it feels to the pupil—what happens to their bodies when they run short and fast, fast and longer, slower and longer, or how it feels when throwing is in progress and goes well or badly, for example. Competition can be developed in ways that don't embarrass pupils and that offer a good chance of some success for everybody (see the partner runs that follow). This early competitive experience serves a useful function in preparing for more formal competition in the next stage. Athletic circuits are equally useful at this stage.

Running

- Exploring and developing more fully the concept of running well, high-lighting parts of the body that are the major contributors; running backwards, sideways and in an odd style, to focus on the inefficient and tiring nature of running incorrectly and so the requirements and advantages of running correctly
- Running over light obstacles, such as canes, with a view to developing hurdling
- Developing pace judgment by running for speed and distance (e.g. using timed runs of 5 to 20 or 30 seconds) with markers at set distances to help evaluate performance and to assess the different demands of various distances and speeds
- Orienteering with string runs or simple maps of the school field
- Standing starts
- Sprint challenges in pairs, working half the class at a time and using the other half to watch their partners and mark where they reached in, say, 5 seconds, then changing over and trying to beat their partners or their own marks
- Relay running with baton changing

Jumping

- Developing more complex jumping routines combining different variations of hopping, stepping and jumping
- Introduction to pole vault with swing and turn exercises on ropes or a pole held by the teacher; swinging for distance in the sand pit
- A variety of jumping challenges over canes on adjustable-height cones onto mats (e.g. competitions in small groups, using two feet to two, one to two or two to one, standing start and then a short approach)
- Tasks to emphasize the key principles of jumping (e.g. jumping two-footed over a cane onto a mat), with conditions imposed (e.g. arms by the sides), leading to questions about the effect of such restrictions to teach, in this case, the importance of the arms for balance and performance; similarly, swinging the free leg straight or bent and examining the effect; developing these into basic matters of approach, takeoff, flight and landing
- Scissors-style high jump and simple long-jump techniques

Throwing

- More adaptation to the throwing requirements of different shapes and weight of implement—long and thin, small and heavier—using a variety of articles, such as wellies, plastic cones, quoits, water-filled plastic balls etc. (e.g., La Boule sets); developing these activities into concepts of slinging, lifting, pulling and pushing
- Setting tasks to bring out the core principles of throwing: exploring as many foot placements as possible to see which is the most effective; combining this with various arm actions and different implements to see which works best
- Using the Schwanbeck throw to develop a core throwing activity
- Working on a variety of related activities such as those outlined in Dick (1987)
- Setting throwing challenges

It is important to develop essential concepts of safety in terms of space and relation to others. This is also a good time to introduce and develop the notion of warming up and cooling down and the effects they have on the body. Moreover, introducing and emphasizing a focus on physical feelings will allow links with other aspects of the curriculum having to do with the functioning and care of the body. In the community, the local athletics club might have a junior section that caters for the upper end of this age range. Where such sections are well organized and the activity is appropriate and supervised by suitably qualified coaches, pupils could be encouraged to attend, and an early appreciation of the value of school-to-community links will be established.

Key Stage 3: Ages 11 to 14

In terms of the developmental stages referred to earlier, pupils will now be progressing gradually towards involvement with the full forms of the various events and to a degree of personal choice. Physically pupils will be capable of responding to more demanding challenges, but it is also an important period for skill development. Moreover, pupils' cognitive development will be such as to allow the teacher to foster their capacity to appraise performance and so to promote in more detail their understanding of specific events. Notice that if the requirements for athletics in the National Curriculum Key Stages 1 and 2 are met anywhere near effectively, teachers in the secondary age range will have to make important adaptations to the current content of their work and the levels at which they now operate.

In essence the focus should be on developing a balanced range of track-and-field events, with an emphasis on the correct technical model as it suits individual physiques and abilities. Some attention should also be paid to the training and fitness demands of the various events and to the rules governing competition. Pupils should appreciate the central concepts of

1. speed,
2. endurance,
3. strength, and
4. mobility

and how these relate to groups of events. Good use can also be made of recording personal progress and performances, which serve a number of functions from motivation to data analysis.

Running

- Performing a range of track events incorporating sprints and middle distance
- Development of challenges in running in line with pupils' better physical development—for example, increased use of orienteering, and keeping a log to see how soon a marathon distance can be reached or the distance between two towns etc.; combining with other pupils to see how few of them can run in relay to beat the 4-minute mile or other records, developing 'slalom' and 'shape' runs to be longer and performed with repetitions etc.
- Monitoring bodily reactions to the various demands of running, and recording improvements over time

Jumping

- Performing a range of jumping events in line with basic technical models
- Developing jumping challenges, such as a jumps decathlon and variations of this idea

Throwing

- Performing specific throws at increasingly more advanced levels incorporating rotation and approach/buildup
- Developing throwing challenges, which can be extensions of ideas outlined previously or adaptations of core throwing exercises that feature critical parts or aspects of throwing actions (see Dick, 1987)

The safe conduct of athletic activities assumes even greater importance with the advent of formal events. This will be useful as well if, as is hoped, pupils are encouraged to join a local athletics club. Particular preference should be given to clubs that make special provision for youngsters and provide experiences relevant to their stage of physical and personal development and competitive experience. To further develop their awareness of the processes and importance of warm-up and cool-down, pupils can be encouraged to plan and lead these parts of the lesson with small groups and to assume more individual responsibility.

Key Stage 4: Ages 14 to 16

The progression towards individual responsibility and choice is a feature of Key Stage 4. Pupils' technical awareness should become more sophisticated, as should their level of analysis, incorporating, perhaps, such things as simple video analysis. For this age range it would seem to be more appropriate to identify the general principles for possible programmes of study applicable to all three groups of events.

* Deeper knowledge of the physiology of exercise related to athletics, building from the introduction of speed, strength, endurance and mobility in Key Stage 3
* Deeper knowledge of how to plan and work to simple training schedules, utilizing knowledge from other areas of the curriculum, such as health-related physical activity modules (see Armstrong and Biddle in this text)
* Further work on the technical aspects of athletics and the application of these to competition, including orienteering
* Greater concentration on performance analysis and using it in simple coaching situations
* Gaining experience of officiating
* Selecting and developing aspects of athletics of personal interest and relevance

Pupils should be offered great encouragement to join a local athletics club or to find an interest in athletics that they can sustain as part of an active lifestyle at whichever level of intensity they wish.

Conclusion

The thoughts offered above are intended as a contribution to the likely development of the National Curriculum in physical education with particular reference to track-and-field athletics. Attention has also been paid to practical examples that may help teachers develop this aspect of their teaching. Of particular importance is the concept of teaching athletics that underpins the programmes of study and the developments and progressions contained in the work. Little mention so far has been made of the various award schemes available in track-and-field athletics, such as the Five Star, Ten Step and Thistle. This is not to devalue such schemes, which can serve a useful purpose in schools as long as they are used in the right way. It is difficult, however, to see them occupying a central place in the National Curriculum in athletics, given the nature of the educational process involved and the sort of progressions envisaged above. They can be a valuable contribution to this process when used to supplement the curriculum, and of course they do offer pupils an excellent opportunity to collect, record and analyse data. Essentially, however, the educational process in the National Curriculum is best served by a process-oriented and progressive curriculum that encourages pupils to explore and refine particular areas of experience in the ways outlined here and in other sources such as Johnson (1988) and O'Neil (1991).

References

Almond, L. (1987). Rethinking athletics. *Physical Education Review,* **20**, 17-20.

British Council of Physical Education. (1990). *Report of the Interim Working Group on Physical Education in the National Curriculum.* London: Author.

Dick, F. (1987). *But first. . . .* London: British Amateur Athletic Board.

Education Reform Act. (1988). London: Her Majesty's Stationery Office.

Fisher, R.J. (1990). Further thoughts on the teaching of athletics. *Bulletin of Physical Education,* **26**, 43-47.

Johnson, C. (1988). A movement approach to the introduction of jumping to 8-13 year olds. *Athletics Coach,* **22**(2), 25-28; **22**(3), 19-21.

Jones, M. (1987). *Throwing.* Ramsbury, Wiltshire: Crowood Press.

O'Neil, J. (1991). Teaching athletics in the primary school, Primary P.E. Focus. *British Journal of Physical Education,* **22**(2), 5-6.

Schmidt, R.A. (1988). *Motor control and learning* (2nd ed.). Champaign, IL: Human Kinetics.

Chapter 6

Gymnastics in the National Curriculum

John Wright

Gymnastics has a substantial pedigree as part of the curriculum in state schools. From a decade before World War I until 1944, it had the official backing of the Board of Education through its Chief Medical Officer; it was promulgated as an important aspect of preventive medicine. Post World War II physical educationists regarded this as undesirably restricting. They modified subject content, teaching and learning procedures and the gymnasium apparatus environment so that wider educational goals could be pursued. By the 1980s, uncomfortable discrepancies between some of these goals and gymnastic curriculum realities were frequently preceived, sparking criticism and reappraisal. The present chapter provides a further contribution to this reappraisal, in the context of the National Curriculum. It focuses first on the wider educational context.

Education in a Democratic Society

I assume that there is a broad consensus among educationists that the formal processes of education in a democratic society should be designed to develop rationally self-determining individuals whose rationality is morally based, individuals who are able to make well-informed judgements about their lives and about a wide variety of issues and who can recognize and accept the consequences of those judgements. I further assume that education should contribute systematically to the well-rounded intellectual, physical, moral, social, emotional, aesthetic and artistic development of individuals, for its more immediate value and for its value in preparing them to become capable and responsible adult members of society.

It follows that education institutions have exacting responsibilities in contributing to these ideals. They need to help their pupils acquire knowledge in a range of disciplines that will lead them to understand principles, so that increasingly they can act independently and solve problems for themselves. Pupils must be helped to acquire expertise in a wide range of skills and the mental and physical capacities to apply those skills for suitable durations of time. Along with knowledge, understanding of principles and mastery of skills, there needs to be a kindling and refining of sensibilities, especially to other people and their needs, to the natural world and its needs, and to the aesthetic and artistic in a variety of their manifestations.

Finally, I assume that the formal processes of education should also be designed to nuture character qualities that are widely deemed to be desirable: self-confidence leavened by an agreeable humility, curiosity, courage, persistence, kindness, gentleness, a care for the less fortunate and a care for other forms of life. This implies the fostering also of a range of constructive attitudes.

If pupils are to be helped to become more rationally self-determining and to have a morally based rationality, it follows that the educational processes in which they are engaged should themselves be consistent with the moral values of a democratic society. They should, as Peters (1966) frequently argued, embody a 'respect for persons'. This implies that all pupils should be treated with dignity and respect, equally so, regardless of age, gender, race, colour, beliefs, social grouping, sexual preference, level of intelligence, ability or disability.

No apology is made for beginning a chapter on gymnastics in the National Curriculum with these statements of broad educational ideals. If gymnastics is to be a legitimate part of that curriculum, PE specialist teachers and primary school teachers need to be clear about the ways it can contribute to the complex web of educational processes and outcomes embodied in that curriculum. To have these insights, teachers must understand the nature of gymnastics as an educational activity and be clear about the movement material it encompasses and the educational processes and outcomes its nature and material make appropriate. This also implies their having insight into, and facility in exploiting, the range of teaching and learning procedures that best attend such processes and outcomes.

Within the limitations of one chapter, it is not possible to consider all these factors thoroughly. Nevertheless, some consideration of them is essential before addressing the crucial issue of progression and discussing the facilities, teaching expertise and time constraints on gymnastics in the National Curriculum.

The Nature of Gymnastics in Education

The recently published recommendations of the British Association of Advisers and Lecturers in Physical Education (BAALPE) Working Party on Gymnastics (British Association of Advisers and Lecturers in Physical Education, 1988), identified 10 principles that it considered should underpin the teaching of the subject in secondary schools. They are very sound and are equally applicable to primary schools. The first 3 are about the nature of several contemporary forms of gymnastics, including the four sport forms, some recreational forms and gymnastics in education. They are that gymnastics is to do with

1. the development and balanced use of the body's physical resources, particularly muscular strength and flexibility;
2. some of the aesthetic aspects of human movement; and
3. the development of skill.

One of the chief ways in which gymnastic skill manifests is in the refined execution of various types of movement (body actions)—some markedly acrobatic—that have come to be seen as characteristic of the still-evolving gymnastic heritage. This is partly because of the natures of many of the movements themselves, partly because of the environment many of them require, and partly because of the aesthetic intentions, expectations and criteria they subserve. The gymnasium environment is itself a distinguishing characteristic of the subject. Movements like climbing, heaving, swinging, circling and balancing with parts of the body below the supporting surface depend for their execution upon the kind of apparatus typically provided by a gymnasium.

A broadly balanced school gymnastics programme needs to make liberal and imaginative use of available apparatus, both single pieces and combinations of two or more pieces in various relationships. This facilitates pupils developing broader vocabularies of movement skills that are not prohibitively difficult or risky and that do not require abnormal strength or flexibility than would be attainable without apparatus. They also make it possible for the teacher to make balanced, nigh all-round demands on the pupils' muscular resources. Such demands cannot readily be duplicated elsewhere in normal PE programmes and continue to be one of the important reasons why gymnastics should form part of a balance programme.

A third major distinguishing characteristic of gymnastics in education as it has evolved by the 1990s is that it is an aesthetic activity. Regrettably, the many implications of this seem not to have been grasped by many teachers. Howard and Laws (1989) lend weight to this view. At least five distinct manifestations of this central characteristic need to be understood.

1. The gymnast engages in gymnastics with a significant degree of aesthetic intention.
2. The spectators, including competition judges, observe gymnasts and their movement with a significant degree of aesthetic expectation.
3. The standards and attention paid to detail in the execution of gymnastic movement skills, regardless of their level of technical difficulty, are in the final analysis the result of aesthetic considerations; what might seem to be exclusively technique refinement, rooted in biomechanics understanding, ultimately subserves aesthetic criteria.
4. The design principles that guide the creation and structuring of gymnastic compositions are essentially aesthetic design criteria appropriately interpreted to a gymnastics context.
5. The judgements made about the merits of a gymnastic performance—as performance per se—and those made about the design and content of the attendant composition and the appearance of the gymnast are significantly aesthetically governed.

The foregoing comments about the nature of gymnastics raise many implications for teachers expected to use the subject as an educational medium in the National Curriculum. The first of these to be examined is the movement material of the subject—the categories of body actions (areas of skills) that are available to form the movement content of programmes of study.

Movement Material for the Curriculum

The movement material of gymnastics is very diverse. It includes many static positions, stable and unstable; the latter are termed balances. All positions are further defined by the body surfaces used as supports and by the overall relationship to the supporting surface or surfaces.

The material also embraces various categories of travelling (locomotion) actions of the whole body: rolling; stepping; assisted springing; springing; other flight—from dropping, releasing from swing, and being thrown; swinging on free-swinging apparatus; sliding and composite actions such as swinging/sliding, stepping/lifting.

There are also various categories of nontravelling actions of the whole body: circling (without or with swinging impetus), spinning, pivoting off balance, step-turning in place, springing in place, lifting, lowering, tilting, swaying, rocking, waving, bending, straightening and composite actions.

All the foregoing are positions and actions of the whole body. They are dependent upon the fundamental actions of body parts, which can conveniently be categorized as bending, straightening, circling (these are the straight-limb movements and circumduction of trunk and head/neck); twisting, untwisting, lifting, lowering and composite actions. These actions of body parts serve a variety of functions, especially in determining body form, applying pull, push, and momentum transfer forces, and in making it possible to exploit or limit the undesirable effects of gravity, friction and strain forces in certain apparatus. Their action function can be described also by many other terms, especially to aid communication when teaching or coaching.

Some of the whole-body actions are necessarily rotational. Some may, or may not, incorporate rotation about one, or more than one, axis; the incorporation of such rotation increases their complexity and, usually, their difficulty. Inverted positions and movements are common in gymnastics, the inversion arising from 180-degree rotation, which can be achieved by several different types of action, such as rolling, stepping, assisted springing, springing, sliding and circling.

The actions of the whole body and of particular body parts are further defined by reference to a range of spatial, dynamic and relationship variables. The spatial ones concern direction, pathway, level, plane and extension. The dynamic variables are time, force and flow dimensions—the rhythmic ingredients of movements.

The relationship variables can have to do with actions, dynamics or spatial features. The last are particularly important in most school work; for example, spatial relationships of body parts each to each that determine body form (sometimes described by convenient shorthand terms such as *tucked, piked, straddle*), and spatial relationships of position and travel relative to the apparatus or another gymnast.

Identical and contrasted relationships are very important in partner and group work. So too are canon and unison timing relationships.

It is important for teachers to recognize that every category of whole-body actions, which can be thought of as areas of skills, embraces many possible single gymnastic movement skills. These can usually range from the technically very simple to very difficult within the same category.

By varying the actions of appropriate body parts, a movement skill can be changed, subtly or radically, in one or more than one of its spatial, dynamic or relationship features. Thus, for example, the long-arm handstand resolved into a symmetrical forward roll is changed radically, in terms of direction and spatial relationships, if only one arm is bent. The body surfaces used in the resolving roll also change, and the roll becomes asymmetrical in a diagonal forwards direction.

Single-movement skills can be elaborated into phrases by blending one movement with one or more other movements of either the same or a different category. Pupils need lots of experience of both types of phrase.

Principles for Selecting Material

What principles can guide the selection of material for a National Curriculum? The following seem apposite.

1. A considerable variety of action categories should be covered over the 11 or 9 years to ensure breadth and balance in the vocabulary of skills practised by each pupil.

2. The actions chosen should make varied and balanced demands on pupils' muscular capacities; movements involving upper body and hip flexor strength are particuarly important.

3. Several of the major categories of travelling actions, together with the simpler nonswinging bar/beam circling and lifting and lowering actions, are so centrally important (in terms of items 1 and 2 in this list) that they should be present in one form or another in almost every lesson from age 7 to 14 or 16. Sometimes they would be the main learning focus; at other times they would be subordinated to some other learning focus—for example, to do with spatial or dynamic variables, or to do with balancing skills or the use of twist actions. Balancing skills are themselves very important. Therefore, gaining, maintaining, deliberately disturbing and appropriately resolving balance positions should be the focus of perhaps two programmes of study in the upper primary school and one, or even two, in the secondary school, and perhaps developed in partner work at secondary level.

4. Material for programmes should be chosen and presented with due regard for progression. This is discussed later in the chapter, but here some key points are noted about the ordering of the broad content of programmes.

Very young children need time to explore moving on apparatus in their own ways at their own pace. They then need lots of practice identifying and mastering many relatively stable weight-bearing positions and finding their own ways of moving smoothly from one position to another; in doing so, they need to note and name the body parts that make contact with the floor and apparatus. They need to practise lots of very basic locomotion movements like running, skipping, galloping, hopping, leaping, jumping, walking on hands and feet (and one foot) and the simpler side rolls. They need to experience, and learn to respond correctly to, various spatial, dynamic and relationship words in the teacher's instructions whilst using basic actions and positions. They need to learn to cooperate in twos or small groups to lift, carry and place apparatus safely, as appropriate to their capacities.

It is progression thereafter, at the junior stage, to focus more closely on a wider range of categories of travelling actions. It is further progression to master some of the simpler balance positions; and further progression still to focus on how balance positions can be disturbed deliberately in various ways. It is also progression to master moving into balance positions from various kinds of travelling actions.

Incorporating twist actions into various stable and unstable positions, and then releasing the twist gently or powerfully into some form of whole-body, long-axis turning, sometimes with simultaneous travelling, is further progression. It is a further stage to initiate twist actions while the body is travelling in various ways.

When any area of skill has been explored and has yielded reasonable control in a variety of single-movement skills and short phrases, it is a progression if movements have to be executed identically in unison timing with a partner; in threes it is even more so.

It is further progression to work in pairs or threes to exploit substantial contact among the pupils. This should be tackled with care. It is work requiring skilful, well-disciplined pupils.

Revisiting areas of skills already tackled at a younger age group is sensible, providing different or more exacting constraints have to be met.

5. Finally, the most important principle determining the selection of movement material for programmes of study is that it must be accessible to every pupil. By accessible is meant that it makes possible movement responses that, by hard work and sound practice, can be refined in the available curriculum time to standards that bring a sense of achievement to each pupil in meeting some of the key agreed criteria of quality execution.

Clearly, this is not only a matter of what categories of actions, or what spatial, dynamic or relationship variables, are chosen for a block of work but is also a matter of how teachers frame their instructions to a class in relation to that material. Tasks frequently need to provide choices that allow pupils to make individual movement responses according to their levels of competence and movement predilections. When tasks are framed to offer no scope for varied response, the particular response required must still be accessible to every pupil.

Given the amount of available curriculum time (this will be further discussed later in this chapter) for any one movement pattern to be practised, most skills and phrases mastered by most pupils will be technically fairly simple.

These then are principles to guide the selection of the movement material—the areas of skills. But educating pupils through the medium of gymnastics should also involve their acquiring knowledge that leads to an understanding of principles. It also requires them to become more rationally self-determining people who are confident in their own individuality, but who are also socially responsible and cooperative. Each of these has implications, which will now be considered.

Knowledge and Understanding Necessary for Gymnastics

If pupils are to be able to tackle their own and each other's technical and aesthetic problems in well-informed ways, are to design their own gymnastic phrases and compositions with some insight into the processes involved, and are to make sound judgements about both the performance and the design features of each other's work, they need to acquire the relevant propositional knowledge. They need knowledge, too, if they are to understand how to prepare and use their bodies and apparatus properly and safely and how to make optimum use of very limited practice time. Ideally, then, a well-conceived gymnastic curriculum should help pupils acquire the following areas of knowledge.

1. *Knowledge about the technical and aesthetic dimensions of gymnastic movements* and about the interpendence that often exists between them. Some of this knowledge would be to do with understanding principles that have wider application than to gymnastics alone: for example, the principles that determine the relative stability or instability of a body position; those that govern safe lifting, carrying and placing of objects; those that identify the variable features of all body movement. Other knowledge would be more specific to gymnastics: for example, how to grip a beam or bar to execute a given bar circle safely; what features contribute to high-quality performance (in part, this would also have implications for some other areas of movement, like dance).

2. *Knowledge about the body* insofar as it relates to these areas: safe and systematic limbering and body preparation for gymnastics and other strenuous movement; safe, efficient ways of increasing strength, flexibility and endurance in specific body areas, and overall circulorespiratory endurance; the physical capacities required, and the body areas where they are required, to facilitate the execution of certain movements; the protection of especially vulnerable parts of the body such as the neck and low back.

For very young children, correctly naming body parts would be part of this area of knowledge. In secondary programmes an important part of this knowledge would be covered during the first, limbering stage of lessons—say, 10 minutes in a 1-hour lesson.

There is clearly a close link here with aspects of health education and health-related fitness (HRF). It can be reinforced and augmented in any programmes exclusively devoted to HRF and to some extent in other aspects of the PE curriculum.

3. *Knowledge about the gymnasium* and how its equipment should be handled, positioned and used safely. This includes knowledge about how apparatus can be used in less usual, imaginative ways without compromising safety.

4. *Knowledge about how to learn efficiently in gymnastics lessons.* This implies knowing the more important factors that aid practice; knowing strategies for tackling open-ended tasks and problem-solving situations systematically; knowing how best to co-operate with peers to facilitate their learning, skill and confidence development and to design duo and small-group compositions and present them in performance. At an advanced level, it implies pupils having the insights to tackle very open, full-scale composition assignments and see them through to performance presentation with knowledge of a wide range of design and performance criteria.

Knowledge of the simpler manual supporting techniques and their underpinning mechanical and psychological principles would be included in secondary programmes when appropriate—for example, in studying the overswing group of springing movements.

5. *Knowledge about individual differences* in physique, physical capacity and temperament. This implies developing self-knowledge and knowledge about one's peers. Teachers need great sensitivity in dealing with this area of knowledge, so that the gymnastics curriculum serves to enhance every pupil's body image and self-image and their sensibility and sympathy to their peers, rather than the reverse. The value of appropriately taught gymnastics as a medium for the positive development of pupils' body images and self-images was persuasively argued by Williams (1974, pp. 6-8).

6. *Knowledge about safety in gymnastics.* Much of this is covered in the previous five areas, but factors like appropriate dress and grooming (e.g. tying long hair and keeping fingernails and toenails at a suitable length) and the dangers of perspiration on the hands when working on beams and bars are important aspects of safety knowledge. Pupils also need to be helped to understand when they should ask for the teacher's help to ensure the safe tackling of a new 'idea' when they are exploring individual responses to an open-ended instruction.

It is, of course, one thing to identify these areas of knowledge and understanding; it is quite another thing to ensure that pupils acquire them. If propositional knowledge is to stand with procedural knowledge (knowing how) and is to inform it at every stage, a number of conditions have to be met.

First, pupils have to be given the appropriate information in appropriate ways at appropriate times.

Second, the information must be reiterated and reinforced frequently.

Third, the information must be applied by pupils, for it is all, in a real sense, useful knowledge.

Fourth, pupils' understanding must be frequently assessed by teachers by the only devices practically available to them, given the available curriculum time and the other objectives and teaching procedures with which they are simultaneously concerned. These devices are drawing inferences from observing how pupils tackle their work and from questioning pupils. Both pose substantial problems. Inferences based solely on observation may simply be wrong; they need checking by teacher/pupil dialogue. The sheer practicalities of this are daunting even for the most methodical, perceptive teacher; several lessons would be needed to question each pupil in a class properly. Even class questioning has to be used discriminatingly because it compromises precious physical activity and skill-practice time. One of the merits of the use of reciprocal pupil teaching is that it partially frees the teacher to devote more time to individual questioning and dialogue.

These, then, are problems that teachers must address if their pupils are to develop even a modest degree of knowledge and understanding.

Individuality

'Human nature is not a machine to be built after a model and set to do exactly the work prescribed for it, but a tree, which requires to grow and develop itself on all sides, according to the tendency of the inward forces which make it a living thing' (Mill, 1910, p. 117). This lofty and beautiful nature analogy is a constant challenge to educationists. Well-conceived gymnastic programmes might well play a modest part in meeting that challenge.

It has already been emphasized that gymnastics is an aesthetic activity involving both performance and composition design; it also involves making informed judgements about both of these, against agreed criteria. Pupils must be helped, gradually and progressively, to develop competence in all of these three dimensions of the activity.

Designing a small phrase of movement at even the most modest level involves the beginnings of creative activity calling forth the expression of the designer's individuality. By the time pupils are able to create full-scale compositions, of up to 2 minutes or so in performance length, that meet a comprehensive range of design criteria, they will be giving mature and exacting expression to their individuality. This is the kind of work one would like to see in General Certificate of Secondary Education (GCSE) programmes.

The processes by which individuality is gradually released and fostered are fascinating and complex. Some are briefly discussed below in the 'Teaching and Learning Procedures' section. Other aspects of pupil development that need simultaneously to take place so that individuality can flower include confidence; curiosity; an increasingly broad repertoire of skills and a willingness to 'play' creatively with any movement pattern as it is being mastered; a capacity for thinking—and moving—fluently, flexibly and originally (i.e. divergent thinking and moving); a capacity to exercise independent judgement and an expanding conception of the range of movement possibilities that each area of material being studied makes possible.

Cooperative Social Behaviour

In the emphasis on the importance of nurturing individuality, it is possible to lose sight of a corresponding nurturing of cooperative social behaviour. This must not be allowed to happen, and teachers need to exploit the various opportunities that gymnastics lessons offer to contribute to this important dimension of pupils' personal and social education.

From early infant days, sympathetic, safe cooperation in handling apparatus needs to be taught. So, too, does the unselfish sharing of apparatus and space.

Assisting a partner in skill acquisition and other learning and safe practice by reciprocal teaching is a particularly important way in which pupils can learn to be sympathetic and sensitive to each other's needs and to be generous and honest in acknowledging progress and problems (Underwood, in press).

The sharing of completed compositions—however short or modest their structure—at the end of a programme of study can also contribute to the general atmosphere of 'respect for persons' and to the sense that every pupil's contribution is valued. This must be sensitively handled by the teacher so that no one is too 'exposed' while performing (this can be achieved by having several pupils performing simultaneously) and so that generous, though truthful, comments on the work are encouraged.

Working on composition tasks in duo, trio and other small groups provides another fertile context for nurturing constructive social behaviour.

So, too, does focus on manual support techniques in secondary programmes, when these are appropriate for safe, efficient learning. All involved must, of course, be helped to understand that these are another kind of movement skill and as such require practice.

Teaching and Learning Procedures

The range of teaching and learning procedures that can be exploited by teachers and pupils can be categorized, continuum fashion, according to the number and type of teacher and pupil judgements they require and make possible. Mosston's (1986) spectrum of teaching styles has brought this continuum concept into more central focus in physical education courses in recent years. Teachers are being encouraged to be more adventurous in their use of various teaching styles. Within the constraints of the present chapter, only a few of the especially important aspects of effective gymnastic teaching and learning can be noted.

1. The adoption of any teaching approach is justifiable insofar as it facilitates pupils' learning and development in ways consistent with a teacher's shorter and longer term curriculum objectives. It is possible to become intoxicated with one's facility in using certain approaches and to overlook this fundamental point.

2. Teaching and learning procedures that best favour the realization of one kind of objective may not be sufficient, or even appropriate, for the realization of another kind of objective.

   * Thus, for example, the most economical approach to enabling a pupil to master the execution of a fairly simple movement skill is for the pupil to be given a good visual model with simple explanations of key

features to concentrate on when practising. This should be followed by practice—with suitable feedback. This procedure is an important part of gymnastic teaching and learning.

✳ Helping pupils to 'play' creatively with some area of skill, or with one particular skill or short phrase of movement, and to develop their capacities to think and move divergently—away from the 'one right answer' mode of behaviour—requires the teacher's instructions to be somewhat open-ended. The teacher needs to guide the pupils' thinking to some of the action, spatial, dynamic, or relationship choices that the task constraints make possible, so that they can experiment with them.

If the teacher also wishes to use such kinds of instructions to enable each pupil to master the execution of one movement, or phrase, arising from their experimentation—and this is usually so—she or he must insist that they select one pattern and then practise to refine it. Without this insistence, they may simply continue to explore different alternatives. A further objective that can be realized through such open-ended teaching procedures is the expansion of the pupils' conceptions of what the area of material being studied makes possible. This is achieved simply by encouraging pupils to note how their peers are responding to the task. They can do this informally while everyone is working and thus increase their storehouse of movement ideas, which is an important factor in the longer term development of creative behaviour. They may also, from time to time, teach each other some of their 'discoveries'.

✳ The development of some aspect of pupils' knowledge and understanding, and the finding of a solution to some technique problem, can often be aided by guided discovery approaches (instead of the teacher simply providing the solution). The teacher thus leads the pupils to discover the one right answer by a series of appropriate questions. This is a process for stimulating convergent thinking skills.

✳ The optimum development of pupils' cooperative social behaviour is likely to be achieved only if reciprocal teaching procedures are properly exploited so that the pupil teachers are helped in their observation; they also need to be helped to be suitably positive, sensitive and truthful in their comments to the learner (Underwood, in press).

Attention must now be turned to the vexed question of progression in gymnastics.

Progression in Gymnastics

The earlier comments on progression were principally to do with the ordering of the major 'bread and butter' areas of skills as the movement content for programmes of study. Several of these areas need to be revisited at different stages of pupils' school lives to extend their learning. It is important that teachers are clear about how they can make progressive demands on their pupils, not only when an area of study is revisited but throughout the programmes and within any one lesson.

The following principles should help teachers to plan progression systematically as well as to spontaneously modify their demands on particular individuals as the need arises.

1. *Pupil's independence of judgement.* This is the notion of progression that should transcend all others. The range and type of judgements that pupils are required to make for themselves and each other should be gradually extended as they mature and gain in confidence, self-discipline, skill and knowledge. By the GCSE assessment stage, their independence should be reflected in their capacities to tackle the following in well-informed ways, even in the absence of any teacher guidance:

* Limbering and bodily and mental preparation at the beginning of sessions
* Technique problems
* The various stages of exploration, selection, elaboration, adjustment/ refinement, consolidation and performance practice in creating full-scale solo and duo compositions (and perhaps trios and other small groups on occasions)
* Reciprocal teaching
* Apparatus handling and design of apparatus relationships for composition work
* Selected manual supporting
* Recognizing when the teacher's help is (a) desirable and (b) essential
* Making judgements about their own work and that of others

These ideals cannot be achieved in a smooth, linear fashion. However, within most lessons and throughout every programme of study, pupils should face learning situations that offer no choice, some that offer a little choice and some that offer rather more choice.

2. *Extending the variety of pupils' movement vocabularies.* This implies each pupil mastering more movement skills—both single actions and short phrases of movement—of approximately the same level of technical difficulty. It applies both to movements within the same area of skill and to movements from different areas. It is a constantly recurring feature of progression.

3. *Mastering movements of increasing difficulty and complexity.* This is the most commonly held view of what progression means. Complexity is here defined as being proportional to the number and variety of actions of body parts occurring per unit of time within a whole-body gymnastic movement. Although action difficulty and complexity often go together, difficulty may increase independently of complexity, as here defined, by, for example,

* an increased physical demand,
* an increased psychological demand,
* limiting available space or apparatus area of support,

✻ using apparatus, or

✻ using the floor rather than apparatus.

The foregoing examples can be further elaborated by imposing additional constraints drawn from spatial, dynamic, relationship or apparatus variables.

Adding rotation to a nonrotating action, where possible and appropriate, necessarily increases complexity. The same holds for an increase in the quantity of rotation. It holds, too, for the addition of rotation about other axes in actions that are already rotational; this can often mean the addition of twist rotation, but there are other possibilities.

4. *Extending the quantity of movement practised as a whole.* This especially means pupils learning to practise short phrases of movement rather than simply single actions (skills). It needs to occur every lesson, with all age groups, so that pupils learn to 'feel' phrases as rhythmic wholes. Phrases may incorporate movements from the same action category or from different categories, and pupils should master many examples of both types of phrase. As they become older and more knowledgeable, confident and skilful, they should be encouraged to elaborate and extend the phrases they practise—and also to practise two short balancing phrases in each practice trial. Some practice of single actions is, of course, also necessary at all stages of development.

5. *Extending the performance quality demands that have to be met.* The normal processes of skill refinement are, of course, implied here. However, because gymnastics is an aesthetic activity with its own aesthetic performance conventions, detailed features of execution are required that go beyond simply getting the mechanics of an action right—crucial though that always is.

In the normal processes of achieving the basic functional requirements of an action—getting round the bar, arriving on the feet, maintaining balance, and so on—teachers must help pupils apply force at the right place, in the right direction, in the right amount, and at the right time or times. Such guidance will always be an important part of improving performance quality and goes on until perfect accuracy and economy are evident—a rare occurrence indeed in curriculum work.

However, experience suggests that the gradual progression towards this rare ideal is reflected in a number of important qualitative features that tend to make movement look good and feel good. Until the first four of these, in the following list, are frequently evident in pupils' execution of a variety of movements, there is little point in directing their concentration to the second group. The same holds, to some extent, with progression to the third group. The performance quality features that pupils should concentrate on, then, are as follows.

Group A

a.   Accuracy and attention to detail in the form of the legs and feet, together with the appropriate muscle tension to bring this about. At first this will

be evident in only parts of a complete action, but ultimately it will be
evident throughout the action.

b. Harnessing and moving in harmony with the natural directional impetuses
of actions of the whole body and of certain body parts. This applies
especially when one movement is resolved into another. It is the first basis
of beautiful movement phrasing and was amply evident in the movement
of such geniuses as Fred Astaire and figure skaters Torville and Dean.

c. Sensitive placing of the feet to achieve lightness in landings and in all
foot contacts with the floor and apparatus. This involves an attendant right
timing and grading of tension changes.

d. Sensitive placing of other body parts on the floor and apparatus, evident
in an overall 'caring' use of the body.

Group B

e. Accuracy and attention to detail in the form of the arms, hands, head and
trunk, together with the appropriate muscle tension to make for crispness
and clarity in body form.

f. Amplitude/expansiveness in stillness and motion. In 'open' body forms,
this will be of the total body; in part 'closed' forms, it may be in only
parts of the body.

g. Accuracy in timing the changes of body form within a single skill or a
phrase of movements to meet both mechanics and aesthetic
requirements—the optimum phased changes that trampolinists and divers
work so hard to achieve.

h. Spatial, temporal and effort accuracy in all force applications, to meet the
mechanics requirements of actions. This implies eliminating all superflu-
ous movement, positioning and effort.

Group C

i. The rhythmic shaping of phrases and compositions beyond what is necessary mechanically, so that climaxes are suitably positioned and highlighted,
and subtle shadings of dynamics are detectable in a beautiful rhythmic
wholeness.

j. The total aliveness/involvement of every body part, in motion and stillness,
throughout the performance of a full-scale composition.

k. Performing in ways that capitalize upon individual strengths and underplay
limitations. This has many implications, too, for the content and design
of a piece of work.

If teachers could only make a major impact on the features in Group A,
gymnastic performance in the nation's schools would rise strikingly. It is certainly

vital that children's awareness of, and sensitivity to, the first stages of quality performance are kindled from their early primary school days.

6. *Extending the design criteria that have to be met when composing smaller and larger scale pieces of work.* Because of space limitations, discussion of this important dimension of progression must await another publication. However, it can be noted that the twin, and in some ways opposing, pillars of aesthetic design are variety and unity. Variety can shade also into complexity. A third pillar concerns the capacity of a composition to grip and hold an observer's interest— sometimes known as its intensity quality. Then there is the contentious issue of orginality. All merit much further thought and discussion.

National Curriculum Realities

Thus far the ways in which gymnastics *could* be a significant medium for the education of pupils from 5 to 16 or, as it will undoubtedly be for some, from 5 to 14, have been discussed. If ideals are to become realities, appropriate facilities, teaching expertise and quantities of curriculum time will have to be available at all the stages. What is the likelihood of this being so?

Facilities

Though far from ideal, available facilities are unlikely to be a major barrier to progress, except in a relatively small number of poorly equipped primary schools in very old buildings. It would, however, be helpful if every primary and secondary school had a minimum of eight benches and 24 suitably sized mats; also, if all secondary schools could replace Swedish beams with round bars and replace all solid-side boxes with the more versatile 'bar' boxes.

Teaching Expertise

Six of the 11 years of the National Curriculum—6 of 9 years for some pupils—will be taught by nonspecialist teachers who are already hard-pressed to meet the requirements of the core and in-place foundation subjects. They will shortly have to grapple with statutory requirements for art, music and PE, this last with five or six components in dance, games, gymnastics, swimming and/or athletics, and perhaps even outdoor activities as well.

From what has been written so far in this chapter, the complexities of gymnastics as a serious educational medium are apparent. Concern about the inadequacy of initial teacher education in preparing intending primary teachers to teach physical education has been a recurring concern of bodies like the Physical Education Association (PEA). The most recent expression of concern has been made by Murdoch (1990). Williamson's (1990) small survey also indicates some of the anxieties of the teachers themselves.

No one doubts that primary teachers are the 'salt of the earth', but it would be dissembling to assert that they are all—yes, all—going to be able to equip themselves to do full justice to the various components of PE and to art and music. Massive in-service training programmes and significant changes in initial teacher education would seem to be essential simply to equip a modest proportion of teachers. Will the funding be forthcoming under the new Local Management of Schools (LMS), when there are other subject priorities to be met?

The arguments for subjects like physical education and music being taught by specialist or semispecialist teachers at primary level must now be very strong indeed. Politicians who pretend to the public that primary teachers can do equal justice to three core and seven foundation subjects are either dangerously naive or deliberately duplicitous.

So far as secondary programmes are concerned, one hopes that the anxieties of Her Majesty's Inspectorate (HMI) and BAALPE about gymnastics teaching in the mid-1980s, and the actions, publications and in-service work that resulted, are beginning to bear fruit in better informed approaches. No doubt much remains to be done, particularly to help those PE teachers for whom gymnastics is not a major strength or interest.

Available Curriculum Time

McConachie Smith (1990) argues for the acceptance of five significantly different learning contexts in PE programmes, following the Alderson and Crutchley (1990) model. If these contexts are accepted, and a more or less even time distribution is given to each, gymnastics would have one fifth of available PE time.

Given two 1-hour PE periods a week, each term, each year in secondary schools (it may, of course be less than this), the most suitable arrangement for gymnastics would be one period each week for either the autumn or spring term, each year, plus two additional half-term blocks devoted exclusively to health-related fitness in, say, years 3 and 4. The location of HRF with gymnastics is simply because, conceptually, by Munrow's (1963) account of 'pure' gymnastics, this is its nearest home. With 12-week terms, gymnastics would then have a total of 72 hours over 5 years from 360 hours of PE time. One complete term would need to be given to each programme of study if any serious composition work were to be done. Dividing the time into dispersed half-term blocks would make a nonsense of significant skill acquisition and knowledge retention; it would make serious composition work unattainable.

So far as primary schools are concerned, a likely arrangement would seem to be four 1/2-hour PE lessons each week, each term, each year. Gymnastics would then have one period each week in, say, the autumn term and two periods each week in the spring term each year—6 hours and 12 hours, respectively. Two, or perhaps three, programmes of study might be tackled each year with the younger children. Thereafter, only two programmes would be tackled each year—one term each.

Even where the teaching is very well informed, it is going to be very difficult for teachers to achieve all of their varied goals in terms of pupil development, namely: high performance in a wide range of skills; confidence and individuality in responding to simple composition tasks; retention of the different areas of knowledge; quickened sensibilities and well-developed social behaviour. A comparison with the time available in only 1 week for English, mathematics or science, or a comparison with the amount of time a child club-gymnast devotes to practising in 1 week, places in stark perspective the problems facing teachers of gymnastics (and all other subdisciplines of PE) in the school curriculum.

The importance of teachers selecting action material that is accessible to all pupils, regardless of their physique and temperament, is now more than ever apparent, given the available practice time in the curriculum.

Conclusion

From what has been written, it is clear that gymnastics has the potential to make a modest but significant contribution to the complex web of processes and outcomes of the National Curriculum.

We must face the limitations to what can realistically be achieved, especially in terms of high-quality performance and composition products, particularly in the primary schools, for the reasons noted. Nevertheless, much can be achieved, given perceptive, demanding teaching and clearly focused, concentrated learning. The realities, therefore, favour as much concern for the processes of learning to perform, of learning to compose, and of learning to appreciate and evaluate gymnastic movement, as for the achievement of high-quality completed products. They lend weight to McConachie Smith's (1990) argument for a process model of the physical education curriculum.

References

Alderson J., & Crutchley, D. (1990). Physical education in the National Curriculum. In N. Armstrong (Ed.), *New directions in physical education Volume 1* (pp. 37-62). Champaign, IL: Human Kinetics.

British Association of Advisers and Lecturers in Physical Education. (1988). *Gymnastics in the secondary school curriculum.* Leeds: Author.

Howard, K., & Laws, C. (1989). Where is aesthetic education in physical education? *British Journal of Physical Education,* **20**, 126-128.

McConachie Smith, J. (1990). A national curriculum in physical education: Process and progression. *British Journal of Physical Education,* **21**, 226-230.

Mill, J.S. (1910). On liberty. In H.B. Acton (Ed.), *Utilitarianism, liberty, representative government.* London: J.M. Dent. (Mill's essay originally published in 1859).

Mosston, M. (1986). *Teaching physical education.* London: C.E. Merritt.

Munrow, A.D. (1963). *Pure and applied gymnastics.* London: Arnold.

Murdoch, E. (1990). Physical education in the National Curriculum: Interim Working Group progress report. *British Journal of Physical Education,* **21**, 223-224.

Peters, R.S. (1966). *Ethics and education.* London: Allen & Unwin.

Underwood, M. (1991). *AGILE—aspects of gymanstics and independent learning experiences.* London: Nelson & Sons.

Williams, J. (1974). *Themes for educational gymnastics.* London: Lepus Books.

Williamson, D. (1990). What are primary non-specialist teachers thinking about the prospective National Curriculum (PE)? *British Journal of Physical Education,* **21**, 251-252.

Chapter 7

Dance in the National Curriculum

Sarah E. Stevens

The place of dance in the National Curriculum is currently the subject of considerable debate. This chapter explores the historical development of dance in the school curriculum from its early place as part of physical education and training to the development of the current 'dance-as-art' model. This perspective provides a framework through which the current National Curriculum debate can be viewed.

The particular role dance can play in the curriculum, at all levels, as a valuable part of an artistic, cultural and physical education will offer a theoretical basis through which current developments and innovations can be addressed. The present role dance enjoys as an art and as an aspect of physical education is addressed through an examination of the position dance presently occupies at a national level.

Dance education faces a dilemma in trying to meet National Curriculum requirements that the subject should be subsumed within physical education (and possibly music). The latter part of this chapter suggests a possible way forward. It proposes a separate profile component for dance that gives scope for dance to be taught, as a formed and performed art, within the framework of PE being a school subject that traditionally groups together a range of complementary and contrasting subject areas.

Historical Perspective of Dance in Physical Education

In the early years of the 20th century, the Board of Education took a lead in recommending that dance should be taught as part of physical education and training. The 1909 *Syllabus of Physical Exercise for Public Elementary Schools* recommended that 'dancing steps should be introduced into many lessons and that they cannot but have good results. The value especially for girls, or even in some cases for boys is becoming more widely recognised' (Board of Education, 1909).

The style of dance that was considered to offer these 'good results' was, in the main, English folk dance—which was enjoying a revival of interest, spear-headed by the work of Cecil Sharp. Later, folk dances from Scotland, Wales, Ireland and Europe were included. Board of Education syllabi published in 1919 and 1933 continued to advocate the value of folk dance and the contribution it could make to the physical fitness and training of young people. An important point emerges from studying these early syllabii. From as early as 1909 there was a public association made between dance and physical education and training. The Gulbenkian Report *Dance Education and Training in Britain* (Calouste Gulbenkian Foundation, 1980) strongly acknowledges this early relationship and suggests that this may also be a key reason why dance in British schools has developed at a greater rate than in many other countries.

Another, perhaps more hidden, point also emerges. In the first part of the 20th century, the value of dance in schools was seen to lie mainly in its contribution to physical health and fitness, although individual dance artists such as Madge Atkinson, Ruby Ginner and Margaret Morris had an influence in schools and colleges. The notion of dance as a fully developed art form, either in its own right or as a significant artistic part of PE, was not on the agenda. This is not surprising, because dance as a serious art form in the British theatre was in its infancy at that time, notwithstanding the individual contributions made by Atkinson and others. It is as well to bear this in mind today when making comparisons between dance in schools and music and drama. Music and drama have enjoyed a longer, more varied and more developed association with the public performing arts arena, and, no doubt, this in turn has influenced and guided their development in schools.

However, in the late 1930s, far from developing and going from strength to strength, dance was at a low ebb. A report by Her Majesty's Inspectorate (HMI), titled *Dance in Secondary Schools*, observed that 'in Secondary schools, time given to gymnastics, athletics and a variety of games increased while that for dance diminished until by 1939 dance had often become a recreational activity used to occupy large groups (mainly girls) in wet weather. Folk dance continued to be taught regularly in many primary schools' (HMI, 1983, p. 1).

Clearly something needed to be done to promote dance in schools and place it firmly on the curriculum. This need for change and innovation came at a time of postwar revitalization and reassessment. Bloomfield (1988) suggests that the 1944 Education Act, which stressed individual needs in education, played a part as well. The main impetus and guiding philosophical basis for dance education came from the theories of a refugee from Nazi Germany, Rudolf Laban.

The Education Model: Rudolf Laban

Laban's theories are very well documented in his own writings: *Modern Educational Dance* (1948), *Principles of Dance and Movement Notation* (1956) and *Mastery of Movement* (1971) and in Preston Dunlop's seminal textbook *A Handbook for Modern Educational Dance* (1963). Foster (1976) provided a perceptive analysis as to why Laban's ideas were so enthusiastically adopted in postwar Britain, by providing a context:

> Laban's work received acceptance because it was essentially an individual approach at a time, after World War Two, when individual differences were being stressed. It was expressive at a time when self expression was becoming fashionable, and it was a non academic outlet when . . . leading educationalists look(ed) for creative outlets. (p. 81)

The 1950s and 1960s provided an ideal background for a theory of movement education that placed an emphasis on individuality, creativity, imagination, feeling responses, and the process of self-discovery and self-directed learning being at the centre of the movement experience. Smith (1988) employs the term *educational model* to describe Laban's theories and comments that 'the essential characteristic of this educational model was its emphasis on the process of dancing and its affective/experiential contribution to the participant's overall development as a moving/feeling being' (p. 257).

It is not the purpose of this chapter to attempt a detailed critique of Laban's impact and influence. Many readers will have had firsthand experience in their own teacher training courses of modern educational dance, as this kind of movement experience commonly came to be known, and witnessed the impact of Laban's work in schools. The fact that modern educational dance was taken up by many, mostly female, PE colleges and school PE departments and subsequently formed the core curriculum at the Art of Movement Studio speaks for itself. It needs to be stressed, however, particularly in the context of the current National Curriculum debate, that one of the main reasons Laban's work had such an impact in schools was because the core of the work reflected a postwar climate emphasizing personal creativity and expression. Also, modern educational dance, both in theory and in practice, offered a unique medium within PE for personal expression (although this was largely confined in practice to women and girls).

The Professional Model: Modern Dance

During the mid 1960s a new artistic development in dance theatre came about that subsequently challenged the educational model of the previous 2 decades. Stevens (1988) suggests that the introduction of American modern dance, through performances given by Martha Graham, Alvin Ailey, Merce Cunningham and Paul Taylor, opened the way for a new contemporary dance theatre aesthetic. Teachers and students began to attend classes in modern dance, and 1966 saw the official opening of the London School of Contemporary Dance. This new development placed the study of dance within a theatrical context, and although contemporary dance was enthusiastically welcomed in the theatre, some of the earlier child-centred principles espoused by Laban and his followers began to be seen less and less in dance classes in secondary schools. The pendulum had swung from the early educational model to a 'professional' training model (Stevens, 1988).

This professional training model placed great emphasis on the development of theatrically derived dance skills, technique and styles. Compositional tasks were often derived from prechoreographed works, and the yardstick for assessment was usually equated with professional dance. It was essentially a method of training that had been devised for the professional theatre. Naturally such a radical shift was not without its critics, and Redfern (1973) was among others who saw this development as more like an indoctrination, with limited educational value.

However, the adoption of a professional training model, which grew out of a consideration of dance as an art, began to raise questions as to whether dance could any longer be viewed as just an aspect of PE in schools. Because dance was viewed as a contemporary theatre art, its profile was raised and made more accessible. Questions were raised as to why dance was not perceived in schools in the same way as music and drama—in other words, as a performing art.

Dance as Art

New courses in dance in secondary schools and at tertiary level came to the fore during the 1970s. Davies (1988) saw this development linked also to the reorganization of many tertiary colleges and a reduction in teacher training places, which provided many opportunities to develop dance in nonvocational degrees. Once it became possible to establish dance courses in nonvocational degrees, the link between dance and PE began to become more and more tenuous. These new courses, most of which focused on the study of dance as a theatre art, offered study of a range of dance styles, dance composition and choreography, dance appreciation and analysis, aesthetics, history and sociology of dance, and notation. The impact was also felt in secondary schools with the introduction of new Certificate of Secondary Education (CSE) dance courses and, later, dance courses at General Certificate of Education (GCE) ordinary (O) and advanced (A) levels. In primary schools, where the emphasis has traditionally been on the 'whole' child, there was less change in teaching methods and pedagogy.

Thus the 1970s and early 1980s saw a major shift and development in terms of dance provision at secondary school level and at tertiary level. As a result of disquiet felt by many teachers that the professional training model was too limiting for the vast majority of pupils, a new model for dance in education began to emerge during the early 1980s. Smith (1977) and, later, Adshead (1981) proposed a model characterized by a three-stranded approach to the study of dance as an art. This approach sought to integrate aspects of the educational and professional training models whilst offering a new organizing conceptual basis underpinning study through the processes and production of performing/performance, composing/composition and viewing/appreciation. This 'midway' model can be seen in various public examination courses in secondary schools, at the present time, and is often utilized with varying degrees of emphasis in primary schools. It also forms the basis of many degree courses, reflecting in a variety of ways the particular aims and objectives of each course.

So, in this all-too-brief look at the historical development of dance in the curriculum, we come up to date. It has been argued here that the relationship between dance and PE, although close in the first part of this century, has increasingly, through the past 2 decades or so, become less clear. The fact that dance has not earned a place in the National Curriculum as a subject in its own right is highly regrettable. Dance in the curriculum has developed along its own lines, and PE, too, has developed distinctive practices and methods of study. Perhaps a way forward can be discerned in the next part of this chapter, which attempts to define the particular contribution dance can make as an artistic, cultural and physically educating medium.

Dance as a Subject and Cross-Curricular Study

The dance-as-art model is found most often in schools today, whether dance is taught as a subject in its own right, within a performing arts context, or as part of physical education. This model contains aspects of both the educational and the professional models referred to previously. A key feature of the model is the notion of integrating the study of dance under a complementary and intercon- nected three-stranded approach.

Performance: Dance Studies

The first strand of the dance-as-art model, *performance*, allows pupils to develop technical and performance skills in a variety of contexts. Technical skills such as control, mobility, coordination and accuracy of execution can be developed from the early years of schooling and gradually refined throughout the later years. Technical skills in all the arts are fundamental tools along the path of personal expression; without them pupils would have a limited range of communication. However, there needs to be a clear appreciation that technical skills are only a means to an end. The Assessment of Performance Unit (APU) 1983 document *Aesthetic Development* sounded a clear warning: 'Technical competence although essential is also a necessary condition. Moreover, too rigid an emphasis on the learning of technical skills may have the unfortunate consequence of destroying creative potential, since these skills are a means to an end' (p. 8).

Besides developing technical skills, pupils at all levels need to develop per- forming skills. Performing skills are a more elusive range of skills but generally encompass such aspects as musicality, stylistic understanding (which necessarily includes a wider understanding of cultural context), fluency, focus and projection. It is a common practice today for pupils to learn both technical and performance skills through prechoreographed dance studies. Stevens (1985a) defined a dance study as 'a prechoreographed technically demanding set of movements which require certain dance performance skills of the executant' (p. 57).

The notion of a dance study is not new in dance education. Dance studies were learnt and taught in the educational model, where pupils learnt to perform 'body awareness', 'effort cube' and 'spatial orientation' studies. In the professional training model, there have always been dance studies in a variety of theatrically derived styles, from ballet through to contemporary dance. Today in schools, dance studies (or technical studies) are used in many General Certificate of Secondary Education (GCSE) courses and at the advanced supplementary (AS) and advanced (A) levels. To prepare pupils for public examinations, teachers often employ dance studies throughout the secondary curriculum and, in some instances, also at primary school level. The distinguishing features of today's dance studies are, firstly, that the study is choreographed with a pupil in mind (rather than using professional dance as a yardstick) and, secondly, that the study utilizes aspects of a contemporary dance style, or styles, and modes of presentation. The dance study also allows for pupils to learn how to perform in a choreographed context, which can underpin their own study of choreography. Moreover, in the later years, dance studies can be drawn from existing dance repertory, which offers opportunities for pupils to begin to investigate style, technique and form in a wide (possibly historical) context. This may involve, possibly at GCSE level and above, viewing dances from a range of sources—much as a drama or theatre—studies pupil may investigate characterization and interpretation.

Cross-curricular links are also possible here. Clearly, learning to dance with confidence, skill, accuracy and stylistic understanding has a central role to play in physically educating young people. In music lessons pupils studying a particular musical style could dance a study in a similar style and study the similarities and differences. Links with geography and history also offer possibilities through utilizing aspects of folk dance and historical dance. Within the broader context of performing arts, there are numerous ways dance performance skills could be used in formal (and informal) performing contexts such as school plays, musicals and operas.

Composition: Creating a Whole

In the second strand, *composition*, pupils develop their own creative and choreographic skills. Crafting principles, principles of form, selection and refinement of movement content in relation to a theme, and knowledge and understanding of compositional style are all aspects that can be developed in this strand. From the early years pupils can begin to perceive and create a 'whole' dance using a simple theme and simple structuring properties; in the later years there could be more emphasis on individual choreographic style and expression.

A method that is often employed by teachers in the teaching of dance composition is the 'dance framework' approach. This method was defined by Stevens (1985b):

[The dance framework approach] is based on the idea that there is always going to be a product or part of a product by the end of the lesson and that pupils understand what the product is. Pupils should be able to come out of the lesson and say, 'We are doing a dance about such and such,' or be able to title the dance. As far as the framework is concerned here, obviously the teacher has structured it so that the pupils can gradually develop that particular dance and be able to perform it by the end of the lesson or lessons. (p. 83)

One can see from this that the teacher plays a key role in structuring material, for simple dances in the primary school through to a more open-ended, stylistic and compositionally demanding treatment of material at upper secondary school level. Links across to professional dance, through viewing, reading, writing and discussion, can be used to provide reference points and exemplify a particular aspect of a professional choreographer's treatment of material and or theme. However, the emphasis should be on the use of professional repertoire as examples and not on producing carbon copies of professional dance works.

The notion of teaching dance composition, again, is not new. There were many instances of individual creative endeavours being fostered in the educational and professional models. However, there are three main differences today. First, today dance theatre repertoire is studied as providing artistic and cultural reference points and as examples of good practice. Second, today the product (i.e. the finished dance) is viewed as a small (or large) work of art. Third, there is an emphasis today on pupils' experiences of life and culture (rather than a predetermined theatrical model) as possible sources for their own creative endeavours.

Parallels with the other arts in education are easy to make in this context. There is a long tradition in music education of teaching musical composition and in drama of the idea of improvisation giving way to a final, finished performance in a theatrical setting. Some performing arts courses in secondary schools look across the arts to see how each individual art addresses and employs some specific concept (such as principles of form) within a range of contrasting cultural contexts. Linking dance composition with current practice in PE is more problematic. Composition in dance is directed towards expression and artistic communication, with the outcome (i.e. the dance) being viewed as a finished work of art. Composition in the field of games and sport, although present to a degree, is markedly different in intention, communicability and outcome. However, in gymnastics, for example, compositional skills are developed in the planning and preparation of gymnastic sequences, where structuring devices such as development and variation of motif, repetition, contrast, climax and unity are used in ways not so dissimilar in kind to practices employed in dance composition. However, where there are fewer links with PE (and many more within a performing arts context) is in the presentation and development of artistic, theatrical modes of expression and communication.

Viewing: Knowledge and Appreciation

In the final strand, *viewing*, pupils engage in developing their knowledge and appreciation of finished dance works, both works created by themselves and works drawn from the professional dance world. This strand has gained in importance during the past 2 decades as professional dance works have increased in availability, and teachers have come to appreciate that by viewing dance works, pupils can gain a wider and deeper perspective of dance. This strand also forms an important part of GCSE, 'AS' and 'A' level courses. The availability of dance works on film and video and in the theatre is essential if teachers are to offer pupils the range of examples that are currently available in the theatre. Also, teachers themselves need to be educated in how to develop and guide pupils' perception and appreciation of artistic and aesthetic qualities present in dance works.

Smith (1987) argues for a fuller understanding of the term *appreciation* in the arts by stressing that

> the word appreciation can be defined as an ability to account the merits or to perceive the qualities in an object. In the arts, however, appreciation means more than this. In fully appreciating an art work one is not only valuing its qualities, its form, its meaningful significance and the cleverness, precision, originality with which it has been wrought perhaps but one experiences a sense of enjoyment sometimes even elation. (p. 103)

For pupils to learn to identify and discuss the salient features of a dance, teachers must develop their pupils' understanding, over a long period of time, of a wide range of choreography and dance performance. This can be started in the primary school by selecting dance works that utilize thematic content appropriate to the early years of schooling. Placing dance works in a wider contextual context through a consideration of historical and cultural factors also plays a part in the process of appreciating dance works. As pupils view a dance work on video, for example, they could discuss how a particular choreographer has used a theme, how the selection of dance material has produced dance motifs, where contrast and climax are used and how the music, design and production elements have been combined to make a 'whole'. Alongside such a discussion, pupils could be reading and exploring how a dance work is a manifestation of a certain time and place, how it breaks or subscribes to traditional choreographic and stylistic boundaries, how differences in individual performances can affect outcomes and so forth. A dance work viewed in this way could also be the starting point for pupils' own choreographic and performance work. The interrelationships in the three-strand approach can also be seen clearly here.

Cross-curricular work could yield a very rich basis for study. A dance work such as 'West Side Story' not only offers a study of a particular kind of dance but also could form the basis for work in the humanities, music, drama and English literature. Viewing dances drawn from Asian and Afro-Caribbean cultures offers valuable opportunities for deepening pupils' awareness of different cultures and opens up a potentially rewarding appreciation of cross-cultural and multicultural concerns. Gender issues, too, could be sensitively addressed through viewing dances that both reinforce and challenge sexual stereotypes. A link with PE may also be possible here through a comparison of salient features in a dance work and those perceptible in gymnastic and skating sequences. However, at the present time, the viewing of sports and gymnastics as cultural and historical manifestations is not fully developed in school courses, where the traditional emphasis has been on physically participating in (rather than reflecting upon) a range of activities.

It has been argued here that use of the dance-as-art model as a basis for school courses across all age ranges establishes dance as a subject in its own right. Other emphases are of course possible—for instance, dance can be seen to contribute to health-related fitness and social and cultural education through a study of folk, ethnic and social dance forms. Cross-curricular links can be made, and in the main these are most successfully achieved when dance is linked with performing and expressive arts, where methods of procedure and assessment and common conceptual bases are most easily definable. A particularly close relationship with music can be seen in many school dance courses, where teachers often employ similar terminology. Swanwick (1983) proposed an integrated three-stranded approach to the teaching of music, based on performing, composing and listening. Drama, too, has distinctive parallel practices in terms of performing, writing plays and studying existing texts.

The next part of this chapter addresses current national developments that have formed a background to the present position and also make a case for dance being a separate profile component within PE.

The Current National Curriculum Debate: Problems and Possibilities

In an ideal and forward-looking National Curriculum, there would be a generic grouping of arts subjects, including visual art, music, dance and drama, within a broadly based common arts curriculum. There would also be a National Curriculum working group in the arts to address both common practices and distinctive differences in a school arts curriculum. The idea of a 'whole' arts curriculum is not new. The Arts in Schools Project in the past 3 years has led the way towards establishing (where appropriate) a common arts language. It has identified examples of good practice within each of the arts and in cross-arts projects and has disseminated current thinking and practice in its many newsletters. However, the National Curriculum, far from building on current combined arts trends and practices, identifies only art and music as foundation subjects and subsumes drama within English and dance within PE (and also possibly music).

Robinson (1989) urged the Secretary of State to coordinate the arts in the National Curriculum, and Almond (1989) made a strong case for dance, in particular, to be included in combined arts practice rather than subsumed as a part of PE. It has been argued throughout this chapter that the relationship between dance and PE is tenuous, and there are many more possibilities for common conceptual bases to be found within expressive and performing arts.

Dance finds itself now in a peculiarly ambivalent position. Despite examples of successful combined arts practice (including dance) in primary and secondary schools and several GCSE, Business and Technical Educational Council (BTEC) and other courses that also include dance as a performing art, dance has not earned a place in the National Curriculum as a subject in its own right or as part of an arts group.

Angela Rumbold, Minister of State with responsibility for the National Curriculum, in a letter dated March 31, 1989, gave a response to the informal dance consortium (composed of representatives from the Council of Dance Education and Training, NATFHE Dance Secton, the National Dance Teachers' Association and the Standing Conference on Dance in Higher Education) who expressed considerable early concern at the exclusion of dance as a foundation subject. She stated:

> We have no intention of squeezing dance out of the school curriculum. We attach importance to the study of it in schools. We recognise that dance makes a unique contribution to the educational process. We believe it can do so effectively as a cross curricular element infusing PE and music in the National Curriculum, and where appropriate as a separate subject in its own right outside the National Curriculum. . . . We shall, however, be ensuring that the machinery established to consider the content of the guidelines on PE and music will address the role of dance in those foundation subjects.

Minister Rumbold is also on record, in a House of Common's debate on the Education Reform Act (reported in *Hansard*, March 23, 1989), as saying, 'As I am sure the hon. Gentleman knows, dance is an important part of physical education'. This view is also endorsed in a recent HMI document (1989a), *Physical Education from 5 to 16* (Curriculum Matters 16), where dance is identified as a significant part of an aesthetic and artistic strand within PE. Thus, as far as present government and HMI policy are concerned, the place of dance is clearly stated. This ambivalent situation is further compounded by the fact that there is no specific HMI Curriculum Matters document for dance education. It could, of course, be argued that as dance is not named as a foundation subject in its own right in the National Curriculum, there is no need for a separate HMI document. However, this has not been the case for drama, which is also not named as a foundation subject in the National Curriculum. *Drama from 5 to 16* (Curriculum Matters 17, HMI, 1989b) provided a clear framework for drama in education. It would have been very helpful indeed, in the context of this current debate, if a similar document had been published for dance—identifying both its separate subject status and its potential to contribute to PE and expressive arts.

Prior to the formal establishment of the Physical Education National Working Group, an important joint British Council of Physical Education (BCPE) National Curriculum Council and Department of Education and Science conference was held in Bournemouth in March 1990. At this conference the BCPE Interim Working Group (which included only one specific dance representative) presented the paper *The Planning, Assessment and Evaluation of Physical Education as a*

Foundation Subject of the National Curriculum From 5 to 16 (BCPE, 1990).
Under a single profile component 'Capability in Physical Education', three
attainment targets were proposed: Performing; Planning and Composing; and
Appraisal and Evaluation, with 10 levels (in each attainment target) and accompanying statements of attainment.

Although these three attainment targets may sound similar to the dance-as-art
model's three-strand approach (performing, composing and viewing), a detailed
reading of the BCPE paper offers little in the way of a conceptual basis for
teaching dance as a formed and performed art. Because the BCPE paper does
not specifically identify a range of physical activities as subject-based starting
points, it is difficult in some instances to identify which particular physical
activity is being addressed in the statements of attainment or to discern clear
levels of progression. There is also very scant reference to dance as an art or to
how, as an art subject, it differs in intention, presentation and communicability
from other physical activities. Another serious conceptual objection to this paper
is that its suggestion that the proposed three attainment targets could operate
separately from one another is mistaken.

Current practice in dance (and music) education has developed a close
interweaving and interdependence among performing, composing and viewing,
with the differences only being in degrees of emphasis. As has already been
argued, a 'good' performance of a dance study (at any level), for example, relies
heavily not only on technical skills but also on pupils showing in performance
an understanding of the choreography—which can be richly informed and
developed through viewing and appreciating a wider cultural and historical
context.

At the same Bournemouth Conference, the National Dance Teachers' Association presented an alternative paper (NDTA, 1990) that made a case for dance as
an art subject within a separate profile component. As might be expected,
performing, creating and viewing were proposed as processes that could exist
within each of the three suggested attainment targets:

1. Show knowledge and understanding of a range of Dance movement.
2. Show knowledge and understanding of structuring Dance movement.
3. Demonstrate critical and contextual understanding of Dance (p. 2).

A detailed reading of this paper identifies dance as the subject area, with the
three-stranded approach being utilized in an integrated manner.

The Secretary for State, in July 1990 (DES, 1990), announced the terms of
reference and membership of the Physical Education Working Group (which
inluded one dance specialist). There was some good news for dance—it was
positively named (more than once) in the guidelines that were issued, and the
Group was charged (amongst other directives)

to take account of:

1) the contribution which PE, including active physical recreation, competitive sport and dance, can make to learning about other subjects and cross

curricular themes including, in particular, expressive arts subjects (including drama and music), health education and PSE and which they in turn can make to learning in PE; and

2) best practice and the results of any relevant research and development (p. 5).

So, what is the best way forward from here? There is clearly profound disagreement between physical and dance educationalists (as can be seen from the papers presented at the Bournemouth Conference), and this should be clearly recognized by the Working Group. A key to finding a workable solution must reside in how the Working Group defines PE. Traditionally PE has encompassed a wide range of complementary and contrasting activities that, seen as a whole, offer young people opportunities for a range of choices. Generic groupings are not easy to find, as the activities PE can encompass do not readily offer common conceptual bases. Perhaps this, too, needs to be recognized.

Maybe rather than having a single profile component (as was proposed in the BCPE Bournemouth paper), there should be three components under an overarching broad definition of PE that takes account of common practice in schools, sporting, cultural and artistic factors and health-based concerns. It is possible to conceive of PE as including competitive sport, active physical recreation and dance, although on the surface these areas have little in common apart from the fundamental use of the body as the means of 'expression'. Furthermore, claims that these activities, in themselves, necessarily induce healthy attitudes to living are difficult to substantiate. There are too many variables in intention and practice for a fitness-based framework to be credible. Without trying to force common ground where it does not readily exist, it may, therefore, be more productive to identify each of these three areas as separate profile components with independent programmes of study and attainment targets.

Competitive sport (as a profile component) could therefore include a range of options, which might include large- and small-team games as individual events—linked together by a common notion of mutually cooperative, interactive and competitive conventions, rules and practices, viewed from a wide cultural context. Active physical recreation (as the second profile component) could include activities such as outdoor education, educational gymnastics, dance and sport-related activities—linked together by a common emphasis on health-related practices and personal and social development, viewed from a wide cultural context. Dance (as the third profile component), within a broadly defined dance-as-art model, could include an emphasis on aesthetic and artistic dance practices and conventions and link across with current thinking in music and drama.

Within each of these proposed profile components there could also be nonstatutory suggestions for programmes of study, offering schools flexibility to devise schemes of work appropriate to their needs.

If PE is conceived by the new Working Group as a wide grouping of related subject areas as outlined above (as the Science and Maths Working Groups did for these subjects in their National Curriculum Guidelines), there could be a logical place for dance as an art, within PE. Moreover, the development of a PE 'midway' model (as has been devised for dance education), with an equal emphasis on 'process' and 'product', may offer an opportunity to combine some of the best practices currently evident within PE in schools.

It is surely in all our interests, at the present time, to be flexible and imaginative and look at other models for guidance and inspiration.

Acknowledgements

Some material in this article is from 'Dance in the National Curriculum: Problems and Possibilities' by S. Stevens, 1990, *British Journal of Physical Education*, **21**. Copyright 1990 by The Physical Education Association of Great Britain and Northern Ireland. Adapted by permission.

References and Suggested Readings

Adshead, J. (1981). *The study of dance*. London: Dance Books.

Almond, L. (1989). New wine in a new bottle: Implications for a national physical education curriculum. *British Journal of Physical Education, 20*, 123-125.

Assessment of Performance Unit. (1983). *Aesthetic development*. London: Her Majesty's Stationery Office.

Bloomfield, A. (1988). The philosophical and artistic tradition in dance education. In I.K. Glaister (Ed.), *Young people dancing. Vol. 1. Dance: Education* (pp. 10-20). London: Dance and the Child International.

Board of Education. (1909). *Syllabus of physical exercise for public elementary schools*. London: His Majesty's Stationery Office.

Board of Education. (1919). *Syllabus of physical training*. London: His Majesty's Stationery Office.

Board of Education. (1933). *Syllabus of physical training*. London: His Majesty's Stationery Office.

British Council of Physical Education. (1990). *The planning, assessment and evaluation of physical education as a foundation subject of the National Curriculum from 5 to 16*. London: Author.

Calouste Gulbenkian Foundation. (1980). *Dance education and training in Britain*. London: Author.

Davies, M. (1988). Of secondary importance and primary concern: Prioritising the study of dance. In I.K. Glaister (Ed.), *Young people dancing. Vol. 1. Dance: education* (pp. 69-78). London: Dance and the Child International.

Department of Education and Science. (1990, July 11). *Circular 231/90, p. 5*. London: Author.

Foster, R. (1976). *Knowing in my bones*. London: Adam & Charles Black.

Her Majesty's Inspector. (1983). *Dance in secondary schools*. London: Her Majesty's Stationery Office.

Her Majesty's Inspector. (1989a). *Physical education from 5 to 16* (Curriculum Matters 16). London: Her Majesty's Stationery Office.

Her Majesty's Inspector. (1989b). *Drama from 5 to 16* (Curriculum Matters 17). London: Her Majesty's Printing Office.

Laban, R. (1948). *Modern educational dance*. London: MacDonald & Evans.

Laban, R. (1956). *Principles of dance and movement notation*. London: MacDonald & Evans.

Laban, R. (1971). *Mastery of movement* (p. 2). London: MacDonald & Evans.

National Dance Teachers' Association. (1990). *A rationale for dance in the school curriculum*. London: NDTA Assessment Working Group.

Preston Dunlop, V. (1963). *A handbook for modern educational dance*. London: MacDonald & Evans.

Redfern, H.B. (1973). *Concepts in modern educational dance*. London: Henry Kimpton.

Robinson, K. (1989, November 24). Whole arts. *London Times Educational Supplement*, p. 25.

Rumbold, A. In a letter to the Dance Consortium, March 31, 1989.

Smith, J.M. (1977). *An investigation to test the parameters of the problem connected with the proposal that dance in the secondary school should be considered an art form, in which pupils may develop their artistic skill in creating and performing dances and their aesthetic judgement in viewing dances*. Unpublished master's thesis, University of London.

Smith, J.M. (1987). New directions in dance education. *British Journal of Physical Education,* **18**, 101-103.

Smith, J.M. (1988). Dance as art education: New directions. In I.K. Glaister (Ed.), *Young people dancing. Vol. 1. Dance: Education* London: Dance and the Child International.

Stevens, S.E. (1985a). The dance study in dance education. *2D Dance and Drama Magazine* (Leicestershire Education Committee), pp. 57-63.

Stevens, S.E. (1985b). Jacqueline Smith interviewed. *2D Dance and Drama Magazine* (Leicestershire Education Committee), pp. 83-93.

Stevens, S.E. (1988). Dance teacher education in Britain in the 1990's. In I.K. Glaister (Ed.), *Young people dancing. Vol. 1. Dance: Education* (pp. 288-296). London: Dance and the Child International.

Swanwick, K. (1983). *The arts in education: Dreaming or awake?* Inaugural lecture as Professor of Music Education, London University Institute of Education.

Chapter 8

Outdoor Education in the National Curriculum

Barbara Humberstone

Thanks for the great time I had. There was plenty to do, so I wouldn't have a chance to get bored. I liked climbing and I thought abseiling was great. . . . I wasn't too keen to come but when it came for the time to leave I didn't want to go home. I thought the staff were great. Like Brenda said, everything's magic! I am looking forward to coming again.(Kate)[1]

With the overload of documentation and the frantic race to ensure that our subject and our values are not overlooked in the melee, with concern about 'delivering' the National Curriculum (NC) and inventing attainment targets, one wonders what has happened to the recipient of all this (cf. Brighouse, 1990). Has the pupil been lost somewhere? Perhaps she or he has disappeared into the 'bustle of the marketplace'! What about areas of the curriculum that attempt to place the pupil at the centre of the learning process—where are their alloted places in the National Curriculum?

One such curricular area, its advocates would argue, is outdoor education (OE). This aspect of the curriculum receives no mention in the National Curriculum document *From Policy to Practice* (Department of Education and Science [DES], 1989a). This is despite OE's past recognition as a valuable medium for personal, social and physical education in reports from Her Majesty's Inspectorate (HMI, 1983, 1989a, 1989b) and others (Inner London Education Authority [ILEA], 1988; Manpower Services Commission [MSC], 1981) and its particular contribution to the enchancement of subject areas concerned specifically with aspects associated with the outdoors and the environment, such as geography and biology (cf. DES, 1979; Schools Council Geography Committee, 1980; HMI, 1986, 1989c). However, OE is briefly mentioned under 'extracurricular activities' in the NC document *The Whole Curriculum*, where, in addition to it contribution to the areas described, it is seen as providing an opportunity for 'education for citizenship' (cf. NCC, 1990, p. 6).

Like dance (also absent from the NC document), outdoor education is 'betwixt and between'. Both have unique subject identities, yet many of their facets can be located in a variety of more strongly bounded curricular subjects—or rather, in those that have been defined as core and foundation subjects in the NC. OE and dance are concerned to empower and educate through the physical, and both are concerned to contribute to the development of pupils' knowledge and understanding of the physical as it concerns the pupils themselves and personal and social relationships.

The Development of Outdoor Education in School Curriculum

In order to consider OE and the dilemmas surrounding its place in the National Curriculum, it is necessary to take a brief look back at the ways in which OE entered school curricula and developed its diverse identity. The 1944 Education Act proposed that

> a period of residence in a school camp or other boarding school in the country would contribute substantially to the health and width of outlook of any child from a town school, especially if care of livestock, the growing of crops, the study of the countryside and the pursuit of other outdoor activities formed the bulk of the educational provision and were handled by specially qualified staff. (Cited in Hunt, 1989, p. 24)

This proposal, a consequence of the government's concern for childrens' health, caused a considerable number of Local Education Authorities (LEAs) to establish their own residential outdoor centres, many based on the Outward Bound concept.[2] OE provision during the 1960s and 1970s burgeoned rapidly. However, despite this expansion, OE was not officially recognized as an 'entitlement' of every pupil, and so not every LEA made OE experience available to all its pupils. Nevertheless, in the greater percentage of LEAs, through the official support and coordination of some of the officers and advisers, particular effort was made to ensure that OE opportunity was made available to the majority of pupils. A further consequence of the 1944 Act, under the aegis of the Central Council for Physical Recreation, was the development of a number of national outdoor residential centres. Use was made of these by various colleges of physical education (PE) in attempts to provide residential outdoor/adventure experience for trainee PE teachers.

An important development in, and a significant dimension of, OE, then, has been the provision of out-of-school and residential facilities. OE experience has been provided by residential or day centres, staffed by centre teachers with a variety of expertise and qualifications. (The clientele of many centres may not be limited to schools but also includes youth and adult groups). Teachers in secondary schools, with a variety of different subject backgrounds, have made use of these centres to provide OE experience for their pupils. Significantly, it seems that it has been PE teachers who have most frequently provided opportunities for pupils to experience outdoor/adventure education (O/AE) and who have made the link between the school and centre-based work. In some cases, schools might not use staffed centres but utilize the expertise of teachers within their school to provide challenging activities. A number of colleges of education have offered O/AE as a main teaching subject. Many of the teachers qualified in OE have tended to move into residential or other centre work, and it has often been through the PE programmes that OE has found a niche in schools. Generally, schools have been reluctant to recognize the possibility of an OE department; rather, where a teacher has been responsible for OE, if not located within a PE department, he or she may frequently be responsible to a PE department.

A consequence of the numerous providers of OE was the development of many national bodies concerned to promote the sectional interests of their members. Until recently, the Department of Education and Science (DES) has played an important part in encouraging the development of OE provision. However, this support appears to be lessening. It is likely that the long-standing OE advisory committee of the DES, the successor of the camping committee (a product of the 1944 Education Act) that had representation from the various national bodies, is to be disbanded, despite considerable concern expressed to the DES by interested individuals and associations. Thus, we see not only the beginning of the rise of OE in the curriculum but also the seeds of its diversity.

What Constitutes Outdoor Education Curriculum Content?

Central to OE is the way in which outdoor/adventure education can provide a powerful medium for personal and social education and change. A qualitative research project undertaken by Roberts et al. in 1974 to investigate residential outdoor/adventure experience clearly showed that the OE providers' objectives to foster social and personal change were, for them, realized and reinforced in the day to day experience of their work:

> Course organizers, often hoping to promote a Utopia social order, . . . receive a feedback sufficient to secure their beliefs that the intended social changes are gradually being actualised in the world around. (Roberts, White, & Parker, 1974, p. 153)

Roberts, White and Parker (1974) found that the OE providers' ideals were largely based on the philosophy of Kurt Hahn, who had been critical of the educational provision of his time. Hahn believed that 'education fails to introduce activities into a boy's [sic] life [which are] likely to make him discover his powers of a man of action: that strong convictions must be built up in a boy [sic] concerning a democratic way of life through meaningful and purposeful experience' (Hahn, cited in Wood and Cheffer, 1978, p. 17) and 'Our claim is to lay the foundation of class peace and religious peace' (Hahn, cited in Roberts et al., 1974, p. 68). Interestingly, despite the considerable passage of time (and change in terminology), OE providers of residential experiences still appear to be committed to similar underlying ideals and believe that these are realized in practice: 'The centre represented a small part of society as a whole. I wanted society to be characterised by the same set of values as the centre' (Nichols, 1989, p. 2).

A consensus view of what constitutes OE was determined and formalized by those present at the 1975 Dartington conference on OE sponsored by the DES. The subsequent report laid down much of the basis for OE: 'Education out-of-doors includes aspects of many disciplines such as geography, history, art, biology, fieldwork, environmental studies and physical education, depending on the context' and 'A means of approaching educational objectives through guided direct experience in the environment, using its resources as learning materials' (DES, 1975, cited in Royce, 1987, p. 12).

These definitions of OE reflect the considerable diversity of interests of those present, and perhaps, on the one hand, a desire on the part of many to make OE 'academically' more respectable and, on the other, a commitment to a holistic approach to education. Nevertheless, when OE is referred to as part of the school curriculum, it tends to be construed as concerned with the utilization of outdoor/adventure-type activities as media for a variety of educational aims, frequently in a residential setting.

The following statement from a recent DES *Safety in Outdoor Education* document captures the present-day practice of OE: 'Traditionally the term OE has been applied to activities which involve some degree of physical challenge and risk. . . . [It] provides opportunities for learning through experience' (DES, 1989b, p. 2).

During the last decade, there has been much published material by outdoor educators concerning the philosophy, values, potential and practice of OE (see, in particular, Royce, 1987). A major influence upon the thinking of outdoor educators is the work of Colin Mortlock, who, in his reflective and stimulating book *Adventure Alternative* (1984), sets out a philosophical framework for OE, based upon progressive adventure education. It is a holistic approach to education, within a framework of safety, in which the ideals of concern for, and awareness of, oneself, others and the environment are paramount. The ultimate educational experience, for Mortlock, is the preparation and execution of some sort of self-sufficient journey.

Unfortunately, as with much published material, equal opportunities and gender issues are not addressed in this work. There is obviously concern that OE should be available to girls, and attention is drawn to their successful participation. However, the philosophical discussions and language usage are male oriented. Interestingly, some of the values espoused might be considered to be traditionally 'feminine' and caring.[4]

Many LEA OE policies and school OE programmes reflect the particular philosophy of OE and its cross-curricular potential. Cumbria LEA's (1984) policy statement on OE in the curriculum describes a developmental programme in which OE is a major focus of pupils' experience from junior school through to further education. This programme, made up of three interconnected aspects—environmental education, residential experience and outdoor pursuits—provides pupils with considerable and varied educational opportunities with a coherent underlying base. The development, over recent years, of the Technical and Vocational Educational Initiative (TVEI), Certificate of Pre-Vocational Education (CPVE) and General Certificate of Secondary Education (GCSE) in the curriculum has had implications for OE (cf. Keighley, 1988, 1989a, 1989b). All are concerned with experience-based and pupil-centred learning and have encompassed aspects such as decision making, problem solving, adventurous challenge, residential experiences and other aspects of OE. A high percentage of GCSE examinations place emphasis upon practical experience, frequently out of doors.

An excellent example of a school successfully utilizing outdoor/adventure residential experience to fulfill some of the aspects of TVEI, geography and biology fieldwork and GCSE English is a secondary school in Hampshire. The head of PE saw the potential, and took the opportunity, to utilize the county's large residential outdoor centre. For 1 week, the whole of the 4th year descends upon the centre to participate in challenging activities such as climbing, skiing, sailing and canoeing, whilst also using the experience to stimulate various forms of writing and using the surroundings for fieldwork. This is evidently seen as a success, not only by the pupils but also by the headteacher and the chair of the governors: 'Staff felt that not only did the experience satisfy the TVEI and TRIDENT objectives but that it was inspirational for pupils and teachers alike' (NCC, 1988, p. 10).

Despite differing views on the relative merits of examinations in OE, there have been a number of Certificate of Secondary Education (CSE) Mode 3, and more recently GCSE Mode 3, syllabi in OE. The East London course required candidates to study and practice five aspects: rock climbing, campcraft, canoeing, mapwork and dinghy sailing. However, it appears likely that the NC will bring the demise of the Mode 3 examinations, because they may well be too costly for the examination boards to continue to administer (Hunt, 1989).

The Education Reform Act's Effect on the Future of Outdoor Education in the National Curriculum

The financial exigencies of recent years have affected OE centres as well as schools. The implications of the restriction on the funding of OE centres since about 1980 and the effects of Local Management of Schools (LMS) are considerable. Following the boom years of the 1960s, the cost of maintaining OE centres has increased, whilst funding from government sources has contracted. Over the last 10 years, some centres have shut or been threatened with closure, whilst monies for the general maintenance of others has been significantly cut, causing the fabric of many centres (like many schools) to degenerate.[5]

With LMS, educational establishments are put under pressure to operate within a competitive marketplace, which, because OE is not mentioned in the NC, has considerable implications for its future in schools. The educational justifications for OE are strong, but they are underpinned by values, some would argue, that are antithetical to the values on which the philosophy of competitive market-led forces is based. As it is possible that most schools will find themselves largely underfunded even in relation to providing the basic requirement for the NC, it will be difficult for heads and governors to claim more monies from LEAs to support an area of work that requires a high teacher-pupil ratio and additional equipment and facilities.

Paradoxically, as schools will also be competing for clientele, a school brochure including outdoor/adventure residential experiences may well be an additional incentive for parents to send their child to that particular school! We can then envisage dangerous and damaging situations in which governors and headteachers, with little experience of OE, and unfamiliar with safety aspects, think it a good idea and support an enthusiastic but inexperienced teacher's request to organize an O/A experience, with the inevitable consequences. The considerable experience of LEA officers and advisers may well become underutilized and disregarded.

Ski trips have tended to receive bad press, not least in the 1988 Panorama documentary on PE. The bad practice of a minority of teachers leading ski trips, and media distortion and sensationalization of the activities of a few school parties in ski resorts, have given the impression that school ski trips are something of a 'jolly'. Skiing is perhaps one of the finest and least problematic ways of providing pupils with access to some of the most magnificent scenery, and most physically challenging activities and skills, around. But these residential experiences need to be made available by qualified and aware teachers, not by teachers who are unfamiliar with the demands placed on them when involved in residential situations or potentially hazardous environments. It is argued that being a member of a ski party can provide pupils with worthwhile, long-term physical interests that can enable them to develop 'healthy and active life-styles' (cf. Styles, 1989). How will skiing and other OE experiences fare in the decade following the Education Reform Act (ERA)?

Far from being despondent, some outdoor educators see ERA, and especially Local Management, as providing greater opportunities for OE experiences, especially through 'the whole-school curriculum'. Thus Styles (1989) views developments in OE hopefully: 'The future successes will not be laid on a plate but [will require] coherent and logical proposals for offsite/adventurous/residential experience to become part of the establishment's overall whole school curriculum' (p. 5). He argues that offsite, out-of-school work could be funded by the school in a number of ways: as part of the core and foundation curriculum, by parental voluntary contribution and by the business world. However, we can only speculate as to which schools will be able to make available OE, to which pupils, under these sorts of conditions. It is, I would suggest, highly unlikely that this type of funding will provide equal opportunities for all pupils to participate in OE.

Many education authorities, OE advisers and other OE interest groups have seen the need to make convincing and rapid responses to the NCC in attempts to ensure that OE does not disappear but gains a more recognized place in the NC. Although much of the content of the post-ERA policy statements on OE reinforces previous statements and continues to be underpinned by original OE philosophy, it has been couched in the terminology of the National Curriculum.

Cumbria OE service, to provide a framework for implementing OE in the NC, is utilizing a 'thematic approach' and drawing upon the ways in which schools, using 'topic webs', are considering published subject attainment targets and how they might be reached through this approach. Activity webs are created linking the activity to core and foundation subjects. This is exemplified utilizing the activity of canoeing. Through a residential stay and canoe activity, it is shown, primary children could cover many of the attainment targets at the appropriate level in mathematics and science (Stansfield, 1989b).

The South West region OE advisers group has shown how OE can be interpreted in terms of the NC learning outcomes and linked with the science attainment targets (cf. Smith, 1989). Their paper, concerned with learning outcomes for outdoor education, was endorsed by the Outdoor Education Advisers' Panel and submitted to the NCC with the request that it be circulated to all subject working groups so that discussion would be initiated about cross-curricular themes. Similarly, other OE policy statements and documents have stressed the cross-curricular nature of OE and emphasized its contribution to personal and social education, TVEI, CPVE, extracurricular activities and community links (Hampshire County Council, 1989; Keighley, 1989b).

An interesting independent initiative undertaken by a group of prominent men, who have been involved for considerable time with the provision of a wide range of O/AE programmes and projects for young people, may have added further positive support for the future of OE in the NC. The group looked at attitudes to, and practices in, OE in Britain. The report of this survey, *In Search of Adventure* (Hunt, 1989), makes a strong proposal that by 1995, 'every young person in the United Kingdom has the opportunity to take part in adventurous outdoor activities' (p. 236). The report makes reference to the underparticipation of ethnic groups and young women. There are short sections concerned with the provision of OA for these groups. Significantly, although it was found that generally participation in OA activities is predominately by white males, over half those involved in the Duke of Edinburgh Award adventure activities are female.

The importance for girls of successful participation in risk-taking, challenging physical activities cannot be underestimated (cf. Humberstone and Lynch, 1990). It is crucial that these types of opportunities are made available to both girls and boys through the school curriculum. This is especially so for girls, because school may well be one of the few opportunities girls have for developing positive self-images and confidence in decision-making and problem-solving situations.

Following the launching of the report, a deputation on behalf of the management team voiced concerns to the Minister of Education, in January 1990, over the exclusion of OE from the NC. Subsequently, a member of the management team, a professor of geography, was called upon to represent OE on the PE National Curriculum working group.

Surrounding OE is a dilemma that is clearly, if implicitly, highlighted by the Hunt report. This is embedded in the view of OE reflected in the following statement, which emphasizes that OE 'is not a subject, but an approach to education' (Hunt, 1989, p. 53). One can ask, if it is not a subject or owes some allegiance to a subject area (or subject areas), what constitutes its associated content, knowledge or skills? For surely OE has all of these, as well as many approaches.

What Is an Outdoor Education Approach?

It is pertinent to consider here what constitutes any particular OE approach. Interestingly, Roberts, White and Parker (1974) pointed out that the OE centre staff of their study were frequently professionals from teaching and youth work who were disaffected with traditional schooling and its inability 'to create the better world that many have expected education to foster' (pp. 152-153). Further, they proposed that encapsulated in all the residential experiences was a 'progressive' philosophy. Within each course, 'is enshrined an ideal that has become prominent in modern educational thought; of presenting to the individual situations of challenge that will enable him [*sic*] to develop and appreciate his [*sic*] own abilities' (Roberts et al., 1974, p. 16).

A significant aim of outdoor educators, it seems, has been to empower pupils to gain confidence to take responsibility for their own learning. Loynes (1984), working with secondary pupils with learning difficulties, implicitly draws attention to the way the social and interpersonal context of traditional schooling may inhibit learning:

It is our view that the only person that can undertake personal and spiritual development is the individual. Our intent is to provide the social and environmental stimuli to bring this about. The biggest step is to get individuals to take responsibility for their own learning. This is made even harder as we are fighting attitudes towards traditional schooling. . . . Through adventure activity and teamwork situations they [the pupils] are faced with situations they cannot ignore. (Loynes, 1984, p. 14)

Moreover, a recent report from a primary school that programmed an outdoor education week, in which all the lessons were focused upon environmental work and problem solving, in locations close to the school, reported its considerable success. Children who generally had problems working in the classroom achieved a great deal during the week, whilst inhibited pupils gained in confidence and became more involved in their work ('New Whittington Primary School', 1989).

Unlike mainstream schooling, where there has been much qualitative research that has explored teaching and learning, there has been little research of this nature within an OE context. However, one ethnographic study within a large OE centre does give an indication of the characteristic features that shaped teaching and learning within OE at that centre and the particular pedagogic approaches through which these features were mediated (Humberstone, 1987). The findings, although exploratory, suggest that, in the OE context, the aims of the teachers were largely realized by the pupils in practice. The teachers' philosophy was underpinned by identifiable OE values and ideals that had much in common with a 'progressive', child-centred ideology. The different form and content of the overt and hidden curricula from that of school had significant and positive implications for pupils' learning and their confidence.[6] An unintended consequence of the 'progressive' approaches realized at the centre was a shift in the construction of gender identities and relations. Girls and boys became more aware of each other's capabilities and sensitivities (Humberstone, 1986, 1990a, 1990b).

Why Is Outdoor Education Not Mentioned in the National Curriculum?

It is considered that the ERA and the NC are the most far-reaching pieces of reform since the 1944 Education Act and that the ERA has substantially curbed teachers' professional autonomy in relation to defining curricular needs (Maclure, 1988). Some argue that the aims of the NC are to reassert 'traditional' values and practice in education whilst shunning the contributions that have been made through progressive approaches: 'Progressive teaching methods, a holistic approach to the development of the individual, a focus on process rather than product, cross-curricular initiatives, democratic participation are all under attack, if not eliminated in the government plans for our schools' (Davies, Holland & Minhas, 1990, pp. 26-27).

I would suggest that OE in its present form did not feature substantially in the NC because it is ideologically incompatible with, and in practice incongruent within, a National Curriculum framework, where knowledge is more rigidly compartmentalized and teaching is likely to be led by tests rather than by the individual needs of pupils.

The NC does mention cross-curricular aspects, personal and social education and equal opportunity issues, and it is through the former two aspects that many physical and outdoor educators have promoted OE. Nevertheless, O/AE opportunities have most frequently been made available through PE programmes. However, as a consequence of the perceived threat to PE in the National Curriculum and the diverse nature of OE, it was initially suggested that OE (along with dance) should not feature in the core of the future PE curriculum but be located somewhere else (cf. Almond, 1989). A number of concerns about the implications of the possible exclusion of OE from the PE curriculum were expressed from a variety of quarters and for a variety of reasons. Humberstone (1990c) argued that

the importance of OE, as an educational media, lies in the opportunities it provides for pupils to experience physical, emotional and intellectual challenges in supportive social contexts and potentially hazardous environ-mental situations. . . . The very foundation and philosophy of OE . . . are firmly embedded within adventure education and upon the physical skills and decision-making potential which underpin the various expressions of adventure education. If OE does not maintain its physical roots and align itself with physical education, at time when both PE and OE are threatened, then OE's valuable potential may be in even greater danger of disappearing and PE will lose a powerful educational ally and resource. (p. 246)

Despite the reluctance of a minority of outdoor educators (largely based in residential centres rather than schools) who felt that OE would not benefit from joining with other professional bodies, many outdoor educators were concerned to collaborate more closely with groups with shared interests. Consequently, and fortunately, OE is now recognized as a valid element of PE by the PE profession and by outdoor educators and is recommended to be included as a dimension of the PE curriculum (cf. British Association of Advisers and Lecturers in Physical Education [BAALPE], 1989a, 1989b; Almond and Dickenson, 1990; DES 1991).

Conclusion

This chapter has sketched the development of OE in the school curriculum, discussed its nature and highlighted the dilemmas surrounding its diversity, particularly within the framework of the National Curriculum.

Generally underpinning the 'delivery' of OE, it has been shown, is a consensual, coherent and powerful ideology, the underlying values of which appear strongly democratic and child-centred. The associated pedagogic approach is concerned to empower pupils and to value individual needs and capabilities. Outdoor educators see the need for this approach, with its experiential and challenging style of learning, to permeate the whole of the school curriculum. But it is unlikely that the necessary material resources, such as higher teacher-pupil ratios and greater access to appropriate training for teachers, will be forthcoming, unless and until *education as a whole* is valued more highly, and financial support is made more readily and equitably available for all aspects of schooling.

Physical education's significant influence in enabling OE to be made available in schools and the physical foundations upon which OE is built have been emphasized. It has been argued that it is of vital importance to the interests of both physical and outdoor education that we maintain collective understanding, dialogue and action. Perhaps, in this way, we may be more effective in promoting our aims and philosophies: to provide challenging physical experiences and equal opportunities that can facilitate the fullest development of the potential of all our pupils within, and towards, a caring and balanced society.

Notes

1. A thank-you letter from an upper primary pupil sent to two staff after a 1-week adventure activity course at a large residential centre in Hampshire.

This centre provides the opportunity for pupils to learn skills related to a variety of adventurous activities, not only in the outdoors (canoeing, sailing and orienteering) but also within a more sheltered undercover environment (skiing and climbing). Overall, the term *outdoor education* can be problematical (there are also urban initiatives associated with OE; cf. McCarthy, 1984), but its concept is in general usage and is discussed in detail throughout this text.

2. The Outward Bound principle was initiated and developed by Kurt Hahn, who escaped from Nazi Germany before the Second World War.

3. The five main bodies that make up the standing committee for OE are the National Association for Outdoor Education (NAOE), Association of Heads of Outdoor Education Centres (AHOEC), National Association of Field Study Officers (NAFSO), Outdoor Education Advisers Panel (OEAP) and its Scottish counterpart (SOEAP). The NAOE has a wide-ranging membership with significant numbers from teachers and teacher educators.

4. Unlike other areas of PE, which have had a strong female tradition (Fletcher, 1984), there have been, and are, few women in decision-making positions in OE (Ball, 1986).

5. The long-term effects of the ERA and LMS on OE centres is still largely speculative, but many heads of centres feel it more beneficial if they could remain under central funding, whereas others are considering alternative options (cf. Association of Heads of Outdoor Education Centres, 1989).

6. The particular educational code (educational message system) realized through the pedagogic and evaluative process at the centre resembled in part the Bernsteinien concept of an integrated code (cf. Bernstein, 1977). Teachers' approaches were interpersonal rather than authoritarian.

References

Almond, L. (1989). New wine in a new bottle: Implications for a national curriculum. *British Journal of Physical Education*, **20**, 123-125.

Almond, L., & Dickenson, B. (1990, July 6). Heads, bodies and legs. *London Times Educational Supplement*, p. 39.

Association of Heads of Outdoor Education Centres. (1989). Local management of schools. *Adventure Education*, **6**, 38-40.

Ball, D. (1986). Gender and outdoor education. *Adventure Education*, **3**, 28-30.

Bernstein, B. (1977). On the classification and framing of educational knowledge. In B. Bernstein (Ed.), *Class, codes and control* (pp. 85-115). London: Routledge & Kegan Paul.

Brighouse, T. (1990). What does it mean to the youngster? In T. Brighouse & B. Moon (Eds.), *Managing the National Curriculum: Some critical perspectives* (pp. 55-84). London: Longman.

British Association of Advisers and Lecturers in Physical Education. (1989a). *Physical Education for Ages 5-16. A framework for discussion.* London: Author.

British Association of Advisers and Lecturers in Physical Education. (1989b). *Physical education in the new era.* London: Author.

Cumbria Local Education Authority. (1984). Outdoor education in the curriculum. *Adventure Education,* **1**, 8-9.

Davies, A.M., Holland, J., & Minhas, R. (1990). *Equal opportunities in the new era.* London: Tufnell Press.

Department of Education and Science. (1975). *Outdoor education in school curriculum, Dartington Conference Report Study Conference N496.* London: Her Majesty's Stationery Office.

Department of Education and Science. (1979). *Aspects of secondary education in England.* London: Her Majesty's Stationery Office.

Department of Education and Science. (1989a). *From policy to practice.* London: Her Majesty's Stationery Office.

Department of Education and Science. (1989b). *Safety in outdoor education.* London: Her Majesty's Stationery Office.

Department of Education and Science. (1991). *Physical Education for Ages 5-16.* London: Her Majesty's Stationery Office.

Fletcher, S. (1984). *Women first. The female tradition in English PE 1880-1980.* London: Athlone Press.

Hampshire County Council. (1989). *Hampshire environmental and outdoor education policy statement.* Unpublished paper.

Her Majesty's Inspectorate. (1983). *Learning out of doors. An HMI survey of outdoor education and short stay residential experience.* London: Her Majesty's Stationery Office.

Her Majesty's Inspectorate. (1986). *Geography from 5-16.* London: Her Majesty's Stationery Office.

Her Majesty's Inspectorate. (1989a). *Personal and social education from 5-16.* London: Her Majesty's Stationery Office.

Her Majesty's Inspectorate. (1989b). *Physical education from 5 to 16.* London: Her Majesty's Stationery Office.

Her Majesty's Inspectorate. (1989c). *Environmental education from 5-16.* London: Her Majesty's Stationery Office.

Humberstone, B. (1986). Learning for a change. Gender and schooling in outdoor education. In J. Evans (Ed.), *PE, sport and schooling* (pp. 195-213). Lewes: Falmer Press.

Humberstone, B. (1987). *Organisational factors, teacher approach and pupil commitment in outdoor activities. A case study of schooling and gender in outdoor education.* Unpublished doctoral dissertation, Southampton University.

Humberstone, B. (1990a). Gender, change and adventure education. *Gender and Education,* **2**, 199-215.

Humberstone, B. (1990b). Warriors or wimps? Creating alternative forms of PE. In M. Messner & D. Sabo (Eds.), *Sport, men, and the gender order: Critical feminist perspectives* (pp. 201-210). Champaign, IL: Human Kinetics.

Humberstone, B. (1990c). The National Curriculum and outdoor education: Implications and dilemmas. *British Journal of Physical Education,* **21**, 244-246.

Humberstone, B., & Lynch, P. (1990). *Girls' concepts of themselves and their experiences in outdoor education programmes. A comparative analysis of the implication for girls of outdoor/adventure education made available in New Zealand and England.* Paper presented at the 7th International Symposium for Comparative Physical Education and Sport, Sheffield, July 8-14.

Hunt, J. (Ed.) (1989). *In search of adventure. A study of opportunities for adventure and challenge for young people.* Guildford: Talbot Adair Press.

Inner London Education Authority. (1988). *My favourite subject.* London: Inner London Education Authority.

Keighley, P. (1988). The future place of outdoor education in the context of the 'National Curriculum'. *Adventure Education,* **5,** 9-12.

Keighley, P. (1989a). Going places. *Adventure Education,* **6,** 18-20.

Keighley, P. (1989b). The future of outdoor education in the context of the 'National Curriculum'. *Adventure Education,* **6,** 26-30.

Loynes, C. (1984). The development of outdoor education at Stanway School. *Adventure Education,* **1,** 14-15.

Maclure, S. (1988). *Education re-formed.* London: Hodder & Stoughton.

Manpower Services Commission. (1981). *The Youth Opportunities programme and the local education authority.* London: Manpower Services Commission.

McCarthy, C. (1984). Inner city challenge. *Adventure Education,* **1,** 15-16.

Mortlock, C. (1984). *Adventure alternative.* Cumbria: Cicerone Press.

National Curriculum Council. (1988). *Physical education: Recent curriculum development.* London: School Curriculum Development Committee.

National Curriculum Council. (1990). *The whole curriculum.* York: National Curriculum Council.

New Whittington primary school—outdoor education week. (1989). *Adventure Education,* **6,** 15-18.

Nichols, G. (1989). What is development training? *Adventure Education,* **6,** 2.

Roberts, K., White, G., & Parker, H. (1974). *The character training industry.* Devon: David & Charles.

Royce, R. (1987). Outdoor education—aims and approaches, an inherent dilemma. *Adventure Education,* **4**(1), 12-14; **4**(2), 12-14; **4**(4), 24-29.

Schools Council Geography Committee. (1980). *Outdoor education in secondary schools.* London: Schools Council.

Smith, B. (1989). Learning outcomes for outdoor education. *Adventure Education,* **6,** 20-23.

Stansfield, D. (1989). A strategy for implementing a thematic approach to outdoor education in the modern curriculum. *Adventure Education,* **6,** 19-23.

Styles, M. (1989, December). Skiing within the whole curriculum. *Educational Skier,* p. 5.

Wood, D., & Cheffers, J. (1978). Analysing adventure education through interaction analysis and participant observation. *Federation Internationale d'Education Physique Bulletin,* **48,** 17-28.

Chapter 9

School to Community—
Progress and Partnership

Bob Laventure

In a society which is being obliged to re-think the nature of work and the meaning of leisure, a fresh look is also needed at the role of education. Local Education Authorities, who have already extended their curricula on leisure related subjects, may need to so further and to continue the breaking down of barriers between schools and the community. Leisure Policy for the Future (Sport Council, 1983, p. 3)

This chapter focuses upon the role of physical education teachers in promoting lifelong participation in sport and recreation activity. In the context of increasing concern for both health- and sport-related levels of participation of young people and the National Curriculum in physical education, it examines a number of developments in education and the sporting community. Lessons from recent innovative work should inform the nature of future curriculum development, which has implications for the role of the physical education teacher. I believe that in seeking a way forward, teachers and people in the sporting community must work in partnership to ensure a future cohesive approach to working with young people towards promoting lifelong participation in physical activity.

School to Community Again?

As education finds itself yet again subject to increased demands for relevance and accountability, particularly with a view to preparing young people for the changing postindustrial and technological society, physical education (PE) is coming under increased scrutiny and is required to justify its unique position within the curriculum. A balanced curriculum must necessarily consider the development of the whole person. Through the process of personal and social education, young people must be given equal opportunity to acquire the skills, knowledge and attitudes that will equip them for all aspects of their lives.

The contribution of physical activity, recreation and sport is not an issue here; it is assumed that enjoyment of activity for its own sake, the experience of challenge with oneself, others and the environment, achievement and opportunities for social interaction have long been recognized as integral features of taking part in activity. We can all identify the immediate feelings of success when a winning goal is scored close to the end of a game or the sense of an achievement that follows a perfect gymnastics sequence or a personal best. We have all experienced the inner glow and relaxation that comes as a result of a vigorous workout and the sense of satisfaction when hours of practice on teamwork bring dividends in a crucially important game.

Yet although it subscribes to the philosophies of physical and mental well-being, achievement, satisfaction, recreation and play, the PE profession finds itself under increasing pressure, unlike most other areas of the curriculum, to demonstrate its specific role in stimulating and promoting lifelong activity. Within the broader arguments as to the value of sport and recreation, which include the contribution to the health of the nation, opportunities for international sporting success and prestige, regeneration of the economy and theories of social cohesion and control, two principal features have recently emerged that have brought increased demands for accountability and relevance to PE and its relationship to life beyond school.

The growth in sporting and recreational opportunities, either through the increasing number of multipurpose and activity-specific sport centres or the increase in the number and variety of activities, has contributed to the growth of 'Sport for All', itself a significant feature of development within the sport and leisure industry. Young people are future participants in these opportunities and consequently should have the opportunity to make informed decisions about them. There have been substantial shifts in the nature of education, and the sporting and recreational community, including the voluntary sector, governing bodies, clubs and the leisure profession, has become increasingly active and vociferous concerning their opinion of what PE should be about. Although curriculum content, teaching styles and philosophies may have changed, there is still a strongly held belief that PE teachers should be producing sport-literate young people with the skills, knowledge and motivation to remain sport participants throughout their lives. Few physical educationalists would disagree with such expectations. But the way in which teachers and those in the world of sport achieve this end have changed fundamentally, and an appraisal of this process is essential for successful future work.

The second important shift relates to increasing concerns about the health of the nation, particularly related to the high incidence of coronary heart disease (CHD). Research evidence suggests that exercise and physical activity help prevent heart disease (Fentem & Turnbull, 1987) and that the intensity and frequency of young people's activity patterns are below the levels they would need, as adults, to produce this effect (Armstrong, Balding, Gentle, & Kirby, 1990). This obligates PE teachers to consider promoting exercise and activity as essential features of all lifestyles, and this should be an integral feature of the curriculum process. Not only are teachers responsible for health-related physical activity as a curriculum process, but they have a responsibility and accountability that such activities should continue.

Moreover, we live in a time in which patterns of physical activity, levels of sport participation and health criteria are more easily identified and measured. PE teachers will still want, and need, to argue for the intrinsic value of what we do, but PE has a responsibility to young people to ensure that they have equal opportunity to chose lifelong participation in the unique experiences offered by sport and active recreation.

We may well claim that PE has always had such concerns as its focus, but evidence suggests that we have not been too successful in the past. The assumption that science, language, the humanities and other aspects of the curriculum are knowledge- and experience-based 'lessons for life' would not be challenged. But such arguments have rarely been articulated with any clarity, regarding physical education, and certainly, to increase its effectiveness, PE will need to consider significant changes in its methods of working in the future.

General demands for PE teachers to consider the place of the curriculum and the school-to-community link are amongst the strategies used to promote the concept of 'Sport for All'. More recently two important thrusts have added considerable force to the debate about physical education and its contribution to lifelong activity.

There has been growing concern about the increase in CHD in the adult population, and research into the activity levels of young people has highlighted the role of PE in promoting the knowledge, skills and attitudes required to adopt an active lifestyle. The work of Armstrong and Davies (1980), Almond (1983), Biddle (1987), and Sleap and Warburton (1989), amongst others, has brought together a research base and curriculum models that focus upon such learning and the continuation of lifelong activity. As a result the emphasis of the physical education profession has substantially shifted to promoting activity and recreation for health's sake rather than for sport.

The second shift of emphasis was brought about as a result of the teachers' industrial action, which involved significant shifts in attitudes and changes in practice regarding their role as providers of sporting opportunities in the extracurricular programme and in interschool sport competitions. If the nature of the ensuing debate was dominated by a largely male, team-sport and vociferous sport lobby, its effect caused sporting organizations to reconsider their role in the development of sporting opportunities and talent.

In effect the nature of the school-to-community link had changed. Previously the sporting world had expected schools to deliver a certain ready-made product: highly motivated, very skilful, sport-specific, competent youngsters. It was the perceived and potential loss of this product that initiated the debate and guaranteed its high public profile. Similar issues concerning the place of competitive experiences, and the increased number of sporting activities available, added to the discussion, which served not only to redefine the nature of the school-to-community link as a structure but also brought about a significant shift in responsibility for future development.

What Has Been Going On?

If increasingly instrumental arguments concerning sport participation and health-related issues have brought increased pressure upon educational practice, it is important to consider the context of sport in the community in which such arguments have appeared. General trends in overall participation saw an increase in sport participation throughout the 1970s and early 1980s, aided by an economic climate that permitted a considerable growth in sport facilities (Sports Council, 1989). However, it was still recognized that the concept of 'Sport for All', as envisaged by the Council of Europe (1976, para. 4.1-4.4), was still far from realized. Certain socioeconomic groups, such as women looking after the home, non-car-owners, the semi- and unskilled and low-income groups, remained underrepresented. The Sports Council, in its role as governmental agent with a brief under its Royal Charter to increase participation amongst all sections of the community, proposed that further increases would depend upon three broad future strategies: first, working with the education system to ensure that young people, and school leavers in particular, maintain one or more of the many sporting skills and interests they developed through the curriculum; second, promoting amongst adults an awareness of the physical, mental and social benefits of sport and exercise and to provide more people with the means of expressing their sporting and recreational needs; and finally, continuing to increase access to facilities, both new and those already existing that were underused. As a result, subsequent development depended upon increasing opportunities for participation, and these, in turn, depend upon strategies that were to involve Local Education Authorities (LEAs), the education sector, sport clubs and, in the long term, the governing bodies of sport. All were called upon to deploy their resources to promote mass participation.

In the early 1980s it was recognized that to futher extend the 'sporting franchise', alternative strategies were needed. These would focus upon innovative attempts to involve nonparticipants from a number of social groups, incorporating a 'target group' philosophy of approach. Such target groups included women, residents of the inner cities, ethnic minorities, the disabled, older and retired people, young people and, in particular, school leavers. Demonstration schemes were initiated that invited partnerships between LEAs, sport clubs, voluntary organizations and commercial operators. These received a high level of grant aid and detailed monitoring. Such demonstration schemes initially focused upon the 'outreach work' concept in selected urban areas and were instrumental in developing new ways of working through a community network approach. Moreover, the monitoring, evaluation and dissemination processes involved led to many LEAs adopting similar programmes and schemes, largely through the appointment of community sport development officers (Sports Council, 1988). But relatively little success had been reported in attempts to work with young people, and it was felt that further impetus was needed with this target group.

Given that the Sports Council at this time was the principal architect of attempts to promote greater participation, it should come as no surprise that little impression had been made upon young people. Co-operation between the Sports Council and the world of education (which were directed by two different governmental departments) had been limited to dual-use development schemes, and the content and process of the PE curriculum remained clearly in the hands of teachers, influenced by Her Majesty's Inspectorate (HMI) and LEA advisory services. The PE curriculum is a significant factor in determining young people's attitudes and motivations towards sport and recreational activity, but little outside influence or focus for change had been brought to bear upon it. Charlton and McIntosh (1985) pointed out a discrepancy between the 'recommended' curriculum (Department of Education and Science [DES], 1979), which suggested five areas of experience common to the European Sport for All Charter (Council of Europe, 1976), and the reality of the actual curriculum, which was heavily dominated by team games (Kane, 1974; Whitehead & Hendry, 1976), as evidence of a lack of movement or change within the curriculum. In turning its attention towards working with young people, the Sports Council saw future work in three separate but related areas, each requiring different approaches and methods of work. There was a need to consider those at the younger end of the 13-to-24 age range who for a number of reasons had been turned off sport and the possibility of gaining youngsters' interest at a younger age than 13. It was also recognized that some with a variety of sporting interests are willing but not always able to try activities and that their aspirations and interests need to be met with genuine opportunities for participation. Persons at the older end of the 13-to-24 age range are involved in a wide diversity of lifestyles and roles, some still in education and training, some in work; a large majority are single, but some are married, with one or more children. Reaching these young people requires providing suitable, attractive programmes for this group.

Attempts to work with young people whilst they were at school proved to be problematic, in that issues of curriculum control, the breadth and depth of experience in PE and the place of sport on the curriculum remained unresolved and in the hands of teachers. As a result the Sports Council saw the need to work with PE teachers in curriculum development. It also saw that working with the education sector as a whole was an important feature of any future strategy in working with young people. At the same time more emphasis was placed upon the need for the sporting world, particularly the governing bodies, to produce appropriate programmes and schemes for this age group. 'Mini' and modified versions of sport were developed to broaden the base for participation in any given sport. This allowed a variety of organizations, in addition to teachers, to become involved with young people. Collectively, this increased the variety of sports and activities available to young people. However, there was little evidence at the time as to how many of these young sport participants remained within such schemes, and it is for debate whether such schemes simply increased opportunities for the same number of people or reached a greater number of participants. There were also some reservations as to the quality of, and standards within, such schemes, as well as questions of whether various practices involved were ethically sound and safe. But more importantly, the nature of such schemes clashed with current educational aims and objectives, which highlighted the need to provide educational experiences that encouraged the development of a range of physical and movement skills rather than sport-specific activities.

Attempts to work with the upper end of the age range were also problematic. The rapid shifts in further education, work and employment patterns and training opportunities meant that reaching these young people to sell and promote sport and recreation was difficult. In addition, this was a time of severe youth unemployment, and there was a danger that exhortations to participate in sport and recreative activities would be seen as attempts to divert attention away from employment issues. Programs to reach this age group, such as the 'Ever Thought of Sport?' campaign (a joint promotion by the Sports Council and Weetabix UK), were based upon promoting sport within adolescent and youth culture, but they met with minimal success (White & Coakley, 1986).

If these two areas of work had yet, for a number of reasons, to make their mark, more success was gained in working with those young people who had aspirations and interests in sport and recreation and providing them with real opportunities for continued activity. The late 1980s saw many school-to-community schemes that focused on the concepts of the Bridging the Gap, School to Community and Sports Link programs. These concentrated upon providing a structural link between young people in school and their postschool life that aimed to provide a continuity of opportunity to participate according to interests, needs and abilities. A significant shift of emphasis had taken place. Up to now, working with young people had been in the context of facility development and community use of schools. Future strategies would be based in the context of sport development and the provision of continuity and progression in sport participation.

The 'Gap' Revisited

Many of these schemes designed to promote continuing participation had their beginnings in the concept of the 'gap' first identified by the Wolfenden Committee on Sport, which drew attention to a dramatic fall-off in sport participation amongst school leavers. It was described as 'the manifest break between on the one hand the participation in recreative activities which is normal for boys and girls at school, and on the other hand their participation in similar (though not identical) activities some years later when they are more adult' (Wolfenden Committee on Sport, 1960, p. 25).

There is a large amount of evidence suggesting that such a concept is now inappropriate. But there is a danger that it remains the most significant feature of attempts to promote continued participation with school leavers. The concept of the gap requires closer scrutiny, which should help to identify a number of issues to be addressed if future efforts in this area are to be more successful than those in the past.

The evidence of the Wolfenden Committee was based upon measurements of sport participation at a time when opportunities to continue depended very much on the voluntary sector, which was mostly small sport clubs. With the exception of swimming, Local Authority provision was in its infancy, and at that time there clearly was a structural inequality of opportunity between PE and opportunities beyond. This inequality was highlighted by the absence of school-to-club links (with the exception of the 'old boy' and former pupil associations related to such team sports as soccer, hockey and rugby football) and the lack of a coaching structure. Expertise was limited to those already involved and committed as players, and coaching practice was based upon adult models of performance.

Increased opportunities in the 1970s and 1980s centred around facility expansion—the growth of Local Authority sport centres, stadia and swimming pools, augmented by sport-specific provision such as ice rinks, golf courses and tennis centres. For those with an interest in outdoor forms of recreation, greater access to the countryside enabled growth in sailing, canoeing, climbing, hill walking as well as the various forms of aid and motor sport. Dual-use policies further increased opportunities by improving access to existing facilities (especially community use of existing school facilities previously unavailable for public use), and encouraging the building of new facilities for shared use. Expansion has continued through greater use of church halls, community centres, industrial premises and defence establishments and the increasing influence of the private sector in developing multipurpose leisure centres and fitness centres as a response to the increased demand for indoor health-related activities from increasingly health-conscious sections of the community.

But facility expansion still left sections of the community (especially non-car-owners and those in rural areas) at a disadvantage, and with the possible exception of swimming (a casual and predominately social activity), it had still to make its mark upon most young people. Perhaps these facilities and the activities presented were largely unattractive to them, or perhaps regular use of sport centres was seen as contrary to adolescent lifestyles. It remains to be seen if the more recent specific marketing and programming techniques of modern sport and leisure centres significantly affect young people. The evidence of the DES survey (Stevens, 1985) showed that using a local sport centre was still a minority activity with 14-year-olds.

The second assumption that determined approaches to bridging the gap concerned the motivation and aspirations of young people in school. It is too simplistic by far to suggest that the gap and cessation of activity coincided with leaving school. There is now significant evidence that health-related activity (Balding, 1988; Dickenson, 1986) and sport-related activity (DES, 1983) declines steadily with age throughout secondary schooling and is significantly more marked with girls than with boys. Thus, solutions proposed as part of a school-leavers programme, by which time activity levels have already declined, may be at the best too late, and therefore remedial, or inappropriate, as being too simplistic.

The third feature of the Wolfenden Report was the assumption that these school leavers returned to participation as adults. In fact they did, although by no means in great numbers. However, it was highlighted by the Wolfenden

Report that the return to participation was a result of club structures being able to accommodate adults and not young people. The generation gap was a significant factor. Although later figures for adult participation in indoor and outdoor activities show an increase, Sports Council (1988) figures by no means match the school-based levels of involvement, and when adults do return to participation, it is often into new activities that often were not available at school. This picture is further complicated by the fact that school-based involvement, in the form of PE lessons, is still compulsory for the majority, whereas out-of-school activity is voluntary. Dropout on leaving school is also about ceasing extracurricular sport (clubs, school teams and casual activities).

The Response From Physical Education

As a response to some of the issues previously identified, a number of demonstration schemes were initiated in the 1980s within the education system with the purpose of forming a structural link between the PE curriculum and opportunities for postschool participation. These focused upon a variety of curriculum-development projects involving health-related exercise and promoting the concept of education or preparation for active leisure. A significant number of school-to-community–link partnership schemes aimed at matching the interests of young people, and especially of school leavers, with locally available opportunities for sport and recreation. At the same time the providers of sport and recreation, within both the local authorities and the governing bodies of sport, became increasingly proactive in their attempts to work with young people and schools. A number of high-profile, nationwide campaigns and initiatives from the Sports Council also have aimed at young people and have sought to encourage and stimulate concerted local action.

Creating Structural Links

Creating the link between school and community in the context of the developments mentioned was perceived as the need to construct a number of structural relationships that would provide freedom of movement and ease of access for young people and those eager and anxious to develop their sport. But a large variety of hurdles had to be overcome to ensure ongoing participation. These included adequately informing young people about the opportunities and facilities and accommodating various levels of ability, competence and maturity. A host of socioeconomic factors also had to be taken into account, including differences in ability or desire to pay or travel and a number of attitudinal factors including the influence of the family, peer groups and close friends.

Solutions to these problems were seen as critical to the process and had been identified by Hargreaves (1982) as a critical area of development for physical education. Consequently teachers and their local sporting organizations examined a number of practical ways of working. These

1. attempted to create structural links between activities that were part of the curriculum and similar opportunities in local clubs and centres,
2. used such local sporting opportunities to introduce young people to activities that would otherwise not be included on the curriculum, and
3. used facilities such as sport and leisure centres as places to learn outside the school environment, in an adult atmosphere.

The strategies employed within such programmes were numerous and varied, but the following are indicative of the sorts of schemes used.

- Club personnel such as coaches, players and secretaries, visiting schools to run introductory and coaching courses
- School visits to sport and lesiure centres
- 'Come and try' or 'taster' activity days run by individual clubs or local authority leisure and recreation departments
- Open evenings or sport conventions at leisure or sport centres
- Information leaflets, school-leavers booklets and sport information databases with details of local activities
- Induction programmes for school leavers into postschool leisure opportunities

Underpinning these and other methods of working were a number of principal considerations that brought such thinking together:

- It is the role of the teacher to raise the awareness and expectations of pupils that these opportunities exist, are available and should be part of a young person's future life.
- That given the logistical problems that inevitably will arise, the work is most likely to be successful if young people at school and the various partners are physically brought together, to not only meet but work together.
- That local providers, their staff, officials and coaches have the required skills, sensitivity and motivation to work with young people in an appropriate manner.
- That there should be sufficient time for these new relationships to develop.
- That teachers actively encourage their pupils to take up these opportunities, recognize their value and see them as positive developments.

Much of the previously described work within education emerged as a result of local-based initiatives. But the picture painted of development in this area would be incomplete without some reference to other areas of development, from the noneducational world, that have greatly stimulated ideas and encouraged changes in practice on the ground.

The Sports Council

In successive policy documents and working papers, the Sports Council throughout the 1980s continued to identify young people as an important target group.

It consequently acted through national and regional structures to stimulate a large number of schemes aimed at young people to increase their participation. The 'Ever Thought of Sport?' campaign (1985), 'What's Your Sport?' (a joint promotion by the Sports Council and the Milk Marketing Board, 1987), and 'Live! Time' (a joint promotion by the Sports Council and the Midland Bank, 1990) were high-profile sponsored schemes aimed at young people. As White and Coakley (1986) observed, the immediate impact of such large-scale schemes left young people untouched, but they gave organizations the opportunity to respond with local initiatives and events, which took the form of sport and leisure fairs, 'come and try it' days, introductory events, coaching schemes and information services.

More significant than the events themselves were the opportunities that were presented 1. to stimulate and initiate collaborative work on the ground and 2. to use such work to further research young people's attitudes, interests and motivation. Such 'action research' has been of great value in informing the direction of future work.

The Sports Council's role in pump-priming local initiatives in the 1980s with targeted grant aid cannot be underestimated. As a result of it, local authorities and other related organizations found ways of establishing permanent structures and links between young people in school and the sporting community. An area hitherto untouched by the Sports Council had been the PE curriculum, perceived by many to be a crucial factor in influencing sporting interests and aspirations. In the mid and late 1980s the Sports Council entered into three national demonstration projects associated with physical education: Active Life Styles (1985) in Coventry, From School to Community (1986) in Cheltenham and Primary Physical Education (1990) in Dudley. These are examining the nature of the PE curriculum in primary and secondary schools as well as in-service and initial teacher training. Each in its own way provides a focus for thinking, research and innovation, but it is for discussion whether the immediate changes in practice have had a greater significance and impact rather than their subsequent dissemination causing others to rethink their own rationales and practices.

The combination of national campaigns, regional strategies and local developments continues to be promoted and disseminated through an extensive programme of regional and local workshops and conferences aimed at teachers, sport governing bodies and organizations and local authorities, all with a view to stimulating change and action on the ground.

Developing Partnerships

Successful innovative work in this area was by no means limited to schools and the education sector. Leisure and recreation departments as well as local clubs and governing bodies were also demonstrating a willingness to both initiate schemes and change their ways of working. At this stage the concept of partnership as a method of working became a reality, demonstrating real potential as a model for future practice. Teachers and a variety of individuals and organizations found new ways of working and developed new relationships, and as a result new structures are emerging that, over a period of time, will provide a context in which the school and community partnership becomes a recognizable and permanent feature of all work in PE, sport and recreation.

Within such a future scenario there will be a number of partnerships that collectively address such issues as continuity and coherence within the development of young people's sporting interests and individually promote and develop schemes and practical ways of working.

At a time of scarce resources, the rationalization of effort, time, enthusiasm and energy through effective coordination and liaison amongst local agencies will require collaborative approaches to addressing young people's needs. But the rationale for such work is more fundamental than the need to use resources effectively. There is now recognition that schools cannot be expected to take entire responsibility for providing sporting and recreative opportunities for young people. Clearly others, such as those already referred to, will take an increasingly active part in providing for young people, but there is a more positive view that such partnerships are an essential feature of the future context of providing a continuum of opportunity activity for young people, without which their interests, motivation and aspirations will remain frustrated.

Partnerships Within the School

The introduction of the National Curriculum has challenged teachers not only to rethink the nature of the core and foundation subjects within the National Curriculum and the whole curriculum but also to identify and define areas that have a cross-curricular focus. Initial concerns for subject overlap and areas of omission have been translated into whole-school approaches to reviewing and planning the curriculum. Physical education teachers will be able to offer a unique and complementary contribution to the area of health-related exercise and activity as a result of PE's collaboration with science, health education and technology. Similar opportunities can also be identified in conjunction with geography and technology.

Physical education must be aware, however, of seeking to justify itself by some form of curriculum 'expediency', by being seen to be everywhere. But the more important issue is PE's real potential to have an impact upon the whole curriculum—and in particular on whole-school approaches to personal and social development, the recording of achievement and the whole life of the school. Those in the primary sector will be more familiar with such approaches and the flexibility of working methods required, but as a clearer picture of the National Curriculum emerges over a period of time, there will be additional opportunities for PE to play a unique part in the whole curriculum and the whole life of the school.

Partnerships With the Community

The relationship between teachers and local sport clubs and centres, between schools and the broader sporting community, will be critical for the future development of postschool participation. From the process of innovation and demonstration, teachers and the local sporting community have established a variety of ways of working together, which have included school-to-club link schemes, coaching programmes and visits to centres. Such partnerships have also considered areas such as policy, development, the sharing of scarce resources including expertise, the exchange and sharing of vital information, joint approaches to training and ways of providing support for the various partners. Recognizing the respective contributions of the voluntary sport club coach, the local authority recreation department and a development officer from a governing body will encourage teachers to clarify their own role within such a partnership. But it will be crucial to the success of such schemes that teachers come to know each potential partner and recognize the unique ways in which they operate and what they can and cannot contribute to the partnership.

Partnerships Within the Community

The appearance of a local sporting network, whilst displaying potential for collaborative work, may also be seen as problematic. In the past, a large number of individual schemes and initiatives, and especially those initiated by the governing bodies of sport, were largely uncoordinated and aimed at the same group of young people, those easily recognized as the competent, well motivated and confident amongst those at school. Following the debate about standards of performance, the governing bodies soon found themselves competing for those youngsters in addition to competing for teachers' valuable time. This is an example of only one of many similar issues concerning continuity, collaboration and cooperation that required a more rational and cohesive approach to development. Figure 9.1 seeks to illustrate some of the local organizations that have the potential to become partners in providing sporting opportunities for young people. It is essential not only that schools and the community should work more closely together, but that all those within such developments should consider the wider implications of such relationships.

Attempts to address this issue have resulted in the formation of local advisory development or action groups for youth sport, where representatives from key agencies, such as education, recreation and the youth service, come together with teachers, professional sport development officers and people in the voluntary sector. Such groups fulfill a variety of roles, including the exchange of information, liaison between the various agencies, the identification of need and the coordination of efforts. If they are properly supported in the future, sport development groups could take on a much wider role and develop a community-wide structure to provide more long-term and cohesive approaches to planning, resourcing and delivering sport opportunities for young people. How teachers can be individually and collectively involved in a local development group will depend to some extent on the group's future agenda and method of operation. However, in the context of the Local Management of Schools (LMS) and the changes in the nature of advisory services that support PE teachers, future

Figure 9.1   The local sport network.

collective action may be much more difficult to achieve, and the opportunity for teachers and others to work together, albeit in a specific context, should not be ignored.

The Governing Bodies of Sport

The governing bodies of sport were originally established to prescribe rules and laws, organize national and international events, arrange competitions and improve standards of performance through organized coaching for those with a commitment to, and well-defined interest in, a specific sport. An overt commitment to increasing grassroots participation was not a prime concern until Sport for All policies began to have their impact and involved the governing bodies in promoting mass participation. This new approach at times may have provided the governing bodies with a conflict of interests, as they may have considered mass participation not as an end in itself but as a means to increasing the broad base of activity, thus increasing numbers to ensure the development of talent for high standards of performance, securing future competition and participants.

The development programmes initiated by the governing bodies to increase grassroots participation demanded regional and local structures; a number of development posts were set up with such a specific brief, and a number of other common features emerged:

- The review and appraisal of coach training and education schemes
- The introduction of various incentives and skills awards for beginners and particularly for young participants
- The further introduction and expansion of mini or modified versions of sports designed to introduce and capture young performers
- The production of resources including videos, posters and coaching information for schools and teachers

Such development programmes are increasingly professional in their approach and often are provided with additional resources by a high-profile sponsor. But all recognize the implications of changes in young people's aspirations and in demographics, which mean that all the governing bodies feel themselves to be competing to attract the same young people into their specific sport.

Community Sport Development

In addition to national and regional development officers working in sport-specific development, a new element of local authority provision has seen the move to employ sport-development officers. Their role is to work with and motivate those who have yet to take the first step into sport participation (Sports Council, 1988). This work focuses on three different, if closely related, areas:

1. Sport-specific development, concentrating on a number of specific sports and the promotion of a programme of activities to create wider participation and heightened performance at a local level. This work has been undertaken in many areas by posts jointly funded by local authorities, the governing bodies and the regional offices of the Sports Council. The sport-specific development officer working in a given locality is involved in working with a range of different target groups but often concentrates upon working with young people in order to initiate and sustain long-term participation.
2. Group-specific development, concentrating on the sporting and recreational needs of specific target groups, such as women, people with disabilities and ethnic minorities. Using the approaches and methods employed by the outreach programmes of the early 1980s, these programmes were designed to take sport and recreation to specific nonparticipant groups.
3. Facilities and programme development. Those involved in the promotion, management and development of sport facilities have become more sensitive to the nature of their programmes and the needs of specific groups, sports and activities. Disabled access, creche provision, off-peak concessions, pricing policies and promotional events all are aimed at providing greater opportunity for persons of different abilities and interests, but particularly low-participation groups.

Sport Leadership

The events and developments previously described have ensured that an increasing number of people now play an important part in providing sporting and recreative activities for young people. Teachers' skills in contributing to the education of the whole child are crucial to planning, teaching and evaluating the curriculum. It is now recognized that many others, including coaches, development staff, sport motivators and leaders (both volunteers and professionals) also must work with young people in an appropriately skilled manner.

Recognizing that increases in sport participation requires a significant increase in the identification and training of sports leaders, both the Sports Council and the Central Council for Physical Recreation developed courses and training schemes that would equip the volunteer with the necessary organizational skills and knowledge to work with nonparticipants in safe and enjoyable sporting environments. The work of the governing bodies in developing leadership schemes for their individual sports also recognized the variety of styles and strategies required to attract and maintain the interest of nonparticipants and beginners. The common ground of the needs of young people, ethically sound and safe practice, and skill development provided a common core of knowledge for all those working with young people.

The National Coaching Foundation developed a nationally coordinated coach education programme to complement the sport-specific programmes of the governing bodies. This helped considerably in ensuring that the status, training and qualifications of the coaching force recognize the needs of individuals rather than the needs of sport. Consequently, over a period of time, more sport leaders and coaches have acquired the necessary skills and sensitivity to work appropriately with young people.

What Did We Learn?

Within a relatively short period of time in the 1980s, a vast amount of grassroots development was undertaken that, in a variety of ways, addressed the issues of young people's participation in sport and recreation. With this evolution of what may be described as a structural relationship between school activities and similar opportunities available in the community, a number of issues, developments and processes have emerged. These should serve as 'action research' and inform and direct the future action of those for whose work the concept of 'school to community' remains an important feature.

The Nature of Community

Through such work, aimed at 'testing the water', a clearer view of the concept and role of the community has emerged. Community was clearly being interpreted in a variety of ways. The most obvious was PE teachers' view of the varied groups, organizations and facilities as valuable resources, providing expertise, leaders and coaches as well as equipment and facilities. In the short term and in the context of the availability of limited resources, the opportunity to identify and make use of such additional resources is important. But these new experiences, whereby young pupils had the opportunity to go off-site to visit sport clubs and centres, took pupils into a different learning environment, which was to be a more realistic and appropriate place to learn a new set of skills and acquire knowledge at firsthand. The sum total of learning in physical education did not take place within the immediate, familiar and sheltered environment of the gymnasium or school playing fields. Most important of all, pupils experienced, and could become part of, a sporting environment, a living and active community that they could expect access to, that they could take part in as young people, and that could play an active role for them throughout their lives.

Issues Related to Age?

The critical theme is that the age at which a young person attempts to move from school based to community based participation is varied and flexible according to a number of issues and circumstances. Many such schemes were initiated as attempts to work with school leavers at the end of their school sporting careers, but for a variety of reasons this does not always seem to be the most appropriate way of working. A number of variables, determined by the specific demands of a particular sport or the standard or frequency of play at a certain club or governing body league, may influence the timing and nature of such schemes. Swimming and gymnastics are obvious examples of sports that are attractive to younger children of primary school age, but it is by no means certain that introductions to clubs at a much younger age ensures more sustained long-term activity and participation.

Many sports, such as rugby, football and tennis, that also have a history of mini and youth development recognize the changes in young people's motivation and the consequent dropout. Clubs also cater for young people in different ways, by running age-related teams within extensive youth sections, or by simply integrating young players into adult teams of varying abilities and motivation.

In larger clubs with a number of youth teams, young players have a chance to play with others of their own age and similar ability, which can enable friendships to develop and flourish. Young players who join adult clubs may well find themselves separated from their friends and perhaps alone in an adult environment. Moreover if the move is to be made whilst young people are still at school, then there may have to be some thought given to the frequency of, and relationship between, commitments at both school and club.

The Context of Participation

The increase in the number of facilities and sport- and health-related activities demands additional thinking about the nature of postschool participation. Competent badminton or tennis players will find abundant opportunities to play, from

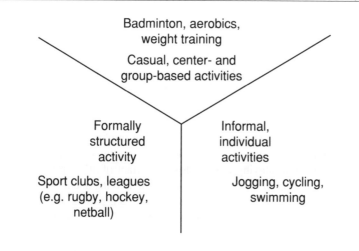

Figure 9.2   The context of participation.

advanced and progressive coaching schemes and local clubs to more casual or centre-based activities requiring less commitment and time. Figure 9.2 identifies the different contexts of participation as casual, informal, and formally organized activities. It may be that these contexts illustrate the motivation for participation—to have fun and to improve, rather than the attraction of the activity itself. Which of these opportunities young people will find attractive will depend upon their reasons for playing, which will vary from the desire to improve and play at the highest level to the need to play and have fun with friends in an informal atmosphere. For more individual and health-related activities, such as jogging, swimming and weight training, no club route is required.

The Sport Careers of Young People

Most of the work developed to date has largely addressed the development of structural links between activity (be it health based, recreative or sport specific) in the PE programme and opportunities for similar activity in the community. There has been an emphasis placed upon developing structures that will provide continuity and progression and in many cases perceived as critical to the long-term development of a particular sport as suggested and modelled by Campbell (1990). See Figure 9.3.

Although they are useful starting points for those sport-specific development schemes, this model does not give sufficient scope for everyone who works with young people, even when structural links have been effectively established. Underpinning such a model is the assumption that all young people want to progress in a single sport. This requires not only the desire to move through the various levels of competence and performance—including having a commitment and desire to practice, improve and perfect skills and train regularly—but also

Figure 9.3   A sports development model. Modified from Campbell (1990).

the confidence to pass through and among a number of structures (e.g. school, club, coaching scheme).

These assumptions must be challenged, because most young people display a diversity of sport participation. They often change from one activity to another and also take part in a variety of activities at the same time. The shifting allegiance of young people as they move from one activity to another (Roberts et al., 1989; Coventry LEA, 1986), understandable at a time of significant change in other aspects of their lives, poses problems for local clubs and organizations that develop youth programmes. They may consider their investment of time and expertise as being wasted when another sport or activity becomes more attractive and their young members leave. In addition, when for a number of reasons a young performer loses interest in one activity or 'dislocates' (Roberts et al., 1989) from a particular sport, the ability to survive such an event and take up another sport or activity will greatly depend upon that young person having acquired a range of skills and competencies and a breadth of sporting experiences. The implications for the nature of the PE curriculum are both enormous and obvious.

Local Sporting Structures

Much of what has been attempted has assumed that the sporting community is ready and willing to cater, and provide opportunities, for young people. Facility expansion in the private and public sectors, which led to an increase in casual sport participation, has provided such opportunities. And large-scale governing body programmes have been partly successful in raising awareness and demonstrating good practice. But given the voluntary nature of sport clubs and organizations in this country, not all such groups are ready or willing to take up the challenge.

It must be recognized that many sport clubs are small organizations geared to participation and competition for their members and may have no desire to become involved with young people. These small clubs operate on very limited resources and, other than accommodating one or two ready-made players, would be sorely stretched to provide sufficient facilities, finance and members to support the additional activities of a youth section. Such clubs would expect younger participants to make a commitment and would find it difficult to accommodate their changes in interest and motivation.

The larger, well-resourced, multisport club is still very much a continental phenomenon and is not yet a feature of our own sporting and recreational life. Some schemes have featured local sport associations or governing bodies that have agreed to work collectively in coaching young players, but such schemes are still very much in their infancy.

Beyond Structural Links

Such developments have been largely successful, in the medium term, at raising awareness and demonstrating what can be achieved by working with a variety of clubs and groups. In addition the process of innovation and demonstration has set the scene for a longer term shift in ways of working, so that a degree of permanence can be established in such structures. There is, however, a danger that the creation of a structural link between school and community would be considered sufficient action to promote life long participation. It is clear that much can be achieved in this way, but if such participation is to be sustained, then two additional features emerge that are crucial to the long-term success of this process.

Given that post- and out-of-school participation in activity is undertaken voluntarily, which activities young people value and are motivated to continue participating in will be based largely upon previous positive experiences in physical activity that may have come from success, enjoyment and achievement. Certainly negative experiences (e.g. the discomfort of a very cold games field, perceptions that one is incompetent compared with others, and other unpleasant memories of physical education) regularly feature in decisions not to continue activity.

Towards a Motivational Link

Physical education experiences are largely determined by teaching styles, process and content. These experiences are the main determinants of young peoples' attitudes to activity. Biddle and Fox (1988) point to the child's perception of future behaviour and argue that such perceptions determine the child's eventual psychological orientation towards physical activity, which in turn will be responsible for her or his adult activity patterns. There are additional crucial factors, besides the PE experience, that have emerged as influencing young people's decisions about sport and leisure participation. White and Coakley (1986) identified competence, external constraints and support from significant others as additional factors, along with a wide range of personal preferences going beyond competitive sport. It is a question not simply of liking PE and sport or activity but more of developing feelings of confidence and competence.

White and Coakley (1986) also refer to a 'participation turning point' when young people have reached a peak in an activity. This occurs when they realize that their skills will not continue to improve or that any improvement will demand more time or energy than they are willing to commit.

But even 'being good' at sport may still be insufficient motivation to continue participating. Biddle (1987) suggests that continued participation is more likely as a result of 'mastery orientation', wherein young people are motivated to play well, seek self-improvement and achieve competence for its own sake. For those that are described as 'ability related' and who measure their success and ability by comparison with their opponents, motivation and desire to participate become more difficult to sustain as the level of competition becomes greater.

In addition, motivation towards competition and performance decreases with age, whereas recreation and relaxation motives become more important. These latter motives may contrast sharply with the expectations of coaches and clubs that have performance-related development activities. Sport can provide many opportunities for competence and mastery for some young people, but equally a wide range of physical activities including noncompetitive and health-related exercise may enable other children to gain confidence and competence previously only available to the successful sport performer.

These deliberations that focus upon the internal motivations that affect young people's decisions about activity must also consider that motivation and attitudes towards activity are rarely fixed for a long period of time and will surely change throughout childhood and adolescence. For example, there is ample evidence that children become less interested in competition as they grow older and that relaxation and recreation become more important. It is clear that if the PE experience is to promote continued participation amongst all young people, it has a duty that all will achieve and grow in confidence and competence. In short, PE teachers and others with similar concerns must address the fact that it is not the activity, but the reason for taking part, that sustains participation.

A Contextual Link

Young people's motivations, whilst subject to change and to some extent dependent upon individual experiences, also depend upon contextual changes in their lives. Context is also of considerable significance in determining levels of sport participation. As teachers know, childhood and adolescence are times of considerable change, wherein young people are constantly redefining and renegotiating relationships with family, friends and peer groups. They also need to establish independent patterns of behaviour and search for identity and have increasing concern for future status with respect to study, vocational training, employment and adulthood. At such times all leisure pursuits and activities become a focus for reappraisal and review, in terms of value, which may well bring about a change in activities, a rejection of some, and a redefinition of priorities.

For some young people, sport and other activities are seen as an important transitional route into adult patterns of behaviour. For others they are related to childish activities and consequently rejected in order to leave childhood behind. The emergence of different friendship and peer-group relationships significantly alters leisure patterns. Moreover, sport and recreational interests compete with other spheres of adolescent leisure activity such as recorded music, fashion and entertainment, in addition to the need to study and take a full- or part-time job. These many and varied changes are responsible for a large amount of conflict, indecision and tension for the young persons involved, which tests affiliation and alliegance to sport participation to the full.

All of this may come at a time when persons in the world of sport are looking for increased commitment, motivation and loyalty from the young person. Teachers and sport coaches alike find it difficult to accommodate the varying degrees of interest and motivation shown at this time, and the established forms of sport organization, such as clubs and coaching schemes, for obvious reasons find it difficult to provide opportunities that are based upon a lesser degree of commitment and enthusiasm.

Long-term participation will depend upon not only developing the structural link that attempts to provide a match of opportunity and activity between school and the community, but also taking into account young people's value systems and their perceptions of activity and motivation as well as the contextual issues involved in the change from childhood through adolescence into adulthood. If we are to progress further in this field, and if sport and recreational participation is to survive this crucial time of change and uncertainty, additional consideration must be given to the nature of both a 'motivational' and a 'contextual' link between school and the community. Decisions about sport participation will be made as a result of young people asking themselves such questions as 'Where do I see sport in my life?' or 'How far do I want to go?' Teachers therefore need to take an individualized approach to young people, by recognizing the process involved and providing what may be a form of personal sport counselling similar to those more frequently used in careers guidance programmes in school.

Partnership and Action

The School Sport Forum

The Sports Council and the governing bodies of sport acted as catalysts for the stimulation of local action to encourage postschool participation. Two events have more recently served to bring an overview and clarity of thought to the role of PE and its relationship with the sporting community. The debate that surrounded the place of competitive sport in schools, the health-related fitness movement and changes in teachers' contracts served to place young people and sport at the front of a political agenda. Consequently the DES and the Department of the Environment (DOE) commissioned a desk study *Sport in School* (Murdoch, 1987) followed by the establishment of the School Sport Forum, which was charged with a brief on ensuring that 'the widest possible range of opportunities for, and thus the benefits of, sport are available to all children of school age' (School Sport Forum, 1988). Through a process of considering issues, evidence and examples of practice and identifying ways of overcoming any apparent problems, the School Sport Forum was asked to recommend courses of action for all bodies involved. Its working document *Sport and Young People* (1988) offered recommendations and strategies for action that could be widely adopted to meet local need and circumstances.

It was recognized at the outset that future action would be supported only within existing resources and that additional governmental support would not be forthcoming. However, the work of the Forum gained wide acceptance and has served as an agenda for many. Not least for all persons in PE, it highlighted the need for coherent statements about physical education and sport. There was a need for a clarity of thought, for an understanding of roles and philosophy that would not only avoid misunderstanding and unrealistic expectations but provide the framework for future collaborative action.

With the title of its report, *Sport and Young People—Partnership and Action*, the School Sport Forum recognized that schools could not be expected to take the entire responsibility for providing sporting opportunities for young people. Effective coordination and cooperation must be achieved at all levels, with a view to

1. harnessing the resources of local agencies, but
2. more importantly, meeting the needs of all young people.

Such debate and thinking drew together many of the examples of practice already referred to and provided a philosophical framework for effective future development.

The National Curriculum

The development of physical education within the National Curriculum has also served to focus upon the relationship between PE, sport and recreative activity and the community. It presents two principal challenges to PE teachers. Through child-centred development of the individual child, from fundamental movement and body management skills to the development of more specific skills within a range of contexts, young people eventually will not only become competent in activities but in addition possess the necessary skills, knowledge and attitudes to make informed choices about the value of such activities that will enable them to have active lifestyles.

Although it is relatively early days with regard to the National Curriculum, the relationship between school and community will be an increasingly integral feature of the development of young people's sporting activity and recreative interests. Physical education teachers will necessarily remain the guardians of the curriculum in educating young people through a range of experiences towards becoming skilful, competitive, and regularly active, but community involvement in this process needs to be carefully considered.

PE teachers will be concerned about the amount of time available for physical education, and there is a danger that opportunities provided by the community are perceived as providing an alternative source of activity or means of supporting the curriculum through additional resources and expertise at a time of change and transition. Such piecemeal and short-term responses must be rejected. Building on the numerous initiatives and programmes that have already been developed, teachers and the sporting community can together progress to what Laws (1990) describes as a 'shared view' of physical education, within which the unique and essential features of physical education will be recognized. With such a view, people in the community will be able to recognize the opportunities they have to provide additional experiences for the development of skills and body management. PE teachers will be able to recognize that, as a result, there is an increasing number of opportunities available for activity, skill development and coaching, opportunities that will meet the diverse needs of young people as they develop specific and general interests.

It is also important that persons responsible for such programmes not only have the sport-specific knowledge required but, through the various available coach education schemes, are able to provide experiences that are ethically sound, safe, enjoyable, and have sufficient flexibility and adaptability to meet young people's needs. This shared view of PE demands not only agreement about what are the essential experiences of content and activity, but also a common view of the process, how young people should be taught and coached.

The National Curriculum has engaged everyone concerned in a debate concerning the nature of PE and the essential areas of experience. It has also focused the minds of teachers and community members alike in defining more precisely the exact nature of the interface between PE and sport, the school and the community. The attainment targets and programmes of study will provide continuity and progression through the phases of physical education. An additional discussion must take place so that the continuum of development will extend into opportunities for participation and performance beyond the curriculum and into the sporting community. Physical education will need to identify the exact and precise nature of how such continuity may be best achieved.

The Way Forward

Implications for Teachers of Physical Education

The processes and development that have been described raise questions for PE teachers that have implications for the way they work in the future. Current changes in education brought about by the National Curriculum and the Local Management of Schools will give teachers time to review the contribution of PE to the whole curriculum. The relationships between school and community, between physical education and sport will inevitably be highlighted as those issues are addressed, areas of critical importance to future development will emerge.

The Physical Education Curriculum

The advent of the National Curriculum will give PE teachers the opportunity to consider anew the question 'Does the school experience adequately prepare young people for postschool participation?' It must be recognized that the school experience is only one of a number of factors (including home and family, peer group, life opportunities) that affect attitudes to regular sport participation. But PE teachers must acknowledge that both curriculum content and curriculum process will have significant effects upon young people's perceptions of the value of regular activity. Questions of curriculum content will be addressed through future programmes of study and activity within the National Curriculum. Clearly teachers must be aware of a supermarket approach that suggests that participation depends upon youngsters having access, and being introduced, to a large number of activities as part of the curriculum. Opportunities and resources previously unavailable to teachers have emerged that will enrich the PE curriculum. These may involve new activities and experiences or provide a level of coaching that extends the horizons and abilities of pupils to foster their success.

It is essential that young people have realistic opportunities to follow up and continue with these activities in their own time. The strategy of bringing young people into contact with local coaches and facilities will be found wanting and raise false hopes unless they can reasonably obtain continued access to these activities.

Questions concerning curriculum breadth must also be asked. Young people must acquire the range of skills and competencies they will need in order to successfully change activities as their interest and motivation shift. This is not to suggest that teachers should revert to a predominately skills-based approach to teaching to satisfy the demands of an increasing number of activities from which pupils will be able to choose. The answer will be found in a critical appraisal of the development of a range of skills and competencies that will meet the collective needs of such activities and provide a basis for the subsequent development of specific skills and abilities according to interest and need.

Finally, the National Curriculum will provide a crucial opportunity to consider the concept of progression of skill and competencies throughout physical education 5 to 16. What is exciting is that the debate and subsequent collaborative action involving both physical education and the sporting community will provide the chance for that progression to be seen in the overall context of broader sport development meeting the needs of those young people who see progress into higher levels of performance as a feature of their personal development. Future collaboration will help free the school curriculum from its past isolation from the 'real' world of sport and recreation.

Permanent Partnerships and Relationships Between Teachers and the Local Sporting Community

The physical education profession has recently been at the centre of a debate concerning the relationship between sport and recreation, the school and the community. That debate brought about a clarity of thinking concerning the unique place of PE (School Sport Forum, 1988) but additionally provided the opportunity for teachers and the sporting community to exchange views and come to Laws's (1990) 'shared view' of PE. Through their involvement in innovative school-to-community link schemes and demonstration projects, PE teachers established a series of new relationships and partnerships with a variety of local agencies such as clubs, governing bodies, sport associations and local authority recreation departments. Many valuable working collaborations have been demonstrated, and it is essential that such approaches become an ongoing and integral feature of local development. As lessons are learned and disseminated, there is a danger that unless they are incorporated into existing structures, or new structures are created that will allow these practices to continue and flourish, the progress of the recent past will be lost, and the future will depend upon additional initiatives and more 'new ideas'. It is important that future methods of work continue to be innovative, attractive and exciting and not simply a repeat of previous successes. There is now sufficient experience amongst all involved to consider building upon those successes and partnerships. In some areas, existing local structures can accommodate these changes, but in the context of the Local Management of Schools, new arrangements may also be required to allow the ongoing interaction between education and the sporting community that has been the essential feature of recent development.

Cohesive Approaches to Local Development

The concept of local advisory or development groups for youth sport was identified as a result of the need to ensure the effective deployment of scarce resources and in response to demands for effective coordination amongst all local agencies concerned. Such coordination could involve policy development, joint training approaches, identifying resources, and interagency liaison (Sports Council for Wales, 1988) but would need to be supported by a youth sport development officer. Teachers need to represent themselves, and be actively involved in the work of the many such local groups already existing, in order to take advantage of the various sporting and recreational networks that will evolve. The opportunities for cohesive and planned approaches to youth sport development will enable areas of overlap and omission to be identified, but crucially will provide an overall framework for local sport development in which teachers and physical education will have a vital role. In the past, different schemes and projects focused upon individual areas of action and innovation, often regardless of similar local practice.

The advantage of a cohesive approach such as that displayed in Active Life Styles (1985), Coventry, was that opportunities for curriculum development, approaches to linking school and community and local sport development were all focused within a single structure.

Meeting the Needs of Young People Through Practice and Research

The action and research that has been described initially concentrated upon ways of developing structural links between sporting and recreational activity for young people who were moving through school towards their future lives as adults. It is clear that structural links that ensure pathways through activities are a necessary feature of developing lifelong participation. However, they do depend upon participants remaining in activities over a certain period of time. Although there is the need for additional research, practice to date indicates that participation is rarely restricted to one activity and that young people frequently change their interests and activities in addition to moving among different levels of participation. 'Decisions to participate in particular sports or physical activities were not made once and for all time. Regular participation seemed to be based on constantly emerging decision making processes' (White & Coakley 1986, p. 13).

Moreover young people are frequently engaged in a range of activities that meet a variety of needs. Greater account must be taken of the various motivational and contextual factors that influence decisions about sport participation. PE teachers must consider how they equip young people with physical skills and competencies and provide a range of experiences that provide the basis for postschool participation. In addition there is a knowledge base about the benefits of activity and local opportunities from which young people can make informed choices about lifelong activity. But the critical feature will be a deeper understanding of the various individual decisions that young people make about sport participation.

It is not the activity but the attitude and motivation of the performer that sustains him. Csikszentimihalyi (1975)

The Value of a Health Focus

The health-based approach to physical education has had a significant impact upon teaching in schools. It was originally perceived as the 'new' PE, posing a threat to traditional programmes and standards of sport performance in schools. That many PE departments were keen to embark upon health-related curriculum development may be attributed to the availability of supporting materials and resources or teachers' recognition of its value as a result of well-documented inadequacies in young people's activity levels.

However, if the momentum is to be sustained and the continuing focus upon health-related PE is to make a real impact upon young people's activity patterns, more than the 'why' and 'how' of PE will have to be considered. Young people will have to develop lifestyle management skills that keep them reflecting and acting upon their needs for activity, and these skills will need to be reinforced with a link into postschool lifelong participation. 'School to community' is not just about relationships among schools, pupils and sport clubs. It is about encouraging all young people to regularly make use of sport and leisure centres, aerobics classes and swimming pools and include in their lifestyles informal activities such as walking, cycling, swimming and jogging.

The Future Role of the Teacher

Current work methods present teachers with an additional challenge as physical educators. Working with local sport coaches and liaising with clubs, identifying appropriate facilities and expertise, and being part of the local sport network calls for additional skills and knowledge of the community. There may be tensions in recognizing that sporting expertise is no longer the sole domain of the PE teacher and that knowledge related to children's physical, personal and social development is also within the thinking of others working with young people in a sporting and recreational context. If teachers are to effectively encourage young people into a range of activities for lifelong participation, they will need to shift their role from being a 'provider' of an activity into being an 'enabler', a person who enables pupils to make the most of the opportunities outside school. Teaching styles and strategies also need to enable pupils to move from being teacher dependent to being able to take responsibility for their own activities.

Futhermore, school management structures will need to recognize the conditions that will allow PE teachers both to respond to local sport-community initiatives and to become increasingly proactive as such local partnerships emerge and develop. The School Sport Forum (1988) recommended that 'schools and their governing bodies should develop closer sporting links with their local communities by designating a member of staff to be responsible for liaison with local sports clubs and organisation[s]' (p. 23). But the opportunity to do so effectively, in a coordinated and systematic development programme, will require resources, particularly people and time. The effects of formula funding under Local Management of Schools may cause departments to consider the use of their time more analytically. But with enlightened management and forward planning, the flexible resource allocation envisaged should allow the PE department to expand its roles in the local community.

Developing the Partnership

Throughout the late 1980s various agencies involved in education, sport and recreation developed the concept of collaborative working under the title of 'partnership'. At the simplest and most immediate level, local sport clubs have worked with teachers, and groups of schools have combined to work with leisure centres. Local recreation departments have appointed sport development officers who see schools as a principal focus for their work and consequently can offer valuable resources in return for the opportunity to work with young people. The governing bodies of sport have similarly found new ways of assisting PE teachers and have developed imaginative leadership and coach-education schemes in order to work more appropriately with young people. The Sports Council has shown itself to be a willing partner with the education sector, assisting small-scale individual schemes as well as national demonstration projects. All of which has identified good practice on the ground and a unique opportunity to learn from experience.

This provides a basis for the further development of partnerships. For most these have been positive experiences that have laid the foundation for further co-operation in the future. Such partnerships have been built upon mutual respect, a willingness to share expertise and experience, and understanding and agreement about areas of mutual concern and trust. The debate has given the participants the opportunity to understand each other's position. From this, long-term partnerships will develop, founded upon the belief that all parties have the lifelong sporting health and recreational needs of young people as their primary concern.

References

Almond, L. (1983). A rationale for health related fitness in schools. *Bulletin of Physical Education, 19*, 5-10.

Armstrong, N., Balding, J., Gentle, P., & Kirby, B. (1990). Patterns of physical activity among 11 to 16 year old British children. *British Medical Journal, 301*, 203-205.

Armstrong, N., & Davies, B. (1980). The prevalence of coronary risk factors in children. *Acta Paediatrica Belgica, 33*, 209-217.

Balding, J. (1988). *Young people in 1987*. Exeter: Health Education Authority, Schools Health Education Unit, University of Exeter.

Biddle, S. (1987). Motivational psychology and exercise: Implications for education. In N. Armstrong (Ed.), *Health and fitness in the curriculum* (Perspectives 31, pp. 47-63). Exeter: University of Exeter.

Biddle, S., & Fox, K.R. (1988). The child's perspective in physical education: 4. Achievement psychology. *British Journal of Physical Education, 19*, 182-185.

Campbell, S. (1990). *Sports development*. Paper presented to the Coventry Sports Development Group.

Council of Europe. (1976). *On the principles for a policy of sport for all* (Resolution (76) 41 of the Community of Ministers). London: Sports Council.

Coventry Local Education Authority. (1986). *School leavers' life styles and sports participation* (Unpublished survey conducted amongst 1,500 Coventry school leavers). Manchester: Sports Council Research Unit.

Csikszentmihalyi, M. (1975). *Beyond boredom and anxiety.* San Francisco: Jossey-Bass.

Department of Education and Science. (1979). *Curriculum 11-16, physical education.* London: Her Majesty's Stationery Office.

Department of Education and Science. (1983). *Young people in the 80's: A survey.* London: Her Majesty's Stationery Office.

Dickenson, B. (1986). Report on children's activity patterns and their perception of PE and activity. *HEA/PEA Newsletter*, No. 2.

Fentem, P., & Turnbull, N.B. (1987). Benefits of exercise for heart health: A report on the scientific basis. In *Coronary prevention group, exercise heart health* (pp. 109-125). London: Coronary Prevention Group.

Hargreaves, D. (1982). *The challenge for the comprehensive school.* London: Routledge & Kegan Paul.

Kane, J.E. (1974). *Physical education in secondary schools.* London: Macmillan.

Laws, C.J. (1990). Towards a synthesis of physical education, sport and community. *British Journal of Physical Education,* **21**, 362-363.

Murdoch, E. (1987). *Sport in schools.* London: Department of Education and Science and Department of the Environment Desk Study.

Roberts, K., Brodie, D.A., Campbell, R., Lamb, K.L., Minten, J., & York, C. (1989). Indoor sports centres: Trends in provision and usage. In *Fit for life—proceedings of a symposium on fitness and leisure* (pp. 83-99). Cambridge: Health Promotion Research Trust.

School Sport Forum. (1988). *Sport and young people—partnership and action.* London: Sports Council.

Sleap, M., & Warburton, P. (1989). Physical activity patterns of primary school children. *Happy Heart Project Survey.* National Children's Play and Recreation Unit.

Sports Council. (1988). *Into the 90's: A strategy for sport 1988-93.* London: Author.

Sports Council. (1989). *Planning for sports development.* London: Author.

Sports Council for Wales. (1988). *Youth and sport. Report on the national conference on the issue of sport for children of school age.* Cardiff: Author.

Stevens, J.E.R. (1985). Developing post school youth participation in school and recreation. *British Journal of Physical Education,* **16**, 134-135.

White, A., & Coakley, J. (1986). *Making decisions.* London: Sports Council.

Whitehead, N., & Hendry, L.B. (1976). *Teaching physical education in England: Description and analysis.* London: Lepu.

Wolfenden Committee on Sport. (1960). *Sport and the community.* London: Central Council for Physical Recreation.

Index

A

American College of Sports Medicine, statement on physical fitness and children, 72

Analysis programs
  applied to physical education, 61-63
  processing student information, 63-64
  used in fitness testing, 62

Arts in Schools Project, 149

Assessment and evaluation, computer-based systems for, 63-64

Athletics. *See* Track-and-field athletics

B

Body composition
  as a function of energy intake and expenditure, 79-80
  assessment of, in children, 80-81
  and control of energy intake, 79-80
  high-energy exercise counterproductive in improving, 80
  and risk of obesity, 80-81

British Association of Advisers and Lecturers in Physical Education, Working Party on Gymnastics recommendations, 124-125

British Council of Physical Education, position on dance in curriculum, 150-151

C

Cardiopulmonary fitness
  of children, 76
  defined, 74
  frequency and duration of exercise for children to achieve, 75-76
  higher training thresholds for children, 76
  maximal oxygen uptake as index of, 76
  physical activity preventing coronary heart disease, 170-171
  positive effect of physical activity on coronary risk factors, 86-87
  studies of, in children, 76, 98-100
  testing, in children, 98-100
  types of physical activity improving, 74-75

Central Council for Physical Recreation, leadership courses provided by, 183

Children's physical activity patterns, 86-89
  difficulty of assessing, 88
  low levels of health-related physical activity in, 88-89

persisting into adulthood, 87
  studies of, 88-89

Coaches, potential for influencing physical education curriculum, 17-18

Cognitive functioning, potential effect of health-related physical activity on, 86

Community sport development, 182

Competence
  nurturing perceptions of, 44
  relationship with self-esteem, 42-45

Computer-assisted learning, 64
  recognized and encouraged by sports organizations, 64-65

Computers, 55-56
  in physical education, 56-58

Cooperative social behaviour, encouraged by gymnastics, 131-132

Coronary heart disease. *See also* Cardiopulmonary fitness
  implications for physical education curriculum, 170-171
  physical activity preventing, 170

Coronary risk factors, positive effect of physical activity on, 86-87

Curriculum. *See also* National Curriculum; Physical education curriculum
  school governors' control over, 6

D

Dance
  appreciation defined for, 148
  as art, 144-145
  changing relationship with physical education, 141-145
  contributing to physical health and fitness, 142
  contributions of, to general curriculum, 149
  dance-as-art model, 145-149
  educational model, 142-143
  encouraging performing skills, 145
  encouraging technical skills, 145
  established as a subject by dance-as-art model, 149
  impact of dance as art approach, 144-145
  included but not recognized in physical education, 150-152
  influence of modern dance, 143-144
  as medium for personal expression, 143

The first volume in the series

New Directions in Physical Education Volume 1

Neil Armstrong, PhD, FPEA, Editor

1990 • Paper • 176 pp
Item BARM0294
ISBN 0-87322-294-6
$20.00 ($25.00 Canadian, £14.50 European)

Volume 1 of *New Directions in Physical Education* is an overview and analysis of current issues in physical education for England and Wales. Each chapter addresses a current topic in physical education with a review of the literature and thought-provoking suggestions for the curriculum.

Educators, tutors, coaches, and sport science practitioners will benefit from the ideas and experience of some of Britain's top physical educationalists and find much to inform and excite them about recent developments in this field.

New Directions in Physical Education Volume 1 is an important reference for physical education professionals and makes an excellent text for teacher training courses for all age groups, and for sport studies courses. It puts present practice and future trends into context for the physical education field.

Contents

Place your credit card order today! (VISA, AMEX, MC)
TOLL FREE: U.S. (800) 747-4457 • Canada (800) 465-7301 **OR:** U.S. (217) 351-5076 • Canada (519) 944-7774
FAX: U.S. (217) 351-2674 • Canada (519) 944-7614

(Access, Visa, AMEX, Diner's Club)
Europe by telephone (44) 0532-781708 • Europe by facsimile: (44) 0532-781709

Human Kinetics Books
A Division of Human Kinetics Publishers, Inc.